Truth is Not of This World: Take Heed, Be Not Deceived

Diana Ketterman

Disclaimer: The author has, to the best of her ability, researched for references to inform Christians about apostasy that has crept into the church. The author has no connection or affiliation with any political, non-political, hate/racist, and/or terrorist groups, entities, and/or individuals.

Readers are encouraged to not take the author's word for material presented, but to do their own research in the Word of God and the Strong's Concordance as well as to seek the Holy Spirit for guidance in all truth (Acts 17:11; 1 John 2:27).

Diana Ketterman is an independent researcher whose sole agenda is to advance truth regarding the world in which we live.

In preparation for writing this book, she traveled and did extensive research, interviewing Jews, Muslims, Catholics, and Christians for the writing of this book. Views and opinions expressed may change as more information becomes available (Daniel 12:4).

Dedicated to

my **Father** God,

my **Lord** and **Savior**, Jesus Christ, and

to the Holy Spirit, who is my **Teacher**.

This book combines knowledge and experience from studying the Bible, pertinent materials and information about the Middle East and the end times and visiting Israel and interacting with people there.

Understanding the current volatile state of the world today is important for every person. The author explains the various situations unfolding in the world and what's at stake for both believers and those who have not answered God's call to become His children and receive His love and protection.

---Barbara Kimble, Editor, *Christian Editor's Network*

JESUS SAID

"I am the way, *the TRUTH,* and the life. **No one comes to the Father except through Me"** (John 14:6).

"My kingdom is *NOT OF THIS WORLD*: if my kingdom were of this world, then would my servants *fight,* that I should not be delivered to the Jews: *but now is my kingdom not from hence"* (John 18:36).

"To this end was I born, and **for this cause came I into the world,** that **I should bear witness unto the truth. Every one that is of the truth heareth my voice"** (John 18:37).

Table of Contents

Preface

The Spirit of Divination

"For we wrestle not against flesh and blood, but against
principalities, against powers, against the rulers of the darkness of
this world,
against spiritual wickedness in high places."
Ephesians 6:12

A black cloud seemed to be hovering. The angels surrounding
me held back the engulfing evil, yet emotional and physical pain was
increasing at a rapid rate. The enemy was coming in like a flood.
Often my eyes filled with tears as I cried out to God, "What is it,
God?" Although I physically never had children, I knew I was in
travail in the spirit (Galatians 4:19). The Holy Spirit reassured me
Jesus was singing songs of deliverance for me (Psalms 32:7).

I often went to the mountain to pray, just as Jesus had (Mark
6:46). One particular time, I invited several prayer warriors to join
me. After extensive time in prayer and fellowship, I approached the
open window to shut out the cool evening breeze. Suddenly, out of
seemingly nowhere, I was struck in the face by something made of
hard iron.

I screamed, "JESUS! JESUS! OH JESUS, please help me." As I
fell to the floor, two remaining warriors ran to me, praying. An
Amish wagon wheel hanging on the wall had fallen. The axle hit my

forehead, broke my nose, and gave me two black eyes. The injury was ruled a concussion. The spiritual warfare was real.

Later, when praying about this incident, asking for revelation, the Lord gave me the verse from Ezekiel 3:9, "Like adamant stone, harder than flint, I have made your forehead; do not **be afraid of them, nor be dismayed at their looks, though they are a rebellious house.**"

Six months later, I awoke early while on a trip out of the country. I stepped into the shower and within minutes I found myself pitching forward. I felt pain as the right side of my body hit the metal ridge of the sliding door and the top of my head hit the shower wall.

Once again, I screamed, "JESUS! JESUS! OH JESUS, please help me." The injury was again ruled a concussion.

It was then I spent some serious time with Jesus. I must know why these two incidents happened! The Holy Spirit said, *"You are under the power of the spirit of divination."* What?!

Wow! I began to mentally scan through my life, analyzing where that spirit had gained access to my life. What did it mean to be under the power of the spirit of divination? Isn't that witchcraft? Exactly, it was. Ignorantly, I had come into agreement with those who had taken oaths not only against Christ, but for Lucifer. In addition, I had unknowingly taken an indirective oath to replace Christ when I joined a community organization.

I realized that I must break off agreements with those who had taken these oaths, renounce the oath I had taken, and resign from the prestigious association.

The very fact that I had ignorantly walked into Satan's line of fire caused me to want to know more. How many others must be making agreements with Lucifer or against Christ and not be aware?

I began to research the origins behind organizations and religions which were antichrist, against, and/or instead of Christ. Often members and followers are not aware. Groups such as these were in Jerusalem over 2,000 years ago when Jesus was there because the beloved Apostle John wrote in 1 John 2:18, "Little children, it is the last hour; and as you have heard that the Antichrist is coming (**future**), even now many antichrists have come (**present**), by which we know that it is the last hour."

I knew that taking on the assignment of writing this book to expose the works of darkness as commanded in Ephesians 5:11 might result in additional spiritual warfare. I stepped away from the assignment for several months to seek God and ensure this was in fact something I was called to do. The confirmation was solid.

The Lord said to start speaking via the Internet and write a book. He said to entitle it, "**<u>Truth is Not of This World</u>**." I wasn't sure what the exact content would be, but in December 2022 the Lord gave me the following scriptures as part of the book description.

Timothy instructs us as soldiers. He said, "Thou therefore endure hardness, as a good soldier of Jesus Christ. No man that warreth entangleth himself with the affairs of this life; that he may please him who hath chosen him to be a soldier" (2 Timothy 2:3-4).

Jesus said in John 18:36, "My kingdom is not of this world." He also said, "I have given them thy word, and the world hath hateth them, because they are **not of the world**, even as I am **not of the world**" (John 17:14).

As we near the end of the age, darkness in the physical world is increasing. However, for those who are living and walking as spiritual soldiers, the Light is shining brighter as all things hidden are being revealed.

Warriors of the light are not of this world. Walking in the Spirit is the life support to endure to the end.

This book presents a contrast between the **physical** and the **spiritual** realms with the Word as the lamp. Come, join the army of the Lord, be a warrior for the light of truth, and separate from the lies of this world as it will soon pass away.

Israel 2023

I felt compelled to take a research trip to Israel. This would be my third trip to the Holy Land. I planned to do specific research on the "unholy" sites. In February 2023, the trip became a reality, and I had a schedule of unholy sites I wanted to visit where evil had occurred, as it was recorded in the Word.

After being in Israel for a few days, I was walking across a parking lot and suddenly something fell and hit me on top of my head. I could not believe I had a third head injury in such a short time. I staggered to sit down and realized the arm of a gate had unexpectedly come down and struck me.

I knew this third blow to the head, later ruled a third concussion, was a sign that I was under direct attack from the enemy and somehow it was connected to the previous two head injuries. I also sensed a revelation was coming.

The satanic attack was confirmed as I learned that the Circle of Freemasonry in Eilat, Israel, was directly in line with the parking lot where the incident occurred. Israel is touted as the cradle of Freemasonry. Jerusalem is where the Temple was built by King Solomon almost three thousand years ago. [212] Solomon's Temple is an idol of Freemasonry. [221]

One week later while I was in Tiberias, the Lord awakened me at 2:30 a.m. to show me an *unscheduled* crescent blood moon over the Sea of Galilee. This sighting was followed by a very distinct word and three warnings for the church. These initial warnings were brought to the church on YouTube at the cited references. [451, 452, 453]

Could the enemy have been trying to take me out before the word of the Lord was given to me? Or could he have been trying to scare me from going forth with this very important word in this book? Whatever the reason, *I am more compelled than I ever have been to write what the Lord is saying to the church today.*

Introduction

The Blood Moon Experience

Protests began on January 7, 2023, against the formation of the thirty-seventh government of Israel, many were and still are against Prime Minister Benjamin Netanyahu's leadership. The escalation of protests, strikes, and hunger strikes continued.

On February 13, 2023, more than 100,000 people gathered for protests in Jerusalem. *(See Photo).* The protests turned into strikes and included individuals from all walks of life, including doctors and tech workers. That day, the Constitution committee at the Knesset voted 9-7 in favor of a reform giving the coalition a majority on the judicial appointments committee, which would give control over the appointment of judges to the government. [420, 421]

On February 14, 2023, at 2:30 a.m. in Tiberias, Israel, the Lord awakened me. I looked out of my hotel glass door to a bright red unscheduled crescent blood moon over the Sea of Galilee. I had never seen a blood moon and was not aware that there would be one while I was in Israel. I wondered why I had not heard about a coming blood moon.

I reached for my new S22 Samsung that I had purchased exclusively for taking photos. I lay in my bed and zoomed with the 100x power through the glass to get a photo. Not wanting to disturb my roommate, but wanting to get a clear shot, I quietly got up, slid open the glass doors, and stepped out onto the balcony into the clear night. The bright red was a reflection onto the soft ripples of the Sea of Galilee. I got several good shots, returned to my bedside, and began to Google when the next blood moon would appear. None were scheduled to appear during this time. (*See Photo*).

At 2:45 p.m., I posted the photos to Facebook and wrote the following,

"It's 2:45 a.m. in Israel. I awoke and looked out my balcony and saw a red moon. It's not supposed to be a blood moon, so I was wondering why is it red? See the red reflection on the water beneath, the Sea of Galilee."

I fell back to sleep. My alarm went off at 5:30 a.m. I looked out the window, searching for the moon as dawn was breaking. There it was! However, it was no longer blood red, but white! I thought, *What in the world? Did I dream I saw a blood crescent moon?* I grabbed my phone and there were the photos I had taken. I dropped to my knees by my bed to pray and to tell my Savior that I love him and ask Him to show me the meaning of the crescent blood moon. Why did I see it, and what was He telling me?

As I asked these questions, I heard in my spirit, "I awakened you to see my warning. This is a sign to my people. The sun shall be turned into darkness, and *the **moon into blood, before the great and the terrible day of the LORD** comes*. And it shall come to pass, that *whosoever shall call on the name of the LORD shall be delivered*: for in *mount Zion and in Jerusalem shall be deliverance*, as the LORD hath said, and in ***the remnant whom the LORD shall call***" (Joel 2:31-32).

I was shaken. I knew this was just the beginning of my special journey. The head injury and now the blood moon were two unique experiences in just a few days. My trip was just beginning!

I felt certain the Lord would reveal more as I spent time with Him and sought His face. From past experiences, when the Lord begins to reveal things to me, it happens like a book; the story unfolds. There is a difference between **revelation** and **knowledge**. We can research and take other people's words to give us answers, but **revelation** from the Holy Spirit is powerful and unique. If we are careful, to hear, to seek, to spend time alone with Him, He will reveal to us things that we did not know. He will reveal Himself, Truth, and things that are to come (Daniel 2:22).

"That the God of our Lord Jesus Christ, the Father of glory, may give unto you the *spirit of wisdom and revelation in the knowledge of him [JESUS CHRIST]*" (Ephesians 1:17).

"Howbeit when he, the *Spirit of truth*, is come, he will guide you into all ***truth***: for he shall not speak of himself; but whatsoever he shall hear, that shall he speak: and *he will shew you things to come*" (John 16:13).

"But the Comforter, which is the Holy Ghost, whom the Father will send in my name, ***he shall teach you all things***, and bring all things to your remembrance, whatsoever I have said unto you" (John 14:26).

Our tour group barely got out of Israel and the protests escalated with many pressing on the outskirts of our vehicle. Protests continued and during the next two weeks attendance at many of these events was well over 100,000.

March 1, 2023, was declared a *National Day of Disruption*, setting off the blocking of highways. March 9, 2023, was declared the *National Day of Resistance*. According to one source, protesters blocked roads and maritime routes, including one of the country's main highways, Ayalon, which connects all the major traffic routes leading to Tel Aviv. Convoys of cars packed the Tel Aviv-Jerusalem highway and streamed toward Ben Gurion Airport's main terminal.

On or about May 10, 2023, Israel and Gaza militants began to trade heavy fire during which dozens were killed.

At the writing of this book, protests have escalated with gunfire, violence, death, fear, confusion, intimidation and war which has gone beyond the Israeli borders. On October 7, 2023, the world changed forever when Hamas was allowed to strike within Israel. Yes, I said "allowed." In my opinion, it was a planned attack.

In previous visits to the Holy Land, I had visited and toured the high-tech electrical fence surrounding the border. (*See Photo*). Israel

Defense Forces of the military boasted that they knew when a cockroach would pass under. I also knew of those who had personally worked on the development of the Iron Dome software. It could not have failed so miserably. Why were these events happening at this time? It leaves much to speculation, but the puzzle pieces are coming together as the mystery of end time events unfold.

Why is there seemingly constant turmoil in the "Holy" land? I will relay my thoughts on this elsewhere in the book. Keep in mind, the Word of the Lord to me and to His people, from Joel 2:32: *"for in **mount Zion and in Jerusalem shall be deliverance,** as the LORD hath said, and in the **remnant whom the LORD shall call**."*

I believe the nation of Israel is the area where there is the strongest spiritual warfare in the world. It is the place on earth where the **spirit of Christ** and **spirit of antichrist** were first at war in the physical and spiritual. It is the place where Jesus defeated Satan! This enmity has rippled throughout the entire world and the escalation is on a global scale.

But, praise God, soon Jesus will return to establish the heavenly city, His bride, the New Jerusalem (Revelation 21:2).

A Call to the Watchmen

"For thus hath the Lord said unto me, *Go, set a watchman, let him declare what he seeth*" (Isaiah 21:6).

"*But if the watchman see the sword come, and blow not the trumpet, and the people be not warned;* if the sword come, and take [any] person from among them, he is taken away in his iniquity; *but his blood will I require at the watchman's hand*" (Ezekiel 33:6).

Thus speaketh the LORD God of Israel, saying, **Write thee all the words that I have spoken unto thee in a book** (Jeremiah 30:2).

Blood Moon Scripture Research

The Lord gave me three distinct revelations of the meaning of my having seen the blood moon. These warnings are covered in the next several chapters of this book.

I am a researcher by nature, so naturally I had a desire to break down the foundational verse the Lord gave me a few hours after the blood moon sighting. I researched Joel 2:31-32 in the Hebrew language using the Strong's Concordance. The word, *Joel*, means "Jehovah is his God." The second chapter of Joel points towards consecration (separation to God), revival, and restoration. This day will be **great** for the **righteous** but **terrible** for the **wicked**. After researching key words, there were indications of many hidden meanings packed in these two verses.

"The sun shall be turned into darkness, and the moon into **blood** *(signifying DEATH, shed by violence)*, before the great and the **terrible** *(powerful, fearful day)* day of the LORD come. And it shall come to pass, that whosoever shall call on the name of the LORD shall be **delivered** *(way of escape)*: for in mount **Zion** *(location, holy place)* and in **Jerusalem** *(place of completion)* shall be deliverance, as the LORD hath said, and in the **remnant** *(survivor)* whom the LORD shall call" (Joel 2:31-32).

The key words were researched in the scripture above. According to Strong's Concordance, the word, *blood*, means "death, blood shed by violence." Could it be possible that the bloodshed which began just a few weeks after the sighting of the blood moon might be the precursor or shadow of the coming great and terrible day of the Lord?

The word, *terrible*, means "powerful, terrible acts, fear, afraid, to stand in awe." Terrible connotes the psychological reaction of "fear," being afraid of something or someone. Terrible also means to "stand in awe, to reverence, recognizing the power and position of the individual revered, to render proper respect, submission to God."

Things in the world are certainly terrible and deteriorating at a fast pace, yet still, many do not, respect, fear, and reverence God.

Those who do will stand in awe and reverence. I believe the great and terrible day is fast approaching. Those who are not in right standing with God have the possibility of having "their hearts fail them for fear" (Luke 21:26).

The word, ***delivered*** means "to escape, to rescue, to release, take away, to save, to escape from danger of an enemy, to give birth, to bring forth, emit sparks." Romans 10:3 says, "Everyone who calls on the name of the Lord will be saved (delivered)." Moses called upon the name of the Lord for the people of Israel to be delivered (Exodus 34:8-9).

When the children of Israel were ***delivered*** out of Egypt, which is a symbol of the world, they saw God's great power. They feared the Lord and believed in Him. They had honor and respect for Him. This honor, respect, and fear can be found in the songs written by Moses. Interestingly, songs written by Moses are found in both the Old Testament (Exodus 20) and the New Testament (Revelation 15)! Both songs are in celebration for those who have been ***delivered out of the world system***.

Songs of Moses and Miriam were written and sung to commemorate their dramatic escape from Egyptian (worldly) bondage.

It is also believed Moses wrote Psalm 91 the day he completed the building of the Tabernacle in the desert. [213] This is a powerful chapter to recite often.

The **Song of Moses** and the **Song of the Lamb** will be sung in heaven in victory for those who have overcome.

"And I saw another sign in heaven, great and marvelous, seven angels having the seven last plagues; for in them is filled up the wrath of God.

And I saw as it were a sea of glass mingled with fire: and them that had gotten the victory over the beast, and over his image, and over his mark, and over the number of his name, stand on the sea of glass, having the harps of God" (Revelation 15:1-2).

The word, *Zion*, means a "holy place, permanent capital, a mountain of Jerusalem, a monumental or guiding pillar in dry places, or drought, solitary and barren places. Think about the children of Israel as they were guided through the wilderness with the cloud by day and the fire by night. They were given hope that came from the mountain. Zion is where the foundation of the Lord is. Isaiah 28:16 says, "Therefore thus saith the Lord GOD, *Behold, I lay in Zion for a foundation a stone, a tried stone, a precious corner stone, a sure foundation*: he that believeth shall not make haste." Zion is a place in Christ, a place in His presence, **the secret place** of the high calling (Psalm 91).

Zion is not only a physical location, but it is **a people**, the glorious, overcoming church, made up of both Jew and Greek in one body. It is a people who proclaim the word of God (Ephesians 2:11-22). [407]

"Strait is the gate, and narrow is the way, which leadeth unto life, and few there be that find it" (Matthew 7:14).

The word *Jerusalem* means "to be safe in mind, body, or estate, to be or make complete, to be friendly, peace, recompense, reward, restoration, repayment, restitution, an end, *finished, full, perfect, prosperous, a condition or action is complete.*"

God is deficient in nothing; He has no shortcomings; His power has no weakness. *Shalam* means "to make peace, to be *complete, perfect.*" God demanded total obedience from His people. First Kings 8:61 says, *"Let your heart therefore be perfect with the LORD our God, to walk in his statutes, and to keep his commandments, as at this day."*

Solomon completed the physical house of the Lord as signified in 1 Kings 9:25, "so he finished the house"; however, Solomon failed to meet the requirements spiritually because his heart was not perfect with the Lord his God (1 Kings 11:4).

One day soon, King Jesus will finish His **house** (the temple) He is building with lively stones (1 Peter 2:5). We are the **temple** (1 Corinthians 6:19-20), in New Jerusalem. He will **tabernacle** among us just as He did with the people of Israel (Leviticus 26:11;

Revelation 21:3). Oh, what a glorious day, that will be when He tabernacles with us and finishes His house!

"And I John saw *the holy city, new Jerusalem*, coming down from God out of heaven, prepared as *a bride* adorned for her husband. And I heard a great voice out of heaven saying, ***Behold, the tabernacle of God is with men, and he will dwell with them, and they shall be his people***, and God himself shall be with them, and be their God. And ***God shall wipe away all tears from their eyes; and there shall be no more death, neither sorrow, nor crying, neither shall there be any more pain: for the former things are passed away***" (Revelation 21:2-4).

But before the New Jerusalem is finished, the remnant will be called and **delivered from death** in that **terrible day of the Lord**.

There is great power in speaking and/or singing the songs of Moses from both the Old and New Testaments. These spiritual songs can be found in the Appendix. I encourage you to meditate on these words.

First Blood Moon Warning

Take Heed, that No One Deceives You

In the hours and days following the crescent blood moon sighting in Israel, the Holy Spirit kept dropping in my spirit a specific verse, Matthew 24:4, ***"Take heed, that no one deceives you."*** This was the first warning I received to disseminate to the church.

Verse five continues, "For many will come in My name, saying, 'I am the Christ,' and *will deceive many."* I noticed that while in Israel there were pictures, displays, and propaganda for false messiahs. *(See Photo).* One promotion was of a dead rabbi from New York who many say will return as the Messiah, the "anointed one." Another "Messiah," who is currently alive, was supposedly performing miracles in Israel with broadcasts on YouTube.

Matthew 24:24 says, "For there shall arise ***false Christs***, and ***false prophets***, and shall shew great signs and wonders; insomuch that, *if it were possible, they shall deceive the very elect."*

Many false Christs and Messiahs will arise. This includes the Artificial Intelligence Messiah and the "other Christ" of the hit TV series *The Chosen. The Chosen* is almost completely man's word as 95 percent of the content is not from the Bible. [231] Many will be deceived through infiltration of truth mixed with lies. We must know Him for ourselves and not what we have learned through a TV show or movie.

The antichrist spirit is anything or anyone that is "instead of" and/or "against" Christ. This includes those who identify as the Messiah (2 Thessalonians 2) and deceive many with signs, wonders, and a false peace. Men of lawlessness are anointed with the *spirit of antichrist.*

Jesus of Nazareth is the only true Messiah, the Christ, our Savior, the Lamb of God, the Prince of Peace, the High Priest, the true King of Israel, and most of all the Son of God (John 1:41, 49). He is the Way. His ways are not our ways (Isaiah 55:8). **Any path we choose that is not His Way, is the way of antichrist.**

The Remnant Whom the Lord Shall Call

I prayed for the Holy Spirit to guide me and was prompted to return to the foundational scripture given to me from Joel 2:31-32. I felt drawn to the words of verse 32, *"and in the **remnant** whom the LORD shall call."*

The entire verse is, "And it shall come to pass, that **whosoever** shall call on the name of the LORD shall be **delivered**: for in mount **Zion** and in **Jerusalem** shall be deliverance, as the LORD hath said, and in the **remnant** whom the LORD shall call."

Deliverance is available for "whosoever" calls on the name of the Lord, but the focus here is the Lord will have a remnant, **spiritual Israel.** All those who believe and call upon the name of the Lord are grafted in, thus **joining** spiritual Israel (Romans 11:24). Remnant status is acquired through faith in Jesus Christ.

Paul illustrates in Acts 15:17, "That the **remnant** of men might seek after the Lord, and all the _Gentiles, upon whom my name is called_, saith the Lord, who doeth all these things." And in Romans 1:16, Paul continues, "For I am not ashamed of the gospel of Christ: for it is the power of God unto salvation to every one that believeth; _to the Jew first, and also to the Greek._"

Jesus was from the tribe of Judah. Those from the tribe of Judah were recognized as **physical** Jews. Abraham was not a physical Jew, but the father of the **spiritual** Jews. **Jesus is the seed of Abraham** (Hebrews 2:16).

Jesus and His disciples preached the gospel of salvation to the Jews, in person, for three and half years. After Jesus died, the Holy Spirit was sent. Over 120 Hebrews in the upper room in Jerusalem and 3,000 more recognized Jesus as Lord on the day of Pentecost. After this historic day, the high priest and the Sanhedrin formally rejected the gospel of Christ. Stephen was then put to death by stoning for his faith in Christ. Paul made the decision to then turn from the Jews in Jerusalem to take the gospel to the Gentiles. The disciples were first called Christians in Antioch Acts 11:26.

"Then Paul and Barnabas waxed bold, and said, 'It was necessary that the word of God should first have been spoken to you: but seeing ye put it from you, and judge yourselves unworthy of everlasting life, lo, **we turn to the Gentiles'**" (Acts 13:46).

I wondered, how does "and in the *remnant* whom the LORD shall call" connect with "Take heed, that **no one deceives you."** Then it clicked. *The remnant will only be the remnant if they are not deceived!* Yes, that was the connection. <u>Those who are deceived will not be a part of the remnant and will not survive.</u>

The word *remnant* means "remaining, alive, survivor, that which is left."

The word *deceive* means "to roam from safety, truth, or virtue, to go astray, to seduce, to lead away from the truth, to lead into error and sin."

Deceiver is the title of the devil. Revelation 12:9 says, "that old serpent, called <u>the Devil, and Satan, which deceiveth the whole world.</u>"

Often, we hear, "The devil made me do it"; however, the Word indicates *sin leads to deception.* *"<u>BE NOT DECEIVED</u>: neither fornicators, nor idolaters, nor adulterers, nor effeminate, nor abusers of themselves with mankind, nor thieves, nor covetous, nor drunkards, nor revilers, nor extortioners, shall inherit the kingdom of God"* (1 Corinthians 6:9-10).

To be a part of the remnant, ***<u>one must not be deceived</u>***, *one must* ***REMAIN*** *and* ***ENDURE***. ***Survival*** is dependent upon not drifting, not going astray, not being seduced, not being led away from truth, and not being led into error and sin. The floodgates of filth have opened, and we can no longer deny the evil and global strongholds in our world, our countries, our cities, our churches, our homes, and many of our lives. It is time the church lifts up a standard against the enemy (Isaiah 59:19).

Deception has crept in through many mediums; what we see, hear, taste, and even what we wear. These are direct attacks, not only on the individual, but on the Word of the Lord. David says, "*<u>Taste and see</u>* that the LORD is good" (Psalm 34:8) and Jesus says, "My sheep <u>hear My voice</u>, and **I know them, and they follow Me**" (John 10:27). **Having eyes, see ye not**? and **having ears, hear ye not**? and do ye not remember? (Mark 8:18).

Demonic forces are at work in the media through songs, news, videos, books, technology, Internet, games, sports, television, phones, and other *devices*. Second Corinthians 2:11 says, "***Lest Satan should get an advantage of us:*** *for we are not ignorant <u>of his devices</u>*."

The word *device* means a **mental** perception, purpose, *<u>itself</u>*, the intellect disposition, thought, an evil purpose, that which thinks, thoughts, or purposes, that which is thought out, translated, of the mind, to exercise the mind, to comprehend, to consider, to perceive, think, understand, to perceive with the mind.

We often think about the above-mentioned devices as being deceptive in the world; however, these same devices are being used to deceive *within* the body of Christ. Many have no idea they are being deceived through songs, sermons, books, Bibles, Internet, videos, games, sports, television, phones, tarot cards, and other *devices*. Some have been made aware but do not care or they do not believe the depths of the deception.

Did you know that devices are developed from human think tanks? Knowledge **from humans** is used to develop devices to please, pacify, and placate self. Human knowledge has given birth to machine learning which is artificial intelligence (AI). AI takes a composite of man's knowledge and combines it with machine knowledge which is then projected through devices. I have been in the technology field for forty years and have witnessed firsthand the takeover of AI in many realms, seen and unseen.

These mediums have polluted our mental, physical, and spiritual environments. One might say that these devices are progress and good for mankind. However, often the initial intent is **to bewitch** the innocent and ignorant. The bad outweighs the good, even to the point of inviting demonic forces to dominate. Yes, witchcraft is in the church in many forms, positions, mediums, and devices. "O foolish Galatians, *who hath bewitched you, that ye should not obey the truth*" (Galatians 3:1).

Bewitched means "to charm, fascinate, by false representation." We must ask, "Are we following men or Jesus?" "Is this a work of man or Jesus?" "Does this ministry involve **men promoting men** over Jesus Christ?"

These antichrist devices are considered leaven. The word *leaven* means mental and moral corruption, viewed in its <u>tendency to infect others</u>. Leaven is applied to that substance, which is small in quantity, *yet* <u>thoroughly pervades</u> a thing ***by its influence***. "A little leaven leaveneth the whole lump" (Matthew 13:33). Do not ignore the small things that brings corruption (Song of Solomon 2:15).

In Matthew 16, Jesus is talking to His disciples about leaven. He says in verses 11-12, 'How is it that ye do not understand that I spake it not to you concerning bread, that ye should beware of *the* **<u>leaven</u>** *of the Pharisees and of the Sadducees*? Then understood they how that he bade them not **beware** of the leaven of bread, ***but of the doctrine of the Pharisees and of the Sadducees.*** <u>What was the</u> <u>*leaven*</u> <u>and the</u> <u>*doctrine*</u> <u>of the Pharisees and Sadducees?</u>

The word ***doctrine***, means "instruction, teaching in religious assemblies of the Christians." ***What we take into our eye and ear gates teaches us***. We must pray for discernment against false teachings. They are antichrist.

The Pharisees and Sadducees were two primary groups of teachers and leaders in the synagogue and members of the Sanhedrin Court, which had 71 members, the one being the chief priest. [214] This is an example of a small minority who pervades a thing by influence. These two groups existed in the priesthood between 159 and 144 BC. The chief high priests of the Sanhedrin were powerful and influential. [423, 425, 426]

The Pharisees valued themselves highly upon the exact skill they had in the law of their fathers and made men believe they were highly favored by God. They were able to make great opposition to kings. They were a scheming sect with displays of open fighting and mischief, who believed they had a foreknowledge of things to come by divine inspiration. [425]

The Sadducees were able to persuade the rich, but the Pharisees had the multitude on their side. The Pharisees had so great a power over the multitude that when they said anything against the king or the high priest, they were generally believed. [199, p. 1331]

The Pharisees were given to fasts, prayers, washing, paying of tithes, and alms, exhibiting themselves on the outward to the people in order to gain favor as self-denying, holy men, zealous for God and the law. However, Jesus exposed them in Matthew 5:20, 15:4, and elsewhere of the reality of who they really were. They were men with lax morals, who loved pleasures of the senses. At an early period, they determined in the Sanhedrin to withstand and to destroy Jesus. Most likely this was instigated by the boldness with which Jesus taught regarding the necessity of personal righteousness and pure worship (Matthew 7:14). [199, p. 1332]

The Jewish people in Jesus' time were under the religious denomination of the Pharisees. This party came about two hundred years **before Jesus** to resist Hellenism. [199, p. 950] Hellenism was the Greek culture, including fusion **with Buddhism**, that arose between the death of Alexander the Great in 323 BC and the death of Cleopatra VII in 30 BC. [410]

The Pharisees were deeply opposed to the cultural and philosophical changes taking place in their society. They saw

Hellenization as a threat to their identity and tradition. They worked to preserve and emphasize the **law** and their customs.

The Sadducees and the Romans were more in alignment with the new Hellenistic culture, causing a rift in the two parties. This caused the Pharisees to hate the Romans. [427]

The Pharisees hated Jesus. Jesus did not respond to their **national pride** and **did not support their political independence from the Romans.** On the contrary, he insisted they fulfill obligations to their Roman masters. Also, Jesus came **to change the priesthood** and therefore, openly criticized the laws, traditions, and religious ceremonies **the Pharisees promoted** (Mark 7:1-13). One example was the issue of the Sabbath (Matthew 12:1-14). Enforcing the Old Testament *laws* was the religion of Judaism. [35, 199, p. 950]

Jesus knew **the hearts** of these law pushers was the issue. He tore off their masks and exposed the evil in their hearts, calling them hypocrites (Matthew 23:13).

The influence of the Pharisees was strong in Judea but did not reach to Galilee where Jesus was from. The common people were faithful to their national religion but were not bound to Judaism. Jesus was one of the Galilean "common people." [199, p. 950]

At the time when the Pharisees used their power against Jesus and His work, there were about 6,000 of this sect who worked out of the capital of Jerusalem. They disallowed the publication of the Gospel, demonstrating their hatred of the kingdom of God (Luke 5:17). [199, p. 1332]

The Pharisees constituted a large portion of the Sanhedrin court, and it was there they put Jesus on trial and condemned him to die. They had the **political and religious power and influence** to convict him when he had not broken any laws (Luke 23). Pilate said multiple times **he found no fault in him**. <u>Should we not consider this to be the pattern and precursor of events prior to the great and terrible day of the Lord?</u> Matthew 24:9 says, "Then ***shall they deliver you up to be afflicted, and shall kill you***: and <u>*ye shall be hated of all nations for my name's sake*</u>."

Sadducees represented the *legal* system and Pharisees the *religious* system. Together they represented the *political system*. They were two wings of the same political bird. One might imagine the Sadducees like the Democrats and the Pharisees like the Republicans. Both groups had individual agendas for power, influence, and status *but the spirit of antichrist was the <u>common ground</u> that brought the groups together.* This same sect of Pharisees in the Sanhedrin still exists today in Jerusalem with an antichrist spirit against Jesus Christ. [215]

The Sadducees represented the wealthy, the elite, the influential, the educated. They made up ninety percent of the 71 members of the Sanhedrin Court. These members were in league with the Romans.

"Pilate sought to release him [JESUS]: but the Jews cried out, saying, *If thou let this man go, thou art not Caesar's friend:* whosoever maketh himself a king *speaketh against Caesar.*

"When Pilate therefore heard that saying, he brought Jesus forth and sat down in the judgment seat in a place that is called the *Pavement*, but in the Hebrew, *Gabbatha.* And it was the preparation of the passover, and about the sixth hour: and he saith unto the Jews, Behold your King! But they cried out, Away with him, away with him, crucify him. Pilate saith unto them, Shall I crucify your King? *The chief priests answered, We have no king but Caesar"* (John 19:12-15).

These political leaders covered each other's sins and joined forces *against* Jesus. "And *Herod with his men of war* set him at nought, and mocked him, and arrayed him in a gorgeous robe, and **sent him again to Pilate**. And *the <u>same day Pilate and Herod were made friends together: for before they were at enmity between themselves</u>"* (Luke 23:11-12). It was the spirit of antichrist that united the enemies. This same spirit is still alive today.

The Sadducees originated from the priesthood of Zadok, the high priest who anointed Solomon as king (1 Kings 1:39-40). Like the doctrine of Freemasonry, they trusted in the authority of King Solomon and rejected the word of the prophets. They were the legal authority; they functioned "as gods" (Elected, "El = god"). Likewise, the elite today function as "gods" controlling the world system. [428]

Pharisee means "separated" as those who are separated from the ordinary person by the correctness of their opinions and the "holiness" of their lives. [199, p. 1330] They were the religious leaders, representing the common people. Their dominant influence was evident during the time of Jesus and today continues in world power. [216, 217]

The Pharisees had outward forms of worship, but the heart was wicked. They were noted for self-righteousness and pride. Jesus said to them, "Woe to you, scribes and Pharisees, hypocrites! For you are like whitewashed tombs which indeed appear beautiful outwardly, but inside are full of dead men's bones and all ***uncleanness***" (Matthew 23:27). The Pharisees bear the burden of having crucified the Lord, who is the giver of life. [199, p. 1330]

The word ***uncleanness*** means "impure physically or morally, the impurity of lustful, luxurious, profligate living with impure motives."

The Pharisees changed the law to suit the times. Oral law was equal to written law, _with interpretation by the Rabbis_. They did not recognize that Jesus was (and still is) the Truth. The Pharisees endorsed a body of traditional interpretations, applications, and expansions of the Old Testament law which was communicated orally. Their trust was in the authority of Moses (John 9:28-29). They believed Moses received the ***ORAL*** law from Sinai and delivered it to Joshua, and Joshua to the elders, and the elders to the prophets and the prophets to the men of the Great Synagogue. However, Jesus cited the ***WRITTEN*** law of Moses and the Prophets and the Psalms (Luke 24:44).

While the Hebrew Torah is in alignment with the Bible, the Talmud is the primary law of the Jewish religious law and theology. Talmud means ***doctrine***. At the time of Jesus, the Talmud was the oral law, recited by heart. Today, it is a written book with many facets of teaching, including the Zohar and Kabbalah, which is Jewish mysticism. The rabbis then and today hold the Talmud as *religious* and *political* authority. The oral law became the Talmud. *The Talmud does not recognize Jesus as the Son of God*. **Parts of this doctrine are law in the United States and other countries**. It has infiltrated under "education" in our schools and seminaries. **If this current law is enforced, Christians will be at risk of losing their lives for professing Jesus Christ as Lord.** The antichrist system in the United States is at work and has been for a long time, actually since the birth of America. The effects of infiltration over the years and the acceptance of false doctrine are almost to complete fruition. [37, 50, 52, 425]

Religious deception has invaded every part of our lives, and one must contend for Truth. What is Truth? Jesus is Truth (John 14:6). Jesus is the Word (John 1:1). The Word is *TRUTH*. Today, there is a famine of the Word and an attempt to wear down the saints (Amos 8:11; Daniel 7:25). Just like there is an inundation of genetically modified food in the physical, there is a stream of polluted food in the spiritual, brought by false teachers with a false doctrine, and a spirit against Christ. Deception abounds. Jesus said, "I, [Truth], am not of this world" (John 8:23). As we research, we find *just about everything we have been taught from the world system has been a lie.*

James 4:4 says, "Ye adulterers and adulteresses, know ye not that the *friendship of the world is enmity with God?* Whosoever *therefore will be a friend of the world is the enemy of God."*

Church leadership today is infiltrated with hirelings who openly profess being Freemasons, witches, and sorcerers. Churches facilitate leading the world in the pagan traditions of men. Idolatry, perversion, and thievery are winked at (John 10:12-13). Why is there not an outcry from the people? Mostly because they want their own sins placated. Soon the mask of "goodly" things which have replaced "Godly" will be ripped off and hearts will be exposed as the husbandman comes *to REMOVE the tares* from the wheatfields. Only the true wheat will be left behind (Matthew 13:24-30). No matter how much wealth, education, and/or influence one has, everything that is hidden will soon be revealed (Luke 8:17). That which is evil will be destroyed (Psalm 37:38).

Many have neglected the Bible for a cellphone, which exhibits the false light of the world. Most do not even own a physical Bible. Just like the oral law was changed with the times, the Bible has been and is changing with the times. Carrying a Bible sends a message to those around. A Bible on the phone is controlled by those who own the application which can be changed at the stroke of a key. Almost no one would know because very few know the Word.

The version of Bibles being used is another form of deception. Many Bibles change the word(s), thus changing the meaning of the content, leaving out words and sometimes even entire verses. Others have witchcraft messages. Some passages in the *Message* Bible are based on the god, Hermes, Messenger of the gods. It contains the formula on which all forms of magic claim to function. The term *As Above, So Below* is a witchcraft oath that when read and spoken in the unclean verses declares a new age, mysticism message, meaning, the universe is the same as God, and God is the same as man. There are tarot cards with this witchcraft quote. Yet, many continue to use adulterated versions of the Bible in direct rebellion against God (Revelation 22:18-19).

Songs are sung about grace, love, and mercy, replacing the blood, redemption, repentance, sin, and hell. It's all about feeling good and being accepted and tolerated without accountability. Unlike the hymns and psalms, many modern songs contain chants violating the Word against vain repetition (Matthew 6:7).

Chanting is a **repeated rhythmic phrase that is sung in unison by a crowd.** In many traditions, chanting is used to induce mysticism. The National Library of Medicine depicts the most common characteristics of chanting, illustrating *how structural features of music,* belief systems, focused attention, and *behavioral aspects of chanting converge to induce mystical states*. Chanting incorporates attention, synchrony, rhythm, repetition, and belief so that the participant will experience mysticism. We must be very careful of the lyrics we hear and what we sing and chant in that we are not drawn into a mystical, occultic experience, mistaking it for spiritualism. [218]

Sermons are canned and often created by artificial intelligence. Teachers are not seeking, prostrate before God on their faces, waiting upon the Holy Spirit to reveal Truth and things they did not know. They are not waiting for a fresh revelation (John 14:26).

Children are taught from the Internet, with games and movies. They are not taught to seek the face of God and how to respond in times of turmoil and distress. We are experiencing the most mental health issues in history and man is turning to more confusion instead of to clarity and the sure foundation of Jesus Christ (1 Corinthians 14:33).

The church has neglected the Sunday night and weekday services for sports and other ecumenical commUNITY events. Union with Christ cannot be found. Time spent with Him is a chore to many. In Matthew 26:40, Jesus says, "And he cometh unto the disciples, and findeth them asleep, and saith unto Peter, What, *could ye not watch with me one hour?"*

Most churches have removed the altars and do not give altar calls anymore. Rarely do you see a church having a weekly prayer meeting. Why is this? Jesus says in Revelation 3:17, "Because you say, 'I am rich, **have become wealthy, and have need of nothing'**— and *do not know that you are wretched, miserable, poor, blind, and naked."*

As a result of the deception that has entered into the church, the leaven has leavened the whole lump. The false doctrine has spread here a little, there a little, and now only four percent of Gen Zs have a biblical worldview as the basis of their decision-making. This generation is more confused and headed to hell quicker than any other generation, maybe even worse than the days of Lot. [429]

This message is a cry to the remnant to get into the Word! *Know* the Word, *speak* the Word, *pray* the Word. Get rid of the humanistic approach of devotional and self-help books. Stop relying on messages from "spiritual" leaders, prophets, apostles and those in the media. Worship Jesus Christ in SPIRIT and in TRUTH (John 4:24). Separate yourself **FROM** the world and **TO** Christ. Spend time in the secret place. Cry out to the Lord for your deliverance, salvation for your families, and get a burden for a lost and dying world. Test every spirit to see if it is of God (1 John 1:4). <u>Those who are deceived will not be a part of the remnant.</u> **Take heed,** *that no one deceives you!*

Second Blood Moon Warning

Hear, O Israel: The Lord Our God Is One Lord

The lady at the cash register squinted her eyes as she held up the $100 bill to the light to see if it "looked right." Her lips twisted in a question as she rubbed the bill between her fingers, then snapped it several times to see if it "felt right." A line was forming, and some were impatient with her taking the time to examine for truth. Reluctantly, she gave in and accepted the bill. Apparently, she did not have a fraud detection pen to verify for truth, and now she was at risk of having accepted something in which she might lose in the end.

Standing in line, I kept busy by reading the signage posted in the Israeli shop. It proclaimed the common Israeli theme as posted throughout the Old City of Jerusalem, *"Three religions, one God"*. [1] I had a check in my spirit as I leaned in to read the fine print justifying this claim. It sounded true, but after prayer and research, I learned it was a very deceptive statement. The Lord had already given me the first warning after the blood moon experience, *"Take heed, that no one deceives you"* (Matthew 24:4). I soon realized this was a springboard to the second warning, *"Hear, O Israel, the Lord our God is One Lord"* (Deuteronomy 6:4; Mark 12:29). It was with great interest as I began to research and seek the Lord for the meaning of the new warning. The verse is in both the Old Testament and the New Testament.

Counterfeits of Satan

A COUNTERFEIT means to COPY or IMITATE something valuable, without authority or rights. The copy is made with the intention to deceive or defraud, by passing the copy or thing forged, as that which is original or genuine.

Satan has many counterfeits. Beware of the false light and false gods. Below is a table outlining a few of the ways Satan counterfeits Christ.

Characteristic	JESUS	SATAN
Jesus is **Light**	Then spake Jesus again unto them, saying, **I am the light of the world** (John 8:12).	And no marvel; for **Satan himself is transformed into an angel of light** (2 Corinthians 11:14).
Jesus has a **City**	And I John saw the **holy city, new Jerusalem**, coming down from God out of heaven, prepared as a **bride** adorned for her husband (Revelation 21:2).	Standing afar off for the fear of her torment, saying, Alas, alas, that **great city Babylon**, that mighty city! for in one hour is thy judgment come (Revelations 18:10).
Jesus is the **Star**	I Jesus have sent mine angel to testify unto you these things in the churches. I am the root and the offspring of David, and **the bright and morning star** (Revelation 22:16).	How art thou fallen from heaven, **O Lucifer, son of the morning [star]**! how art thou cut down to the ground, which didst weaken the nations! (Isaiah 14:12).
Jesus is the **Seed** (Offspring)	And I will put enmity between thee and the woman, and between **thy seed** and **her seed**; it shall bruise thy head, and thou shalt bruise his heel (Genesis 3:15).	
Jesus is a **Son**	Whosoever shall confess that **Jesus is the Son of God**, God dwelleth in	Let no man deceive you by any means: for that day shall not come, except there come a

	him, and he in God (1 John 4:15).	falling away first, and that man of sin be revealed, the **son of perdition (destruction)** (2 Thessalonians 2:3).
Jesus **has Power, Performs Miracles**	Then began he to upbraid the cities wherein most of his mighty works (**miracles**) were done, because they repented not (Matthew 11:20).	Even him, whose coming is after **the working of Satan with all power and signs and lying wonders** (2 Thessalonians 2:9).
Jesus has a **Mystery** (Secret)	Without question, **this is the great mystery of our faith:** Christ was revealed in a human body and vindicated by the Spirit. He was seen by angels and announced to the nations. He was believed in throughout the world and taken to heaven in glory. (1 Timothy 3:16).	For this **lawlessness is already at work secretly**, and it will remain secret until the one who is holding it back steps out of the way (2 Thessalonians 2:7).
Jesus has **Beauty, Perfection, Wisdom**	The LORD reigneth, he is clothed with **majesty**; the LORD is clothed with **strength** (Psalm 93:1). Be ye therefore **perfect**, even as your Father which is in heaven is perfect (Matthew 5:48). For the LORD giveth	Thine heart was lifted up because of thy **beauty**, thou hast corrupted thy **wisdom** by reason of thy **brightness** (Ezekiel 28:17).

	wisdom. (Proverbs 2:6).	
Jesus is a **Prince**	For unto us a child is born, unto us a son is given: and the government shall be upon his shoulder: and his name shall be called Wonderful, Counseller, The mighty God, The everlasting Father, The **Prince of Peace** (Isaiah 9:6). And from Jesus Christ, who is the faithful witness, and the first begotten of the dead, and **the prince of the kings of the earth** (Revelation 1:5).	for the **prince of this world** cometh, and hath nothing in me (John 14:30).
Jesus is a **Lion**	And one of the elders saith unto me, Weep not: behold, the **Lion of the tribe of Juda**, the Root of David, hath prevailed to open the book, and to loose the seven seals thereof (Revelation 5:5).	Be sober, be vigilant; because your adversary the devil, **as a roaring lion**, walketh about, seeking whom he may devour (1 Peter 5:8).
Jesus has a **Woman** (Wife)	And there came unto me one of the seven angels which had the seven vials full of the seven last plagues, and talked with me, saying, Come hither, I will shew thee **the bride, the Lamb's wife**	Upon her forehead *was* a name written, MYSTERY, BABYLON THE GREAT, THE **MOTHER OF HARLOTS** AND ABOMINATIONS OF

	(Revelation 21:9).	THE EARTH (Revelation 17:5).

Religions are intertwined with many ideologies that are counterfeits of truth. Often, we accept hook, line, and sinker what someone tells us, especially if the person has power, status, or influence. How could a "good" person(s) lead us in an "ungodly" path?

First, <u>we must assess our **connections** to the person</u>. Are we connected physically or emotionally, such as in a family or through influence to one such as an employer or pastor? Does the person have wealth, leadership, or are they admired in society?

Second, <u>what is the **social status** of the person presenting the information</u>? How can we know when something we are told or taught is true? We ask the Holy Spirit to guide us. The Word of God is our plumbline. His Word is Truth (John 17:17). When we know the Word, we are unshakeable. The Word is the lamp unto our feet and a light unto our path; straight, perfect, and true (Psalm 119:105). We must be connected to the Word on a daily basis. The Word must have top status and stand above all other authorities.

The quote "three religions, one God" insinuates that three major religions, Judaism, Christianity, and Islam, are under the domain of "one God". However, this is deceiving.

First, we note that not everyone has the same definition of Christianity. When the name "Christianity" is lumped with religion, the reference is usually to Catholicism, [4] which is not the same as Christianity. This will be discussed later in this book.

None of these three major religions are not considered under the umbrella of Christianity, even though they are all monotheistic religions, meaning they **each** have **one** God. Each of these religions worships a **different** God, and **none** of these three religions worships Jesus Christ as <u>the one and only true God</u>.

There is much deception and misunderstanding interwoven into the worldview, church doctrine, and belief systems. Many believe all religions lead to the same God; however, this is not biblical nor in alignment with the Word of God.

Judaism, Christianity, and Islam are often denoted as the "Abrahamic religions" with the false projection that all have descended from Abraham. [430, 431]

The expression "Abrahamic religions" originates from the Quran's (religious scripture of Islam) with repeated references to the "religion of Abraham." [29]

The "many or all religions, one God" concept is now integrated into the worldview through the churches as well as many global leadership organizations, ideologies, mandates, and movements. This ideology is being touted as the foundation for peace. You may be familiar with the examples below where this concept is being touted.

- Abraham Accords
- Abrahamic Family House
- The Third Temple
- Interfaith
- Coexistence
- Tolerance Trainings
- Diversity, Equity, and Inclusion
- Church Doctrines
- Government Control
- Education mandates
- Seminary Theology
- CommUNITY Events

False doctrines originate from the father of lies, the devil (John 8:44). These lies and assumptions have infiltrated our society, churches, education, entertainment, media, and heritage, making it almost impossible for those who are not in the Word to know "the Truth." Many just accept whatever someone tells them without studying to show themselves approved and rightly dividing the word of Truth (2 Timothy 2:15). Let's take a look at each of these examples to understand the connection to the global initiative to herd all toward the "Abrahamic religions."

The Abraham Accords

The Abraham Accords is a series of treaties normalizing diplomatic relations between Israel, the United Arab Emirates (UAE), Bahrain, Sudan, and Morocco. The agreements were facilitated by the U.S. Administration and are called "The Abraham Accords" in honor of Abraham, whom they recognize as the patriarch of Judaism, Christianity, and Islam. [29] I will leave the reader to his own opinion after reading this book and praying for the Holy Spirit's guidance in all Truth (John 16:13). I doubt that Abraham would approve of having his name connected to this effort.

On September 15, 2020, the official signing ceremony for the Abraham Accords was hosted by the United States at the White House.

The accords were signed by Bahraini foreign minister Abdullatif bin Rashid Al-Zayani and Emirati foreign minister Abdullah bin Zayed Al-Nahyan vis-à-vis and Israeli Prime Minister Benjamin Netanyahu. American President Donald Trump was the witness. They were negotiated by Trump's son-in-law and Senior Advisor Jared Kushner and Kushner's assistant Avi Berkowitz. [39]

On June 15, 2023, a special envoy bill passed the House of Representatives. The legislation called on the State Department to create an ambassador-level position. "The addition of a special envoy will be critical for bringing **Saudi Arabia** into the Accords and continuing to strengthen and expand them," stated Rep. Mike Lawler (R-N.Y.), who sponsored the bill. **"We are closer to a <u>lasting, long-term peace</u> in the Middle East than we have ever been."** [40]

We know there will not be a **lasting, long-term peace** until Jesus Christ returns. First Thessalonians 5:3 says, "For when they shall say, **peace and safety; then sudden destruction cometh** upon them, as travail upon a woman with child; and they shall not escape."

The Abrahamic Family House

The Abrahamic Family House is an interfaith complex located on Saadiyat Island in Abu Dhabi, United Arab Emirates. It hosts a synagogue, a mosque, and a church. Representing the **three religions, Judaism, Islam, and Catholicism** at these facilities are the Rabbi, Imam, and Pope. Followers of these religions must go through their representative to hear from their god. These leaders administer the Talmudic Law, Sharia Law, and Canon Law to those who are of these faiths. These laws incorporate oral law, mysticism, and traditions of men.

The idea for the Abrahamic Family House was born long before the signing of the Abraham Accords. In a first for the Middle East, an **interfaith complex** has been built in Abu Dhabi. Under one roof, the Abrahamic Family House provides a place of worship for the three "so-called" monotheistic (one God) religions: Christianity, Judaism, and Islam.

The announcement of the opening of the Abrahamic Family House was made on February 15, 2023, **the day after the blood moon experience**. The facility opened to the public on March 1, 2023.

The Third Temple

The Third Temple references the nonbiblical rebuilding of the defiled and destroyed temple of Solomon. The Temple Institute has launched a campaign to raise funds for plans of the temple, which, if built, it says, would "usher in **universal harmony**'." The organization has recreated the vessels to be used in a Third Temple, including a menorah which is located in Hurva Square, within the Jewish Quarter of Jerusalem's Old City. (*See Photo*). Priests are being trained and preparations were being made to sacrifice a red heifer on Passover, 2024. [220] However, this has yet to happen. I do not believe that God will allow it to happen. It would be an insult to our Savior and would trample His sacrifice.

"For it is not possible that the blood of bulls and of goats should take away sins" (Hebrews 10:4).

Those supporting the building of the temple believe it would "usher in a new era of **universal harmony and peace.**" (222)

This effort is supported by Freemasonry. Of all the objects which constitute the Masonic science of symbolism, the most important, the most cherished, by the Mason, and by far the most significant, is the Temple of Jerusalem. (221) This is affirmed in the Encyclopaedia of Freemasonry, Albert Mackey, MD, and Charles T. McClenachan, both of whom are 33rd degree Freemasons.

Interfaith

Whenever you see the word *interfaith*, it refers to relations with members of the "Abrahamic faiths." Some interfaith dialogues have included atheists, agnostics, humanists, and others with no religious faith but with ethical or philosophical beliefs. The intermixing of faiths is not a Biblical concept.

Interfaith can include secular agencies, chaplains, organizations, and events. Chaplains are being restrained from praying in the name of Jesus. (397) A driving quote behind the interfaith message is: "There will be no peace among the nations without **peace among the religions**. There will be no peace among the religions without dialogue among the religions." (223) We know peace comes only from Jesus Christ and Jesus spoke against religion and traditions of man (John 14:27).

Coexistence

You have probably seen the coexist symbol on bumper stickers and other places, representing the three "Abrahamic religions." It has the crescent moon representing Islam, the star of David representing Judaism, and the cross which most often represents Catholicism.

The word *coexistence* is often used to represent different religions existing together peacefully. This sounds like a wonderful concept.

"Why can't religions coexist peacefully?" The short answer is because the various religions are **each competing for the hearts and souls of men**. The very makeup of religious belief is restricted in that each religion makes claims about truth that are at odds with the claims of truth of other religions. [224]

Coexistence policies are established to help diminish escalating conflict between religions and politics. In reality, there may be an opposite effect. At some point, there could be an uprising, depending on the fairness shown toward each religion. For example, those who promote Jesus Christ are not shown the same tolerance as other religions. It is because there are many religions but only **two spirits**, Christ and antichrist.

Tolerance

The 1828 Webster's Dictionary said the word *tolerance* meant "the act of enduring." Today in the Merriam Webster Dictionary, the definition is much different. The new meaning is "sympathy or indulgence for beliefs or practices differing from or conflicting with one's own" or "the act of allowing something." [225]

Pressure to tolerate may mean that one must accept practices which do not align with their faith. **This hinders freedom of religion** for the individual. For example, if a parent is not comfortable with the education of their children in areas such as sexuality, they should not have to tolerate or allow these practices as taxpaying citizens. When parents are forced to comply with someone else's belief, it shows a lack of tolerance for the parents' religion by the other party, thus the conflict.

Diversity, Equity, and Inclusion

Diversity, equity, and inclusion (usually abbreviated DEI) are organizational frameworks which seek to promote "the fair treatment and **full participation of all people**." This spells CONTROL. The key point is, who are the groups defining these frameworks? What are their biases? Are the frameworks being developed to represent and consider Christian views as well? I hardly think so.

Diversity refers to gender, culture, ethnicity, religion, disability, class, age, and opinion. There are groups in charge who are controlling others to be "re-educated" on the opinions of the group. Those who are being "re-educated" are apparently not allowed to have their opinions as part of the definition.

Equity pertains to fairness and justice, especially in allocating resources. This draws a parallel to communism and socialism. Many think they want this, and while it may look good in theory, these ideologies are not why people are clamoring to get to America.

Inclusion is promoted as creating an atmosphere where everyone feels included and their voice is heard, yet those who stand for Christ are often marginalized.

While these have good points and are often areas of concern, we must be conscious of going too far in the opposite direction where God's laws are limited. While God is no respecter of persons, He has set an order for the church. When the world's definitions override the church and the government of God, then we have problems (Acts 10:34, Titus 2). [226]

Church Doctrine

For many churches, church doctrine is entangled with the traditions of man and the doctrine of the government. It has become evident over the last decade that church doctrine, which was once thought solid in alignment with the Word, has now separated from the Word to the world.

Across the board, regardless of denomination, most churches are under 501c3 guidelines. This regulation is deceptive. Religious bodies have been led to believe that they must have 501c3 status to be tax exempt. *This is a lie.* Rather, when a church acquires this status, **they have put limitations on themselves**. These limitations include the following for 501c3 churches: [107]

- Prohibition from supporting political candidates.
- Subjection to limits on lobbying.

- Violation of the 501c3 rules means a risk of losing tax-exempt status.
- An organization that loses its 501c3 status due to being engaged in political activities cannot subsequently qualify for 501c3 status.

These are deceptive muzzles on the church as a whole. The truth is that the annual federal gift tax exclusion allows an individual to give up to $17,000 each in 2023 to as many people as one wishes without those gifts counting against a $12.92 million lifetime exemption. [227] What this means is that one does not need 501c3 status in order to write off gifts to **individuals**. The 501c3 status provides a way for one to write off gifts which are not to individuals, but rather instead for gifts written to **churches**, such as to the 'First Baptist Church". Gifts to individuals, such as pastors, leaders, or others can be written off without the 501c3 status.

Government Control

In times past, society viewed government as being for the good of the people, especially in keeping peace. However, bad governance is producing anything put peace due to the struggle for global control in many areas such as information, technology, religion, money, food, medicine, and transportation. This global control is an effort to put in place the New World Order.

The New World Order has been surmised to be brought in through the plan involving "Order out of Chaos." Order out of Chaos is also the motto of the 33rd degree mason and is associated with LIGHT from DARKNESS. [229] This ideology is in direct conflict with the Word. John 1:5 says, "And the light shineth in darkness; and the darkness comprehended it not." Jesus was the light who **brought a new order** and his order was rejected.

The world is a dark place, but there is light in the realm of the spirit. We must stay in the light and walk in the light. First John 1:7 says, "But if we walk in the light, as he is in the light, we have fellowship one with another, and the blood of Jesus Christ his Son cleanseth us from all sin." **Those who unconditionally love God,**

walking by faith, will stay in the light in the time of gross darkness.

George Orwell wrote, "The price of order" always entails a handing over of control and loss of freedom on the part of the citizenry." It appears that his assessment can be seen in many situations, for example, the control of food consumption to force the eating of bugs. He says order out of chaos is a method of "creating chaos and then seizing power under the pretense of putting things back in order is a tried-and-true method of deception and manipulation." [228]

The Bible outlines this methodology as the strategy of the beast system where a one world government enforces a global worship and commerce (Revelation 13).

Education Mandates

According to the Merriam-Webster Dictionary, the word *reeducate* means "to train again; especially to rehabilitate through education." The goal of reeducation is to **change a mindset** to conform to a **new way** of thinking.

Education mandates are in every sector of the world system. Continuing education is set for government employees, teachers, and professionals. It is a requirement for anyone who wishes to stay licensed under the world's regulation system. It sets a standard.

Should an entity wish to change the mindset of their employees, they simply require mandatory training, and often new learning is tied to incentives. For example, in the educational system, the federal government uses a complex system of funding methods, policy directives, and significant power of the presidential platform to bully and shape what, how, and where students learn. [234] The Word says, "And be not conformed to this world: but be ye transformed by the renewing of your mind, that ye may prove what is that good, and acceptable, and perfect, will of God" (Romans 12:2).

Seminary Theology

Educational mandates flow into the seminaries where new age and emergent church doctrine and theology are taught.

Due to the education of seminary theology, church leaders are now more open to adopt the principles of **social justice**, liberation theology, and collective salvation. Some leaders also incorporate elements of Universalism, the Seeker-Friendly Movement, and even New Age Spirituality. [236]

Social justice means fair balance in the distribution of wealth, opportunities, and privileges within a society where individuals' rights are not recognized and protected. This is a **dangerous tightrope philosophy which might possibly lead to imprisonment** for having a politically incorrect or religious view. [235] Television and movies play a big role in reeducating the masses in this area. Many emergent churches will incorporate Hollywood into the message, such as *The Chosen* TV series or *The Purpose-Driven Life*. Nonbiblical doctrines, movies, and study guides are found in many churches.

Members of the emergent church movement often place a high value on good works or social activism, including missional living. This theology leads to a very liberal, loose translation of the Bible. This doctrine values experience more than truth. Truth becomes relative. Relativism opens all kinds of problems, as it destroys the standard that the Bible is the plumbline for absolute truth. [237]

CommUNITY Events

The word *ecumenical* refers to the concern with establishing or promoting unity among churches or religions. The Merriam-Webster Dictionary says it means, "promoting or tending toward **worldwide Christian unity** or cooperation." The 1828 Webster's Dictionary defines it as "**universal**." This concept is rooted in new age theology and in the religions of Catholicism and Judaism as well as Freemasonry ideology. The overall concept is that there are many ways to God.

Jesus said, "I am the way and the truth and the life. **No one comes to the Father except through me**" (John 14:6).

Loving and acknowledging others as individuals is one thing, but when it comes to walking in the Spirit, the Word says, "Can two walk together, unless they are agreed?" (Amos 3:3). Joining in unison with doctrines outside the doctrine of Christ is preparation for a one world religion and the New World Order is the antichrist system.

The doctrine of Christ is a personal, father-son relationship. The formalities of Christianity were founded by the Apostle Paul (Matthew 11:27).

There has been a fierce undermining of Biblical doctrine in the church in the last few decades. In the past, many of today's ecumenical stances would have been unacceptable. For example, the North Carolina state council of churches has joined with the LGBTQ movement, and they support bringing together Christians, Muslims, and Jews. [241]

The Bible warns us that today's most effective enemies of Christ are those who claim to be Christians but who instead have a counterfeit Christianity. Examples of Christian Ecumenical Movements are: Evangelicals and Catholics Together (ECT), the Pro-Life Movement, Promise Keepers, and Freemasonry.

The primary test is whether Jesus Christ is promoted as the ONLY way to God. Many who profess Christianity actually deny certain fundamentals of the faith as outlined in the Word, which is Truth. Another test is to assess the goal of the venture. Colossians 3:17 says, "Whatever you do, whether in word or deed, **do it all in the name of the Lord Jesus, giving thanks to God the Father <u>through him</u>**." The Gospel of Christ must be the main priority and Jesus must be glorified.

The Catholic Church promises salvation apart from the finished work of Christ on the cross. It has been reported that Promise Keeper founder Randall Terry is the latest Protestant pro-life activist to join the Roman Catholic Church. [239] The Roman Catholic and Mormon churches have officially declared that they find no conflict between Promise Keepers' teaching and their own doctrines. [17]

Most churches, schools, and government are run by Freemasons. [240] Freemasonry teaches there is salvation through all religions. "The true Mason is not creedbound. He realizes with the divine illumination of his lodge that as a Mason **his religion must be universal**: Christ, Buddha or Mohammed, the name means little, for he recognizes only the light and not the bearer. He worships at every shrine, bows before every altar, whether in temple, mosque or cathedral, realizing with his truer understanding the oneness of all spiritual truth." (Manly Palmer Hall, *The Lost Keys of Freemasonry*, p.65).

Albert Pike says, "Masonry is a search after Light. That search leads us directly back as you can see, to the Kabalah. In that ancient and little understood medley of absurdity and philosophy, **the Initiate will find the source of many doctrines . . .**" (Morals and Dogma, p. 741). [238]

Paul warns, "But I fear, lest by any means, **as the serpent beguiled Eve through his subtilty**, so your minds should be corrupted from the simplicity that is in Christ. For if he that cometh **preacheth another Jesus**, whom we have not preached, or **if ye receive another spirit**, which ye have not received, or another gospel, which ye have not accepted, ye might well bear with him" (2 Corinthians 11:3-4).

Now that you are aware of the many "doors" to the "Abrahamic" religions, we will find out who Abraham was and from there delve into each of the so-called "Abrahamic religions."

Who Was Abraham?

Genealogy

Abram was born in the Babylonian city of Ur of the Chaldeans [8, 199, p. 23] He was a Gentile, born into a family of moon worshippers and idolators. There were no Jews at that time. He was a non-Jew chosen by God to be the founder of the spiritual Jews.

Ur, also known as Babylon, was a day's journey from Bagdad, the capital of Iraq. [198, p. 3039] Physical Babylon in the Bible is modern day Iraq. Abram's racial background was Mesopotamian (Arabian), which is modern day Iraqi. [23, 198, p. 18]

Abram was a descendant of Noah's son, Shem. Noah had three sons, Ham, Shem, and Japheth. Semitic is a name used since the 1770s to refer to the **language** of those who currently live in West Asia, North and East Africa, and Malta. [279] Shem's descendants spoke the Semitic language.

The Canaanites were the descendants of Ham and were living in the land that God had promised to Abram. Ham had violated his father, Noah, by looking at his nakedness. As a result, his descendants were cursed. Shem and Japheth received Noah's blessing because they had covered their father's drunken nakedness. [201]

Abram's father was Terah. His brothers were Nahor and Haran, and his nephew was Lot.

Abram is a type of Christ. His story is a shadow of many other stories found later in the Bible. At the time of Abram's birth, Nimrod was King. Nimrod was the great grandson of Noah and grandson of Ham. Nimrod is a type of antichrist.

Nimrod was a mighty hunter with a rebellious, evil heart. He built the city of Babel in the land of Shinar or Babylon and was king over Babel. There he built the tower of *Babel*, which means "the gate of the gods" (Genesis 10, 11). [199, p. 203, 1579] But the one true God blew down the tower and brought **confusion** to the language.

Interestingly, the Chaldean tradition states the tower blew down during the Autumnal Equinox. [199, 203] The Autumnal Equinox is the two moments in the year when the sun is exactly above the equator and day and night are of equal length. In the Northern Hemisphere, the autumnal equinox falls on about September 22 or 23, and in the Southern Hemisphere occurs on March 20 or 21. [202]

Abram's father, Terah, was a prince of Nimrod's court. He was very great in the sight of the king and his subjects. The king and princes loved Terah, and they held him in high esteem.

The book of Jasher, a non-canonical Hebrew book, mentioned in the King James Bible (Joshua 10:13 and 2 Samuel 1:18) tells about the night Abram was born. It says in Jasher chapter eight, that all the servants of Terah, and all the wise men of Nimrod and his conjurors came and ate and drank in the house of Terah, and they rejoiced with him on that night. It says, "When all had come out from the house of Terah, they lifted up their eyes toward heaven to look at the stars, and they saw one very large star came from the east. They were astonished at the sight and understood the meaning.

And they said to each other, 'The child that has been born to Terah this night will grow up and be fruitful, and multiply, and possess all the earth, he and his children forever, and he and his seed will slay great kings, and inherit their lands.' They felt obligated to go and tell King Nimrod this news."

King Nimrod brought Terah before him and said, "Give me the child, that we may slay him before his evil springs up against us, and

I will give thee for his value, thy house full of silver and gold." In other words, King Nimrod was threatened by Baby Abram much like King Herod, who was also a type of antichrist, was threatened by Baby Jesus.

Terah asked for three days to consider the request. On the third day, Nimrod threatened Terah. He said, "Send me thy son for a price as I spoke to thee; and shouldst thou not do this, I will send and slay all thou hast in thy house, so that thou shalt not even have a dog remaining."

Terah took a child from one of his servants and took it to the king, **posing the child as Abram** and receiving money for him.

Jasher 8:34 says, **"And the Lord was with Terah in this matter, that Nimrod might not cause Abram's death,** and the king took the child from Terah and with all his might dashed his head to the ground, for he thought it had been Abram."

The text says, "Immediately Terah secretly took Abram, his mother, and his nurse and hid them in a cave and brought provisions to them until the king had forgotten the incident."

When Abram came out from the cave, he went to live with Noah and his son Shem, and he remained with them to learn the instruction of the Lord and his ways. **This is how Abram learned about the statutes, judgments, and ordinances of Jehovah God.**

Abram was in Noah's house thirty-nine years, and Abram knew Yehovah from three years old, and he went in the ways of Yehovah until the day of his death, as Noah and his son Shem had taught him." (Jasher 9:5-6) [197]

Abram **learned the instruction of Jehovah and His ways.** Abram served Noah and Shem, his son, for a long time. **It was from Shem that the holy line, the holy seed descended, Jesus**. [199, p. 1570]

In those days there was great transgression and rebellion against the Lord. They made and served gods of wood and stone, which could neither speak, hear, nor deliver.

Idol Worship

Abram's father, Terah, was an idol maker, and he worshipped many gods. [199, p. 23] He had twelve gods of favor. The gods were of large size, made of wood and stone after the twelve months of the year. He served each one monthly, and every month he would bring a meat offering and drink offering to his gods. [219]

Although Terah had thousands of other gods he worshipped, his primary god was Nanna, <u>the moon god</u>. He made many different gods from stone, brass, wood, iron, gold, silver. Abraham helped his father in the idol making shop.

In this wicked and perverse generation, Abram knew the Lord was with him for the Lord had given Abram an understanding heart. Abram had doubts about idol-worship and his father's business. He knew all the works of this generation were vain, and that all these gods were vain and were of no avail. [219]

Abram thought, *If my father is the maker of these idols, he is greater than the idol. Why don't people worship him instead of the idols?* Soon, he discovered that the gods of his father had no power. [6]

Ancient texts tell about an incident when Abram was watching his father's shop alone. He destroyed all of the idols in his father's shop, except the largest one, next to which he put a stick.

When his father returned, Terah was furious, and according to tradition, the exchange went something like this: "What happened here, Abram?" his father demanded.

Abram replied with, "Well, the big idol got angry at all the other idols, and he destroyed them."

To which his father answered, "That's impossible. He doesn't move. It's just stone."

"Exactly, Father," Abram said. "It is only a stone. There is but one true God." [41]

The Apocalypse of Abraham [42] describes an experience with God from Abram's childhood similar to what happened with Samuel. It has a connection to the directive God later gave Abram in Genesis 12 to leave his family.

The ancient text says, "And it came to pass while I spake thus to my father Terah in the court of my house, there cometh down the voice of the Mighty One from heaven in a fiery cloud burst, saying and crying: "ABRAHAM, ABRAHAM!" And I said, "Here am I."

And He said: "Thou art seeking in the understanding of thine heart the God of Gods and the Creator. I am He. Go out from thy father Terah, and get thee out of the house, that thou also be not slain in the sins of thy father's house."

"And I went out. And it came to pass when I went out, that before I succeeded in getting out in front of the door of the door of the court, there came a sound of great thunder and burnt him and his house, and everything whatsoever in his house, down to the ground forty cubits."

This happened in Ur. Ur means fire. Fire is often the element God uses for judgment. Fire is what God says will burn up this world in judgment in the last day.

"But the heavens and the earth, which are now, by the same word are kept in store, reserved unto **fire** against **the day of judgment** and perdition of ungodly men . . . But the day of the Lord will come as a thief in the night; in the which the heavens shall pass away with a great noise, and **the elements shall melt with fervent heat**, the earth also and the works that are therein shall **be burned up** . . . Looking for and hasting unto the coming of the day of God, wherein **the heavens being on fire** shall be dissolved, and the elements shall **melt with fervent heat**? Nevertheless we, according to his **promise**, look for new heavens and a new earth, wherein dwelleth **righteousness**" (2 Peter 3:7,10, 12-13).

As with Abram, our focus must remain not on what is, but what is to come. Abram's focus was not on the things of this world, but rather "he looked for a city which hath foundations, whose builder and maker is God" (Hebrews 11:10).

Physical Babylon

Ur of Babylon, Canaan, also known as Palestine, and Haran, was where Abram grew up. "Canaan" refers to an area encompassing all of Palestine and Syria.

Abram lived during the time of period of 1996 BC to 1821 BC. [207] The Apostle Paul was still speaking about Abraham in 63 AD, over 2000 years after Abraham died. It is estimated that Abraham died around 1942 BC. [209]

Babylon was the capital city of the southern Mesopotamia region. Babylonians were scholars in the study of astronomy. The temple in Babylon was crowned by an astronomical observatory where the stars could be studied. This temple was built by King Nimrod and later finished by King Nebuchadnezzar. [199, p. 203]

The god, Sin, was the Mesopotamian god representing the moon. The city of Ur where Abram was born, was presided over by the moon-god, Sin. [198, p. 1337, 199, p. 1692]

Sin's lunar character refers to the **CRESCENT**. (Wow! A connection to the blood moon sighting?) In Mesopotamian art, **Sin's symbol was the crescent.** His daughter was Ishtar. Ishtar was the ancient Mesopotamian goddess of love, war, and fertility. She is also associated with beauty, sex, divine law, and political power. [200] Ishtar is the god of **Easter. Ishtar is transgender**. [242]

Haran was the name of Abram's uncle, Lot's father. Haran died in Ur of the Chaldeans, the land of his birth, while his father, Terah, was still living. Meanwhile, Abram and his brother, Nahor, both married. The name of Abram's wife was Sarai, and the name of Nahor's wife was Milcah (Genesis 11:27-29). Abram became a surrogate father to Lot, son of Haran.

Abram and his father left Ur (Babylon) and settled in the land of Haran where Sin was the seat of worship.

"And Terah took Abram his son, and Lot the son of Haran his son's son, and Sarai his daughter in law, his son Abram's wife; and they went forth with them from Ur of the Chaldees, to go into the land of Canaan; and they came unto Haran and dwelt there" (Genesis 11:31).

The Call and the Covenant

God put a call on Abram's life. The call included a command for Abram to leave **his country** and **his family** to go to a land where God would lead.

"Now the LORD had said unto Abram, Get thee out of thy **country**, and from thy **kindred**, and from thy father's house, unto a land that I will shew thee: And I will make of thee a great nation, and I will bless thee, and make thy name great; and thou shalt be a blessing: And I will bless them that bless thee [ABRAM], and curse him that curseth thee [ABRAM]: and in thee **shall <u>all families</u> of the earth be blessed** (Genesis 12:1-3).

This important promise consists of two parts, one **temporal** and one **spiritual**. The temporal was the promise of posterity, blessing, and becoming the founder of a great nation. The spiritual was that Abraham was the chosen ancestor of the Redeemer, and **<u>through</u> <u>CHRIST</u>** the blessings would be extended to **<u>all the families</u> of the earth**. The implied condition on his part was that he should publicly profess the worship of the true God. We see this demonstrated often as Abraham built altars to Jehovah. [199, p. 24]

This Genesis promise is known as the **Abrahamic Covenant**. The Abrahamic Covenant was an **unconditional** covenant that God made with **Abram**. In this covenant God defined **His people**, who would later be called **Israel**. Jesus is the seed of Abraham (Galatians 3:16). Those who believe on Jesus are his people (Romans 2:28-29).

The promise is for **all who will to possess.** Paul tells us in Romans 4:13-17, "For the promise, that he should be the heir of the world, was not to Abraham, or to his seed, through the law, but through **the righteousness of faith.**

"Therefore it is of faith (not the Rothschild's nation of Israel as misinterpreted by many), that it might be by grace; to the end the promise might be sure **to all the seed**; not to that only which is of the law, but to that also which is of the **faith** of Abraham; **who is the father of us all,** As it is written, I have made thee a father of many nations,) before him whom he believed, even God, who quickeneth the dead, **and calleth those things which be not as though they were."**

God announced **all the heirs** of the future before they were born. He declared those of us who have faith in Jesus Christ as God **before we were born to a part of his promise to Abraham!**

Esaias also crieth concerning Israel, "Though the number of the children of Israel be as the sand of the sea, **a remnant shall be saved**" (Romans 9:27).

"And it shall come to pass, that **whosoever** shall call on the name of the LORD shall be delivered: for in mount Zion (the spiritual city of God, (199, p. 1751) and in Jerusalem shall be deliverance, as the LORD hath said, and in the **remnant** whom the LORD shall call" (Joel 2:32).

Abraham and his seed are accounted to God through **righteousness** of **faith** (Romans 4:3, 9, 13, Galatians 3:6, James 2:23).

Righteousness means "holiness, justice, obedience, integrity, and purity." Examples of unrighteousness are outlined in 1 Corinthians 6:9-10. Paul said, "Know ye not that **the unrighteous** shall not inherit the kingdom of God? Be not deceived: neither fornicators, nor idolaters, nor adulterers, nor effeminate, nor abusers of themselves with mankind, Nor thieves, nor covetous, nor drunkards, nor revilers, nor extortioners, shall inherit the kingdom of God."

Faith means "a heart issue, a frame of mind, resting in God, confidence in Him, a humble trust, to commit the keeping of our souls into His hands, His ability and willingness to save us." [199, p. 646-647] "Now the Spirit speaketh expressly, that in the latter times some shall depart from the faith, giving heed to seducing spirits, and doctrines of devils" (1 Timothy 4:1).

The Scriptures tell us, "Abraham believed God, and God counted him as righteous **because of his faith**" (Genesis 15:6). Abraham kept his focus on the spiritual and eternal. Genesis 11:10 says, "For he [Abram] looked for a city which hath foundations, whose builder and maker is God."

Abraham is the father of physical Israel, the children of God. He provided an example to us to **separate from his physical family** who had the baggage of moon worship and idolatry. We see this command echoed to all of us in the New Testament by the Apostle Paul.

"Therefore, **come out from among unbelievers,** and **separate** yourselves from them, says the LORD. Don't touch their filthy things, and I will welcome you. And I will be your Father, and you will be my sons and daughters, says the LORD Almighty" (2 Corinthians 6:17-18).

The condition to be a part of the **Israel of God** is to separate from the world to God. The promise of **blessing** is unconditional to those who have faith in Jesus Christ.

Separation is sanctification. Sanctification is a requirement to be in the family of God. Hebrews 2:11 states, "For both He who **sanctifies** [is separated] and those who are **sanctified** [separated] are all from one Father; for which reason He is not ashamed to call them brethren [brothers]." God will not allow those with a heart for sin in His family.

The Seven Separations of Abraham

Following are seven separations God called Abram to make in order to come into full obedience and blessing. My uncle, Dr. Kelley Varner, a world-renowned Bible teacher, preached this message many years ago when I was much younger in my walk with the Lord. As I got into the research for this book and started researching who Abram was and his background, God reminded me of this teaching. I have paraphrased it the way I learned it from his teaching. His message of this subject can be found on YouTube. He passed away fifteen years ago, but much of what he wrote and taught is relevant to the hour in which we live. [246]

Separate from Country

Every time we obey the Holy Spirit in separating from the world, we will grow in our spiritual life. When God calls us out of our way to His way, and we obey, He will raise the bar and challenge us to even greater separations.

The first separation that Abram was asked to make was, **"Leave your country."** How many people would be willing to leave their country? How important is your country to you? Is it an idol? Could you leave it if God commanded you to do so?

A country has: boundaries, limitations, surroundings, and familiarity. It provides a comfort zone, and many, of course, have their national pride.

Babylon was the country that Abram had to leave. He was born and raised in Ur of the Chaldees, which is in modern Iraq. Ur was ruled by the Chaldean Dynasty of Babylon.

Ur of the Chaldees was a place where the focal point was trade. It was the center of a wealthy empire that drew traders from as far away as the Mediterranean Sea, which was 750 miles to the west and 1500 miles to the east. A massive, stepped pyramid rises above the city and still dominates the landscape today.

The word *Chaldean* more often referred to **a social class** of highly educated people than to a race of men. At that time, Chaldees was the commercial capital of the highly developed civilization.

During the time of Abram, it is believed that about 60,000 people lived in Ur (2000 BC). Recent digs have found large factories producing wool clothes and carpets with evidence they were exported abroad. [206]

It was a city **full of idolatry** and **moon worshiping**. Ruins have included masks of Humbaba, a Mesopotamian demon associated with giants. [205]

The Apostle Paul tells us in 1 Corinthians 10:14 to flee idolatry. "Wherefore, my dearly beloved, flee from idolatry." **What exactly is idolatry?**

Paul defines it for us in Colossians 3:5-6 and tells us what happens when we participate in this evil. He says, "Mortify therefore your members which are upon the earth; **fornication, uncleanness, inordinate affection, evil concupiscence, and covetousness, <u>which is idolatry</u>**: For which things' sake <u>the wrath of God cometh on the children of disobedience</u>."

Idolatry and sensuality are generally associated. Hosea 3:1 says, "Then said the LORD unto me, Go yet, love a woman beloved of her friend, yet **an adulteress**, according to the love of the LORD toward the children of Israel, who **look to other gods**, and love flagons of wine."

We learn more about Babylon from the Book of Daniel. Daniel was from the tribe of Judea (the same tribe as Jesus) and was taken captive to Babylon around 605 BC for seventy years. [208] At the time of Daniel, Babylon was the intellectual center of western Asia. Daniel talks about the Chaldeans. He says in Daniel 4:7, "Then came in the **magicians, the astrologers, the Chaldeans**, and the soothsayers: and I told the dream before them; but they did not make known unto me the interpretation thereof." The Chaldeans were influential and highly sophisticated. Evidently there were historical records handed down to Daniel from the time of Abram (over 1600 years).

Daniel said the Chaldeans were connected **to science** and that they had great influence over the King of Babylon in Daniel's time. He describes them as "Children in whom was **no blemish, but well favored,** and **skillful** in all **wisdom**, and **cunning in knowledge**, and **understanding science**, and such as had ability in them to stand in the king's palace, and whom they might teach the learning and the **tongue of the Chaldeans**" (Daniel 1:4).

He went on to write that the Chaldeans influenced Nebuchadnezzar's decision to throw Shadrach, Meshach, and Abednego into the fiery furnace. "Wherefore **at that time certain Chaldeans came near and accused the Jews.** There are certain Jews whom thou hast set over the affairs of the province of Babylon, Shadrach, Meshach, and Abednego; these men, O king, have not regarded thee: they serve not thy gods, nor worship the golden image which thou hast set up" (Daniel 3:8,12).

The word *Chaldean* became synonymous for **Babylon**, and we see many verses in Scripture where the word *Chaldean* was used to refer to Babylonians in general. Babylon in the Strong's Concordance refers to Babel, meaning **confusion** (by **mixing**) (Fear + Confusion = Controllable). **Does this sound like today's society?** The church has mixed the world with Christianity and many Christians are full of **fear** and **confusion**. This puts them in a state where they are controlled by every **wind** of doctrine (Ephesians 4:14) such as the doctrine of men (Colossians 2:22), the doctrine of **devils** (1 Timothy 4:1), doctrine of the **Pharisees and Sadducees** (Matthew 16:12), doctrine of **Balaam** (Revelation 2:14), doctrine of the **Nicolaitans** (Revelation 2:15) and/or **strange** doctrines (Hebrews 13:9).

The confusion of modern-day Babylon will soon see the mighty hand of God just as Isaiah warned in Isaiah 13:9. "And Babylon, the glory of kingdoms, the beauty of the Chaldees' excellency, **shall be as when God overthrew Sodom and Gomorrah.**"

Isaiah goes on to warn the <u>**Israel of God**</u> to flee from those who practice idolatry in Isaiah 48:1, "Go ye forth of Babylon, **flee ye from the Chaldeans**, with a voice of singing declare ye, tell this, utter it even to the end of the earth; say ye, The LORD hath redeemed his servant Jacob." The children of God are the **Israel of God. Jacob is Israel. Jesus (the seed) is Israel.**

This warning regarding idolatry continues in the New Testament. Revelation 17:5-6 says, "And upon her forehead was a name written, MYSTERY, **BABYLON THE GREAT**, THE MOTHER OF HARLOTS AND **ABOMINATIONS OF THE EARTH**. And I saw the woman drunken with the blood of the saints, and with the blood of the martyrs of Jesus: and when I saw her, I wondered with great admiration." [16]

The word *woman* in the Bible refers to the church (Ephesians 5:23). An interpretation of this verse could be that **the church** will be responsible for the **true saints** being martyred. How could this be? **Every wind of doctrine brings confusion.** John tells us in John 16:2, "**They shall put you <u>out of the synagogues</u>: yea, the time cometh, that whosoever killeth you <u>will think that he doeth God service.</u>**"

Abram received the calling to leave his country, but he did not initiate the leaving – his dad did! This is recorded in Genesis 11:31. "And Terah took Abram his son, and Lot the son of Haran his son's son, and Sarai his daughter in law, his son Abram's wife; and they went forth with them from Ur of the Chaldees, to go into the land of Canaan; and they came unto Haran and dwelt there."

Abram **half listened**. He had left his country as God instructed, but his relatives, his father's house went with him. Dad and his nephew would become key players in his journey.

Abram should have only taken his wife, as they were one flesh. The command was for him to **leave his family** as recorded in both the Old and New Testament (Genesis and Acts). Sarai, his wife, had a major role to play in God's plan.

"For this cause shall a man leave his father and mother, and cleave to his wife; And they twain shall be **one flesh**: so then they are no more twain, but one flesh. What therefore God hath joined together, let not man put asunder" (Mark 10:7-9).

His father Terah headed for the land of **Canaan**, but instead they stopped at **Haran** and "settled there." There were many issues as a result of Abram following his earthly father. The word *Terah* means **Loiterer**. Terah caused Abram to delay his calling and delayed the journey by stopping at Haran. Have you ever intended to do something, but instead you settled for something else?

See, God's call on Abram's life was never Dad's calling. Dad stopped the family journey and settled for a place just as wicked as **Ur**. Could it be possible Dad stopped at Haran because his son who died was named Haran? Could it be that Dad was controlled by his emotions or thoughts of his dead son?

Haran as a land means "parched, mountaineer." Haran was very similar to the city of Ur. It was where the **Temple of Sin** was located. It was also a city where the Moon god was worshipped. It was a place like they had just left, **full of idolatry**.

Abram's days in Haran were wasted days, delayed days, and useless days. They were days outside of God's plan. His family was a hindrance to the plan of God and the call on his life. As long as we cling to the life *we* want to live, we will not live the life that God wants us to live.

Terah, Abram's father, died in Haran (Genesis 11:32). After Terah's death, God once again instructed Abram to go. There were seven promises in Genesis 12:2-3 God made **to Abram** if he would obey. They were:

1. I will make of thee a great nation.
2. I will bless thee.
3. I will make thy name great.
4. Thou shalt be a blessing.
5. I will bless them that bless thee.
6. I will curse him that curseth thee.
7. In thee shall **all families** of the earth be blessed.

Satan may have whispered to Abram, "If you would have stayed in the land of Ur of the Chaldees, you would have inherited your family's business. You could have depended on the wealth of your father. You would not need to trust God. It would have been easier." But **God separated Abram from the land of idolatry to the Kingdom of His Son**, to a place of freedom, **away from the bondage of sin.**

We must not put limitations and boundaries on God. So many in our nation are touching and partaking in unclean things, but God is **calling us out of a land of idolatry**. We must separate from the world and unto Him.

Below are sample personal questions one might ask in order to test for idolatry in our lives.

1. How much time, attention, and money goes into this diversion?
2. What is my passion, intensity of devotion, and depth of my loyalty?
3. At what expense do I put this diversion above other things?
4. Am I willing to step back from my diversion and question my loyalty?
5. Where is the line drawn between interest and worship?
6. How does my diversion align with the Bible?
7. What do I advertise publicly through my behavior, clothing, and emblems?

8. When I put my diversion in comparison to Jesus Christ in time, attention, money, and interest, what is first?
9. What are the effects of my devotion to my diversion?
10. How does the diversion affect my relationship with Christ and others?

Paul tells us in 2 Corinthians 13:5-6, "Examine yourselves as to whether you are in the faith. Test yourselves. Do you not know yourselves, that Jesus Christ is **in you**? —unless indeed you are disqualified. "

Separate from Family

Most likely one of the most difficult separations Abram had to make was when God told him to **separate from his kindred** in Genesis 12:1. The word *kindred* means: nativity or birthplace, lineage, offspring, or family.

The direct order to Abram from God was "Leave your family." Who was Abram's family?

Jesus answered this question when His family tried to keep him with them rather than going about His call in the ministry.

This incident is recorded in Mark 3:31-35. Jesus' mother and brothers came to see him. They stood outside and sent word for him to come out and talk with them. There was a crowd sitting around Jesus, and someone said, "Your mother and your brothers are outside asking for you."

Jesus replied, "Who is my mother? Who are my brothers?" Then He looked at those around him and said, "Look, these are my mother and brothers. **Anyone who does God's will is my brother and sister and mother."**

We see another example when Ruth left her family for the calling of ministry. Ruth represents the church and Boaz represents Jesus.

"Then she [Ruth] fell on her face, and bowed herself to the ground, and said unto him [Boaz], Why have I found grace in thine eyes, that thou shouldest take knowledge of me, seeing I am a stranger? And Boaz answered and said unto her, It hath fully been shewed me, all that thou hast done unto thy mother in law since the death of thine husband: and **how thou hast left thy father and thy mother, and the land of thy nativity, and art come unto a people which thou knewest not heretofore. The LORD recompense thy work, and a full reward be given thee of the LORD God of Israel, under whose wings thou art come to trust"** (Ruth 2:10-12).

Psalm 45:10 presents a royal wedding song calling us **away from our family and into our father's house**. "Hearken, O daughter, and consider, and incline thine ear; **forget also thine own people, and thy father's house**. So shall the king greatly desire thy beauty: **for he is thy Lord**; and **worship thou him**."

We addressed Abram's father, Terah. Terah was an idol worshipper. His lifestyle put **a generational curse** on his family. Later in the generations, Joshua sought to break the generational curse of Terah. He urged the people to make a clean break from their pagan heritage.

"And Joshua said unto all the people, Thus saith the LORD God of Israel, Your fathers dwelt on the other side of the flood in old time, **even Terah, the father of Abraham, and the father of Nachor: and they served other gods**…Now therefore fear the LORD, and serve him in sincerity and in truth: and **put away the gods which your fathers served** on the other side of the flood, and in Egypt; and serve ye the LORD" (Joshua 24:2, 14).

Because Abram followed in the footsteps of his father, **his calling was delayed.** God called Abram AWAY from his father and his gods. When God calls, we have to be willing to leave behind that which causes us to procrastinate or delay or STOP or SETTLE, even if it is our family.

Nahor, the name of Abram's brother, means "one who snorts or blocks vision or is critical of others." Often our family members do not share the vision that God has given us. We have to **separate ourselves from criticism** so that our vision will not be blocked, and we can move forward in clarity. It was a blessing that Nahor was not on Abram's journey. Later I will address the issues of having Lot, his nephew, along on the journey.

After Terah's' death, Abram set out as God commanded, away from the darkness of idolatry, out of the country where he was confined within the boundaries of a system of darkness.

"Abram departed [Haran], as the LORD had spoken unto him; **and Lot went with him**: and Abram was seventy and five years old when he departed out of Haran" (Genesis 12:4).

Abram was still unwilling to give up his nephew, Lot. He also hung onto his wealth, his livestock and all the people he had taken into his household at Haran. He had a lot of BAGGAGE!

Abram had become very rich in Haran. Genesis 12:5 goes on to say, "And Abram took Sarai his wife, and Lot his brother's son, and **all their substance that they had gathered, and the souls that they had gotten in Haran**; and they went forth to go into the land of Canaan; and into the land of Canaan, they came."

Abram had acquired servants and wealth. Acquiring wealth doesn't necessarily mean it came from God; in this case it was acquired **outside of the will of God**.

One might imagine neighbors, servants, and other family members taunting Abram as he started out. **"Where are you going, Abram?"** "I don't know"; **"What will you find when you get there?"** - "I don't know"; **"What will you do when you get there?"** - "I don't know." **Taking the step of FAITH is where righteousness is** (Romans 4:9).

Abram and his entourage headed for the land of Canaan. When they arrived in Canaan, Abram traveled through the land as far as Shechem. There he set up camp beside the oak of Moreh. At that time, the area was inhabited by Canaanites.

Then the LORD appeared to Abram in Genesis 12:7 and said, "Unto **thy seed** [**JESUS**] will I give this land." Abram built his first altar there and dedicated it to the LORD, who had appeared to him. After that, Abram traveled south and PITCHED HIS TENT in the hill country, with Bethel to the west and Ai to the east. There he built another altar and dedicated it to the LORD, and he worshipped the LORD. Then Abram continued traveling south by stages toward the Negev (Genesis 12:6-8; 13:3).

This is the first recorded altar that was built to Jehovah and the first on Abram's journey. It's interesting that **Abram had to let go of his earthly father to embrace his heavenly Father**. In contrast, Jesus left his heavenly Father to go to His earthly father, Joseph.

Abram's altars were built on pagan lands. This is an example for God's people to raise up a standard on enemy territory. Abram was going to possess land, Canaan (Palestine), that was inhabited by a cursed people who were his relatives. Canaan was where Jerusalem was. **Physical Jerusalem was birthed from the land of Canaan or Palestine**, a neighbor of the Ishmaelites.

"Thus saith the Lord GOD unto Jerusalem; **Thy birth and thy nativity is of the land of Canaan**; thy father was an Amorite, [Giants – Amos 2:9] and thy mother an Hittite [Tribes of Canaan who sold the tomb at Hebron to Abraham, Cave of Machpelah] (Genesis 23:7-9). And **as for thy nativity**, in the day thou wast born thy navel was not cut, neither wast thou washed in water to supple thee; thou wast not salted at all, nor swaddled at all" (Ezekiel 16:1).

Abram built his second altar between *Bethel* which means the "house of God" and Hai, which means "heap of ruins". Lot is still with him.

Genesis 12:8-9 says, "And he removed from thence unto a mountain on the east of Bethel, and pitched his tent, having Bethel on the west, and Hai on the east: and there he builded an altar unto the LORD, and called upon the name of the LORD."

The three sons of Noah were still alive when the call of God came to Abram. Interestingly, God had Noah **take his family with him** on the ark, and Abram was called to **separate from his family**.

We may not always understand why God calls one to one purpose and another for another purpose. The important thing is to be open to God's personal call on our lives.

Noah's calling was a calling of **salvation**. He was to enter the ark. It was the right thing to bring the whole family. Unsaved people can come along when we are under the calling of salvation. That is a calling **for all people**.

Abram's calling was a calling of **ministry**. He was to enter the land of Canaan. It was wrong to bring the whole family. Unsaved people or those without a calling cannot come along with us in our calling of **ministry**. That is an **individual calling**.

"But without **faith** it is impossible to please him: for he that cometh to God must believe that he is, and that he is a rewarder of them that diligently seek him.

By **faith** Noah, being warned of God of things not seen as yet, moved with fear, prepared an ark to the **saving** of his house; by the which he condemned the world, and became heir of the righteousness which is by faith.

By **faith** Abram, when he was called to go out into a place which he should after receive for an **inheritance**, obeyed; and he went out, not knowing whither he went" (Hebrews 11:6-8.

Abram was **the first person** to be called a Hebrew (Genesis 14:13), and **the first person** to **worship one God**, YAHWEH or Jehovah. YAHWEH means, "self-existent or eternal." [9] Colossians 1:16 says, "For **by him [JESUS] were all things created**, that are in heaven, and that are in earth, visible and invisible, whether they be thrones, or dominions, or principalities, or powers: all things were created by him, and for him."

We can think of Abram as the halfway mark from Adam to Jesus. There are approximately 2,000 years from Adam to Abram and 2,000 years from Abram to Jesus.

God put Adam here to start a family and rule with God in the earth, but Adam's family was put out of the garden of Eden because of sin. Adam's family could not go back to the garden of Eden until the last Adam (Jesus) came. *Eden* means paradise.

We need to leave Adam's family by dying to it (SIN) and taking on a new family with a new name, Jesus, who is the last Adam. (1 Corinthians 15:45).

With a new name and new family, we can enter back into Paradise. Luke 23:43 says, "Verily I (Jesus) say unto thee (thief on the cross), **today thou shalt be with me in paradise."**

Paul tells us in Romans 8:15, "You received God's Spirit when he adopted you as his own children. Now we call him, 'Abba, Father.' For **his Spirit joins with our spirit to affirm that we are God's children**. And since we are his children, we are his heirs." Jesus, the **last** Adam, represents the **spiritual** family; the **first** Adam represents the **physical** family.

Jesus adopted us into His spiritual family and freed us from the bonds of our physical families Galatians 4:4-5 says, "But when the right time came, God sent his Son, born of a woman, subject to the law. God sent him to buy freedom for us who were slaves to the law, so that he could adopt us as his very own children." In the **physical** we are bound to this **world**, but when we are born of the **Spirit**, and live and walk in the Spirit with **Christ**, we have freedom from the chains of sin.

Again, in Ephesians 1:5, our adoption into the family of Jesus through Jesus is confirmed. "God decided in advance **to adopt us into his own family** by bringing us to himself **through Jesus Christ**."

This adoption **separates** us from the physical world and its bondage to sin. We have a command to separate **from** the world and **to** Christ. Second Corinthians 6:17-18 says, "Wherefore come out from among them, and **be ye separate**, saith the Lord, and **touch not** the **unclean thing**; and I will <u>receive you</u>, and will <u>be a Father unto you</u>, and ye shall be my **sons** and **daughters**, saith the Lord Almighty."

Abram started out as a follower of his **earthly** father, but thankfully ended up being a follower of his **heavenly** Father. His critical life decisions set an example for us and became the pattern for separation. Paul tells us in Colossians 1:13-15 we are to leave the place of darkness and come into the kingdom of God.

As children of God, **we are Abram's kin** and <u>heirs to the same promises</u>. Galatians 3:9 says, "And now that you belong to Christ, **you are the true children of Abraham**. You are his heirs, and **God's promise to Abraham belongs to you.**"

A country has boundary lines; we must likewise set physical and spiritual boundaries. We must determine that "I WILL NOT LET **ANYTHING** KEEP ME FROM GOD." The only place that is boundary free is our relationship with God. We must not set boundaries or limitations on God. He can take us to places we never believed we would have gone.

A family has ties. We must break any ties or constraints that separate us from God. We must determine, "I WILL NOT LET **ANYONE** KEEP ME FROM GOD."

Stephen testified of Abram's journey in Acts 7:2. He said, "Brothers and fathers, listen to me. Our glory of our God appeared to our ancestor **Abraham in Mesopotamia** before he settled in Haran. God told him, 'Leave your native **land** and your **relatives**, and come into the land that I will show you.' So **Abraham left the land of the Chaldeans** and lived in Haran until his father died. Then God brought him here to the land where you now live."

Abram kept his mind set forward and did not look back. Hebrews 11:8-10 says, "<u>By faith</u> **Abraham obeyed** when **he was called to go out to the place** which he would receive as an inheritance. **And he went out, not knowing where he was going**. <u>By faith</u> he dwelt in the land of promise as in a foreign country, dwelling in tents with Isaac and Jacob, the heirs with him of the same promise; **for he waited for the city which has foundations, whose builder and maker is God. "**

Abram was looking for a new country. He would have a new family and soon God would give him a new name. Abram was on a journey. Abram was walking in the Spirit in a physical world. He had a **mind of separation**. He separated from his past, moved forward, not knowing where he was going, but waiting on God to give him what he could never obtain in a world of idolatry.

Separate from the World

God separated Abram **from** the land of idolatry **to** God, **to** the kingdom of His Son, **to** freedom. God separated Abram **from** his earthly family **to** the family of God.

Abram's journey took him to and from Egypt. **Egypt represents the world.** Abram went to Egypt due to a famine being in the land. Instead of turning to God, Abram turned to the world to solve his problem. While Abram was in Egypt, God had to intervene for Abram to save the Holy Seed. Abram ended up in a situation of **fear**, which caused him to **lie**. He almost lost his wife, Sarai, in Egypt. Through Sarai the holy seed was to come. In addition, he picked up the servant woman, Hagar, the bondwoman, which represents the beast system.

Jesus said in Matthew 4:4, "It is written, 'Man shall not live by bread alone, but by every word that proceedeth out of the mouth of God.'" Abram had to feed his family and instead of turning to God to supply his need, he went *DOWN* into Egypt. Anytime we turn to the world, we will go down spiritually.

God did not tell Abram to go down to Egypt. The story is in Genesis 12:10, "And there was a famine in the land: and Abram went *DOWN* into Egypt to sojourn there; for the famine was grievous in the land. And it came to pass, when he was come near to enter into Egypt, that he said unto Sarai his wife, Behold now, I know that thou art a fair woman to look upon: Therefore it shall come to pass, when the Egyptians shall see thee, that they shall say, This is his wife: and they will kill me but they will save thee alive."

If the Egyptians knew that Abram and Sarai were married, then the Egyptians might conclude that the only way to have Sarai for themselves was to kill Abram. However, if the Egyptians thought that Abram and Sarai were siblings, then the Egyptians would have no reason to kill Abram.

Fear of being a target of the Egyptians (the world) set in with Abram and then he compensated, covering himself by telling a half-truth. Abram said, "Say, I pray thee, **thou art my sister**" (Gensis 12:13). Uh, oh, *half-truths are lies*. **Lies** and **deception** go hand in hand. Getting caught up in lies makes one the tail and not the head. "The prophet that teacheth lies, he is the tail" (Isaiah 9:15). Lying puts us out from under the umbrella of God's protection.

Abram continued, "**But they will save thee alive** for thy sake; and **my soul shall live because of thee.**" This in turn leads to Abram thinking about himself. When one turns their attention to the world, the focus becomes about me, me, me. See how when fear was present, the situation escalated?

This was the influence of Satan. John 8:44 says, "He [Satan] is a liar and the father of lies."

"And it came to pass, that, when Abram was come into Egypt, the Egyptians beheld the woman, Sarai, that she was very fair. The princes also of Pharaoh saw her and commended her before Pharaoh: and **the woman was taken into Pharaoh's house. And he entreated Abram well for her sake**" (Genesis 12:14-16).

At this point, Abram received a *very nice pay-off for his wife*. Sarai was taken into the king's house. Pharaoh was looked at as the "god of Egypt." He was a type of Satan, the prince and the god of this world. The Egyptians believed that Pharaoh was the "key" to the cosmic gods of the universe. He was deemed to be the son of the Canaan god, Ra, and the incarnation of their god Horus. They believed Horus provided protection through Pharaoh for the people. Pharaoh's word was law and he owned everything. The people were slaves to the system. [443]

Pharaoh's actions of bringing Sarai into his palace showed he honored Sarai more than Abram. The Word goes on to say that Abram was given "sheep, and oxen, and he asses, and menservants, and maidservants, [*Here comes Hagar, the bondwoman!*] and she asses, and camels" (Genesis 12:16).

So now God had to intercept for Abram and Sarai as the holy seed was at risk. They had a call on their lives and Abram had led them to a point of jeopardy. Thankfully, God's protection brought him and Sarai back, but there would be **lifelong consequences** that continue to affect all mankind.

"And the Lord plagued Pharaoh and his house with great plagues **because** of Sarai, Abram's wife" (Genesis 12:17).

God intercepted Abram's lie on Sarai's behalf to *save the seed*! God sent plagues to Pharoah after Sarai was brought into his palace. This made Pharoah realize something wasn't right. God intercepted Abram's lie by sending the plagues in order to save Sarai from the intentions of Pharaoh. Pharaoh did not appreciate the lie Abram had told him.

"And Pharaoh called Abram, and said, 'What is this that thou hast done unto me? why didst thou not tell me that she was thy wife? Why saidst thou, 'She is my sister?' so I might have taken her to me to wife: now therefore behold thy wife, take her, and go thy way.' And Pharaoh commanded his men concerning him: and **they sent him away, and his wife, and all that he had"** (Genesis 12:18-20).

"And Abram went *UP* out of Egypt, he, and his wife, and all that he had, and Lot with him, into the south" (Genesis 13:1).

Abram was the first recorded rich man. "And Abram was **very rich** in cattle, in silver, and in gold. And he went on his journeys from the south even to Bethel, unto the place where his tent had been **at the beginning** between Bethel and Hai; unto the **place of the altar**, which he had made there at the first: and there Abram **called on the name of the Lord"** (Genesis 13:1-4).

Abram had to go back to his starting point and **start all over with God**. When we turn to the world, and God rescues us, we need to make an altar, get on our knees, call on the name of the Lord, and thank Him for His protection, grace, and mercy.

Abram identified as a pilgrim by two invariable symbols: a tent and an altar. We need to be able to move when God commands. There are no altars or praying that have been recorded as taking place in Egypt. Abram had to move out of Egypt and return to a place where he could worship His Lord.

The Bible is full of types and shadows. Abram is a type of both God the Father and Jesus. God and Jesus are one. Jesus said in John 10:30, "The Father and I are one."

We as believers in Jesus Christ are the children of Abraham. We are the children of God. Paul said, "For Abraham is the father **of all who believe**" Romans 4:16b, and in Galatians 3:29, "And now that you belong to Christ, **you are the true children of Abraham**. You are his heirs, and **God's promise to Abraham belongs to you.**"

Sarai had a major role in the promise given to Abraham. She would give birth to Isaac and in Isaac would be the seed to the lineage to Christ (Romans 9:7; Hebrews 11:18).

Sarai was an important woman in the Bible. She represents the freewoman. She is a type of the church, an example of the New Jerusalem. Galatians 4:22-26 says, "For it is written, that Abraham had two sons, the one by a **bondmaid**, the other by a **freewoman**. But he who was of the bondwoman was born after the flesh; but he of the freewoman was by promise. Which things are symbolic: for these are the two covenants; the one from the mount Sinai, which gendereth to bondage, which is Hagar? For this Hagar is mount Sinai in Arabia, and answereth to **Jerusalem which now is, and is in bondage with her children. But Jerusalem which is above is free, which is the mother of us all.**"

Jesus is the husband of the church. The church are those whose hope is in Jesus Christ.

"For a husband is the head of his wife as Christ is the head of the church. He is the Savior of his body, the church"(Ephesians 5:23). This scripture could be interpreted as: For a husband [**Abram**] is the head of his wife [**Sarai**] as Christ [**Jesus**] is the head of the church [those **who hope** in Christ]. He [**Christ**] is the Savior of his body [**Woman** came from **man**], the church [**Woman**, those who hope in **Christ**].

"So the LORD God caused the man to fall into a deep sleep. While the man slept, the LORD God took out one of the man's ribs and closed up the opening. Then the LORD God made a woman from the rib, and he brought her to the man" (Genesis 2:21-22).

"This explains why a man leaves his father and mother and is joined to his wife, and the **two are united into one**. Since they are **no longer two but one**, let no one split apart what God has joined together" (Mark 10:7-9).

Jesus is the Head and the Bridegroom (Man) and the Church is the Body and soon to be the Bride (Woman).

One may look at John the Baptist as the best man at the wedding. John said, "A man can receive nothing, except it be given him from heaven. Ye yourselves bear me witness, that I said, **I am not the Christ, but that I am sent before him**. He that hath the bride is the bridegroom: **but the friend of the bridegroom, which standeth and heareth him, rejoiceth greatly because of the bridegroom's voice**: this my joy therefore is fulfilled. He must increase, but I must decrease" (John 3:27-30).

Christ is the **Savior** of the body. What is a Savior? This is what the husband (Christ) is to the church (those who hope in Christ).

The word, *Savior,* means "to save, keep safe and sound, to rescue from danger or destruction, to make well, to restore health, to deliver from penalties of Messianic judgment."

Abram was to be the Savior of Sarai, but he listened to the wrong Father when he went *down* to Egypt and turned to the world to meet his needs. Abram put his wife in danger and risked the promise and the seed.

Remember Satan is a liar and the father of lies (John 8:44b). A number of commentators blame Abram for receiving booty at Sarai's expense, based upon clear deceit, and then for not returning it when his trick was discovered. Many believe this is evidence of Abram's pagan background, the old man, showing through.

Abram lied about his wife for **self-preservation**. He decided if he had Sarai pose as his sister, the Egyptians would not kill him. Abram had already been promised a son by God. Did he lose his faith while in the world? One thing we know; he picked up Hagar, the future mother of Ishmael, the bondwoman, while in Egypt.

Abram was to remain in the land of Canaan. He failed this test when he went down to Egypt. Some commentaries say that the Jews from this point afterward always looked to Egypt (the world) for help instead of God. Abram had set a standard that was **passed down**. He did it **his way.** He became an example. As we know, often the bad example becomes prominent and remains in our heritage.

John says, "Love not the world, neither the things that are in the world. If any man love the world, the love of the Father is not in him. For all that is in the world, the lust of the flesh, and the lust of the eyes, and the pride of life, is not of the Father, but is of the world" (1 John 2:15-16).

"Is not of the Father" means it does not come from Christ, and is not on His side, but **stands in opposition to Him**. He created the world and gave it to men to be used in His service, not to be abused as the minister of fleshly lust.

"Is of the world" refers to something which comes from the world as the nourisher of earthly lust. It is opposed to God and His service. It is antichrist.

"Lust of the flesh" means feeding the desires of the body, such as sexual appetites and food. Satan tried this temptation on Jesus. The need and desire for physical food (famine) is what drew Abram down to Egypt (the world).

Then the devil said to him [Jesus], "If thou be the Son of God, command this stone that it be made bread" (Luke 4:3).

"Lust of the eyes" means feeding on the outward things of the world: wealth, greed, or to gaze upon.

"And the devil, taking him [Jesus] up into an high mountain, shewed unto him all the kingdoms of the world **in a moment of**

time. And the devil said unto him, 'All this power will I give thee, and the glory of them: for that is delivered unto me; and to whomsoever I will I give it'" (Luke 4:5-6).

I believe Satan showed Jesus Rome at that **moment in time**, as it was the kingdom of the physical world and spiritual Babylon. One can stand on Palatine Hill in Rome (palace, hill of royalty) and look out over the physical remains of a kingdom that once stood. It is an example of the world system that will be brought to nothing (1 John 5:8). (*See Photo*).

"Pride of Life" means power and selfish ambition.

"And he [Satan] brought him [Jesus] to Jerusalem, and set him on a pinnacle of the temple, and said unto him, If thou be the Son of God, cast thyself down from hence: For it is written, He shall give his angels charge over thee, to keep thee: And in their hands they shall bear thee up, lest at any time thou dash thy foot against a stone" (Luke 4:9-11).

"And when the woman saw that the tree was **good for food**, and that it was **pleasant to the eyes**, and a tree to be **desired to make one wise**, she took of the fruit thereof, and did eat, and gave also unto her husband with her; and he did eat" (Genesis 3:6).

It appears no harm was done by Abram going down to Egypt. There was no **immediate** consequence to his disobedience. He was still very wealthy in livestock and in silver and gold. However, Sarai and the Holy Seed were put at risk in Egypt. Interestingly, Abram did not have to go through any hardship. As a matter of fact, he came out with **more** servants and **all** his possessions.

Have you ever strayed from God and things worked out well, and maybe you even came out ahead and you said, "See God actually blessed me," although deep down you know you disobeyed God? Hidden beneath the "blessings" is a worldly attachment that will bring a curse or bondage to your family and lineage.

Abram going down to Egypt was a big mistake, and it altered **God's plan**. Hagar, a female servant, came back with Sarai from Egypt. We will discuss the consequences that remain today later in this book. Sometimes, we do not realize the damage we cause by our disobedience.

When we are in a famine of life, we must first seek guidance from God or we may end up going down to Egypt and picking up a Hagar, a bondwoman.

Genesis 13:2-4 shows **redemption** for Abram. He *started over* and *repented*. The experience was not wasted. He learned something, and he **set an example** for us to turn to God for redemption when we make wrong choices. When we turn to the world before turning to God, we need to back up, start over, humble ourselves, thank God for His protection, and repent.

Abram and Paul had the same mindset. Paul said in Hebrews 3:13-14, "Brethren, I do not count myself to have apprehended; but one thing I do, **forgetting those things which are behind** and **reaching forward to those things which are ahead**, I press toward the goal for the prize of the upward call of God in Christ Jesus."

Separate from Co-Dependents

Have you ever had a family member who made your life difficult? Lot was that family member to Abram. Lot was a long-term problem. Abram was emotionally connected to Lot. It was hard for Abram to let go of Lot and his problems. Lot was the monkey on Abram's back.

Remember, Egypt represented the world. Lot represented a worldly faith. Lot believed in **profit** more than **principle**. Because of his covetousness, Lot lost his testimony, he lost his family, and he lost his character. [210]

Lot and Abram were both wealthy. Genesis 13:5-18 outlines the strife that came between Abram's herdsmen and Lot's herdsmen. This strife eventually forced Abram to separate from Lot. Let's take a look at this situation.

The wealth of Lot and Abram came between them to the point where they could no longer live together.

"And Lot also, which went with Abram, had flocks, and herds, and tents. And the land was not able to bear them, that they might dwell together: **for their substance was great, so that they could not dwell together**" (Genesis 13:5-6).

Abram and Lot had "too much stuff!" The more we have, the more it can cause problems. It's easy to get attached **to the things** we have and soon it will cause a separation **from God** and possible problems in the family.

In Hebrews 12:1 Paul tells us, "Let us lay aside **every weight**, and the sin which doth so easily beset us, and let us run with patience the race that is set before us." Abram and Lot's things became weights that would soon easily beset Lot.

The land could not bear them both and all of their "baggage." Abram could not live with Lot. Lot was walking after the flesh. His actions indicated that deep in his heart he wanted to turn back to his idols.

Lot couldn't care less about the promise of God; he was just along for the ride. If his uncle Abram prospered, he prospered. When the famine came (Genesis 12:10), Lot went down in Egypt with Abram. He went along for what he could get out of it.

There are a lot of Christians like Lot. They are only Christians for what they can get out of the Christian experience. They want to be blessed, healed, saved, and filled with the Holy Spirit, but buried in their heart is a lust for Sodom. How do we know this? When we separate from them, their hearts are exposed.

Having Lot along brought strife. There was too much "baggage" between them, and it caused arguments.

"And there was a strife between the herdmen of Abram's cattle and the herdmen of Lot's cattle: and the Canaanite [PEDDLER] and the Perizzite [VILLAGE PEOPLE] dwelled then in the land. And **Abram said** unto Lot, **Let there be no strife**, I pray thee, between me and thee, and between my herdmen and thy herdmen; for we be brethren [RELATIVES]" (Genesis 13:7-8).

Unsaved people (heathen) in the area were watching Abram and Lot to see us how they handled their conflict. Likewise, the unsaved are watching how Christians resolve their conflicts.

Proverbs 28:25 says, "A greedy man stirs up strife, but the one who trusts in the LORD will be enriched."

Abram was unselfish and wanted the strife to end. Lot was greedy. Abram gave Lot the opportunity to take his choice of the land.

"Is not the whole land before thee? **separate thyself, I pray thee, from me:** if thou wilt take the left hand, then I will go to the right; or if thou depart to the right hand, then I will go to the left. And Lot lifted up his eyes, and **beheld** all the plain of Jordan, that it was well watered everywhere, before the LORD destroyed Sodom and Gomorrah, even as the garden of the LORD, like the land of Egypt, as thou comest unto Zoar" [Insignificance, Dead Sea] (Genesis 13:9-10).

Essentially Abram said to Lot, "Let us not fight, nor let our friends fight because of us and our baggage, because we are family."

Abram gave Lot the first choice. He asked him, "What would you like to have, Lot? You take what you want, and I'll take what's left."

Lot looked out over the land with his **senses**. He lifted up his eyes and gazed on what **looked** the best. He was a flesh man. He was walking after sight (flesh) instead of faith.

Matthew 6:22-23 says, "The light of the body is the **eye: if therefore thine eye be single,** thy whole body shall be **full of light**. But if thine eye be evil, thy whole body shall be full of darkness. If therefore the light that is in thee be darkness, how great is that darkness!"

Lot was looking at the lush, green grass. You've heard the saying, "The grass is always greener." He wanted the best for himself. He chose Sodom and Gomorrah, a place that ended up losing its vitality, blessing, and fruitfulness.

"Then Lot chose him all the plain of Jordan; and Lot journeyed east: and they separated themselves the one from the other. Abram dwelled in the land of Canaan, and Lot dwelled in the cities of the plain, and pitched his tent toward Sodom" [A place of BURNING] (Genesis 13:11-12).

Lot *beheld* the territory. The lust of the eyes, his flesh, was the basis for his choice. He was walking in the *physical* instead of the *spiritual*. Lot did not pray about his decision.

First John 2:15-16, says, "Love not the world, neither the things that are in the world. If any man love the world, the love of the Father is not in him. For all that is in the world, **the lust of the flesh**, and **the lust of the eyes**, and the **pride of life**, is not of the Father, **but is of the world.**"

Lust of the eyes is feeding on the outward things of the world, wealth and greed. Lot gazed upon the land and chose with his eyes and heart. Abram and Lot were not spiritual kindred! Abram walked by **faith** (spiritual) and Lot walked by **sight** (physical).

Hebrews 11:8, says, "**By faith** Abraham, when he was called to go out into a place which he should after receive for an inheritance, obeyed; and he went out, not knowing whither he went."

Lot chose the plain with the greenest grass. Abram and Lot separated. Lot journeyed east. East was toward Hai, the "Heap of Ruins." Abram went west, built an altar, and called upon the name of the Lord.

"And he [Abram] journeyed unto a mountain on the east of Bethel, and pitched his tent, having Bethel on the west, and Hai [HEAP OF RUINS] on the east: and there he built an altar unto the LORD, and called upon the name of the LORD" (Genesis 12:8).

Lot made a *choice* to live in Sodom. Lot represents people who are not interested in serving God with their whole hearts. He looked to what was pleasing to the eye. When given a choice, many pick the closest thing to Babylon. Babylon is the *seat of idolatry, confusion*.

Like Abram, Lot was born in Babylon. But **unlike** Abram, Lot could not leave Babylon behind. Lot chose something that was familiar to him. He chose Sodom. Sodom resembled Babylon.

Something that looks good may be in reality a heap of ruins. Remember, where the grass is greener indicates where the septic tank is! Lot pitched his tent toward Sodom because that is where he wanted to go all the time. Lot *chose* Sodom [BURNING] that would become a burning heap of ruins.

This is where we get our word *sodomy*. It was where the familiar Babylonian spirits were. Like Abram, Lot's family ancestry was idol making and idol worship. The difference was Lot chose to continue in the path of his heritage. Abram chose the call of God.

What do you think the churches were like in Sodom? Do you think Lot became an elder in a church that supported homosexuality?

"But the men of Sodom were wicked and sinners before the LORD exceedingly. And the LORD said unto Abram, after that Lot was separated from him, Lift up now thine eyes, and look from the place where thou art northward, and southward, and eastward, and westward" (this included what Lot had just chosen) (Genesis 13:13-14).

Joshua 24:15 says, "But if serving the LORD seems undesirable to you, then choose for yourselves this day whom you will serve, whether **the gods your ancestors served** beyond the Euphrates, or the gods of the Amorites, in whose land you are living. **But as for me and my household, we will serve the LORD."**

Paul said in Romans 1:24-27, "So **God abandoned them to do whatever shameful things their hearts desired.** As a result, they did vile and degrading things with each other's bodies. They traded the truth about God for a lie. So they worshiped and served the things God created instead of the Creator himself, who is worthy of eternal praise! Amen. That is why God abandoned them to their shameful desires. Even the women turned against the natural way to have sex and instead indulged in sex with each other. And the men, instead of having normal sexual relations with women, **burned** with lust for each other. Men did shameful things with other men, and as a result of this sin, they suffered within themselves the penalty they deserved."

Lot *dwelt* [SETTLED, ESTABLISHED, HAD HABITATION] in Sodom. He lived there. Lot wanted to be with the wicked and the sinners. **No altars or praying was ever recorded in Sodom.**

Separation brings **revelation**. After Abram had the courage to separate from Lot, God said, "Abram, look all around, all the land you see is yours and your seed.

"For all the land which thou seest, to thee will I give it, and to thy seed forever. And I will make thy seed as the dust of the earth: so that if a man can number the dust of the earth, then shall thy seed also be numbered" (Genesis 13:15-16).

The land God showed Abram included the land Lot had chosen. **Abram would possess all of it.** Satan is the god of this *world*; but the *earth* belongs to the Lord, and we are joint heirs (1 Peter 3:7) with Christ in ownership of the earth.

God told Abram to "Arise and walk through the land." The land wasn't his yet, but **God had him walk it and claim it.**

"Arise, walk through the land in the length of it and in the breadth of it; for I will give it unto thee. Then Abram removed his tent and came and dwelt in the plain of Mamre [STRENGTH], which is in Hebron, and built there an altar unto the LORD" (Genesis 13:17-18).

Abram built an altar. Separation brought revelation, and **revelation** brought Abram to **worship.**

Have you ever heard anyone say, "I have 'a lot' on me." or "I'm going through 'a lot.'"? I can imagine that must be how Abram felt. However, Abram brought Lot with him when God had specifically commanded him to leave his kindred behind.

Lot became Abram's baggage. Often our baggage is rooted in family members to whom we are emotionally tied. This is called codependency. We may say, "I love him" or "I feel sorry for him." However, a "LOT" will keep you from your divine destiny. We can't bring our "lots" to the place where we have been called by God.

Timothy tells us, "For **there is one God**, and **one mediator** also between God and men, the man Christ Jesus" (1 Timothy 2:5).

Our relationship with Christ is **vertical**. Our relationship with others is **horizontal**. We must test our relationships, whether it be marriage, friends, business. Some possible questions to answer about our relationships include:

- Does this relationship stimulate, provoke, or correct me?
- Is it a Godly relationship?
- Are the people that I am in relationship with "yes" people, men pleasers or God pleasers?

Lot's relationship with God was primarily through his Uncle Abram. He was dependent upon his uncle to maintain his relationship with God. We cannot have a relationship through anyone else. It must be a personal relationship.

Often people will respond to the question, "Are you a Christian?" with "My daddy was a preacher." This is the same concept. However, we must know Him personally for ourselves. Our family members cannot get us to the throne room. We cannot get to God through anyone other than Jesus. Abram had a direct connection to God. Even though Jesus had not come in the flesh yet, Jesus was in every step of the plan (Genesis 22:13).

Lot represents the carnal or **pertaining to the flesh**. Christian carnal co-dependent relationships are draining and are a distraction.

Lot represents a relationship that Jesus didn't arrange. He was on Abram's journey due to human sympathy. His dad had died, and he wanted to hang with his uncle, and his uncle could not refuse him.

Lot knew God through his uncle. He was riding on his uncle's coat strings, but that will only take one so far.

So, what happened to Lot? After Lot moved to Sodom, we find that he held an important job in the sinful city.

Genesis 19:1 says, "And there came two angels to Sodom at even; **and Lot sat in the gate of Sodom**: and Lot seeing them rose up to meet them; and he bowed himself with his face toward the ground."

The gate of a city is often where the elders and leaders of a town would gather to discuss the issues of the day. His seat in the city gate also was a place where he would welcome visitors. This shows that Lot clearly held a place of importance in Sodom. It speaks volumes about Lot's relationship to the culture he chose to live in. Those who openly challenged the sins of Sodom would not have been respected enough to sit at the city gate.

Paul says in 2 Timothy 3:4-5, "[For men will be] **lovers of pleasures more than lovers of God; Having a form of godliness, but denying the power thereof:** from such turn away."

The sinful culture chosen by Lot led his daughters to deceive their father into drunkenness and incest.

"And they made their father drink wine that night: and the firstborn went in and lay with her father; and he perceived not when she lay down, nor when she arose. And it came to pass on the morrow, that the firstborn said unto the younger, Behold, **I lay yesternight with my father**: let us make him drink wine this night also; and **go thou in, and lie with him**, that we may preserve seed of our father. And they **made their father drink wine** that night also: and the younger arose, and lay with him; and he perceived not when she lay down, nor when she arose. Thus were **both the daughters of Lot with child by their father**" (Genesis 19:33-36).

The Moabite people came from the eldest daughter, and the Ammonites came from the youngest daughter.

"And the **firstborn** bare a son, and called his name Moab: the same is the father of the **Moabites** unto this day. And the **younger**, she also bare a son, and called his name Benammi: the same is the father of the children of **Ammon** unto this day" (Genesis 19:37-38).

The god of the Moabites and the Ammonites was the sun god, **Baal**. The Moabites called Baal **Chemosh**. The Ammonites called it **Moloch**. The worship of this god was **introduced into Jerusalem** by **Solomon** and abolished by King Josiah of Judah, but later crept back in.

"Then did **Solomon build a high place for Chemosh**, the abomination of Moab, in the hill that is before Jerusalem, and **for Molech**, the abomination of the children of Ammon. And likewise, did he for all his strange wives, which burnt incense and sacrificed unto their gods" (1 Kings 11:7-8).

Akeldama is a valley outside the old city of Jerusalem. (*See Photo*). It is known as the place where children were sacrificed during the times of King Solomon, and where Judas Iscariot hanged himself after selling Jesus for thirty pieces of silver. It was identified as a place of hell on earth [233] (Jeremiah 19:1-6; Acts 1:19).

The pagan god Molech required his devotees to toss their children into his fiery belly as an act of worship. [211] Molech has been associated with human abortion for thousands of years. The Bible warned the Israelites repeatedly to have nothing to do with Molech, "You shall not give any of your children to offer them to Molech, and so profane the name of your God: I am the Lord" (Leviticus 18:21).

And yet, Solomon and other kings continued to revere or fear this horrible god. His statues were repeatedly put on display in "the high places" (1 Kings 12:31), or places regularly visited by ancient day tourists. This statute is still honored by many.

From Autumn 2019 to March 29, 2020, a large statute of the Canaanite god Molech was on display at the Roman Colosseum (232). The Roman Colosseum is where many early Christians were slaughtered at the hands of the Roman emperor. (*See Photo*).

The Roman Colosseum is one of the new Seven Wonders of the World. After the Romans *destroyed Jerusalem* and the Second Temple in 70 AD, they brought many of the Jews back to Rome and made them slaves.

It is estimated that 60,000 to 100,000 Jewish slaves were employed in the construction of the Colosseum. After the Romans conquered Jerusalem, *Christians* had a choice to either sacrifice to the Roman gods or die. Many were eaten by lions or killed by gladiators at the **Colosseum**.

It is believed St. Ignatius of Antioch was the first Christian who died in the Colosseum. He was saved under St. John, and Peter and Paul made him the first bishop of the church in Antioch. He chose to die for his religion in front of tens of thousands of people. He was eaten by lions.

"And it came to pass, that a whole year they assembled themselves with the church, and taught much people. And **the disciples were called Christians first in Antioch**" (Acts 11:26).

About 3,000 Christian martyrs in all died in the Colosseum.

With the fall of the Jewish state in Jerusalem, the Sadducean party disappeared as there was no more opportunity for politics. As of this day, the Pharisees have remained, carrying on the traditions of Judaism. [198]

The Catholic church previously recognized the Colosseum as a sacred site to honor the Christians who were martyred there for their faith. The church placed Stations of the Cross inside the Colosseum as a reminder. Placing the Molech statue, a symbol of the sacrifice of children, at the entrance, was not a welcome sight for Christians. [211]

This promotion of evil is an abomination Often we may shrug off or not speak up when evil is elevated. Often it is because of laziness, but some people are like Lot. Buried in their hearts is a lust for Sodom and the idol worship they left.

If there were no heaven to gain or hell to avoid, how many still serve Christ? If there were no eternal damnation, many would live the evil in their hearts outwardly. Serving God is a life insurance plan for many.

One of the main hindrances to the gospel of the kingdom is the hypocrisy of those in the church who have a form of godliness on the outside but buried in their hearts is lust for Sodom.

We have to separate from those who have the character of Lot. Lot represents those Christians who are walking after the flesh.

Abram was a faith man. Faith is a spiritual force; faith goes beyond the flesh; faith goes beyond the natural senses; faith calls those things which are not as though they are.

While living in Sodom, Lot ended up in a situation where he was seized by four kings.

Genesis 13:12-13 says, "Lot dwelled in the cities of the plain, and pitched his tent toward Sodom. But the **men of Sodom were wicked** and sinners before the LORD exceedingly."

We usually end up living where we pitch our tents. Lot pitched his tent among the sinners and the wicked. He ended up needing Abram's help to get out. Four kings went to war and ended up kidnapping Lot and all his belongings during the combat.

"And the vale of Siddim [SALT SEA] was full of slimepits; and the kings of Sodom and Gomorrah fled, and fell there; and they that remained fled to the mountain. And they took all the goods of Sodom and Gomorrah, and all their victuals, and went their way. **And they took Lot, Abram's brother's son, who dwelt in Sodom, and his goods, and departed"** (Genesis 14:10-12).

Jesus said if a man seeks his life, he will lose it. If he loses it, he will find it. Lot lusted after the things of the flesh and lost it all.

Separate from the Love of Money

When Abram found out about Lot's kidnapping situation, he gathered an army together to go in and rescue Lot and *all of the goods*.

"And there came one that had escaped, and told Abram the Hebrew; for he dwelt in the plain of Mamre the Amorite, brother of

Eshcol, and brother of Aner: and these were confederate with Abram. And when Abram heard that his brother was taken captive, he armed his trained servants, born in his own house, three hundred and eighteen, and pursued them unto Dan. And he divided himself against them, he and his servants, by night, and smote them, and pursued them unto Hobah, which is on the left hand of Damascus. **And he brought back all the goods, and also brought again his brother Lot, and his goods, and the women also, and the people"** (Genesis 14:13-16).

Abram defeated five heathen kings of Sodom and Gomorrah and all of their armies were taken out. Abram got the booty. He was a rich man to begin with, but now he was a *very rich* man.

This brings us to another characteristic of Abram. He did not love money! One doesn't have to have money to love it, but Abram had it. What would you do if God brought you into unlimited finances? Would you tithe, give an offering, help widows, orphans, or the poor?

Abram did not have a love of material possessions and money. He was spiritually minded instead of money minded. Paul tells us in 1 Timothy 6:10, "For the love of money is the root of all evil: which while some coveted after, they have erred from the faith, and pierced themselves through with many sorrows."

The king of Sodom and **Melchizedek** king of **Salem** met with Abram after his victory. Melchizedek brought forth **bread and wine.** He was the **priest of the most high God. He blessed Abram** and said, **"Blessed be Abram** of the most high God**, possessor of heaven and earth**. And blessed be the most high God, which hath delivered thine enemies into thy hand." And **Abram gave Melchizedek tithes of all** that he had taken [booty from the war]" (Genesis 14:18-20).

This was the first recorded meeting in Jerusalem. **It was the first Passover meal**. Abram and Melchizedek, king of Salem, partook of bread and wine representing the **Holy Seed, Jesus**. The last Passover meal was with Jesus, King of Israel, and His disciples in Jerusalem in the upper room, representing the **Seed of Abraham, Jesus**.

Then the king of Sodom made Abram an offer. He suggested to Abram that he keep the booty from his successful raid. "He said unto Abram, 'Give me the persons, and take the goods to thyself'' However, Abram refused. He said to the king of Sodom, 'I have lift up mine hand unto the LORD, the most high God, the possessor of heaven and earth, That I will not take from a thread even to a shoelatchet, and **that I will not take any thing that is thine, lest thou shouldest say, I have made Abram rich**. Save only that which the young men have eaten, and the portion of the men which went with me, Aner, Eshcol, and Mamre; let them take their portion'" (Genesis 14:21-24).

Sodom's offer to share the spoils from the battle with Abram was unlike Melchizedek, in that he brought no blessing with him. If Abram were to accept this offer, the king of Sodom could enhance his reputation, claiming that he enriched Abram.

Abram said, "No way, I don't belong to anybody." Abram separated from a *desire* to get wealth and be connected to the evil King of Sodom. Abram's separation was not from wealth itself or God's plan to make him wealthy, but rather he separated from **the desire for** or **the love of money.**

Abram **refused to take support** from the King of Sodom. Most preachers can be bought. There are those who try to take control of the church through finance. Many churches have been bought off through government programs and partnerships. The way **to Christ** and the **way out of the world** cannot be bought. Financial influence should not dictate what is preached.

What would you do if someone offered you wealth? Would you conform to the world and compromise or stay true to God?

What did Abram do? He said, "I have lift up mine hand unto the LORD, the most high God, the possessor of heaven and earth" (Genesis 14:22). In other words, he said, **"I don't need your money."**

Interestingly, after Abram met with Melchizedek, he was rejuvenated. Afterwards Issac was born, **the physical seed** which would bring forth **the Holy Seed**. Jesus, the Holy Seed, was God. He was flesh and blood wrapped and laid in a manager.

"After these things the word of the LORD came unto Abram in a vision, saying, 'Fear not, Abram: **I am thy shield, and thy exceeding great reward.'**

'And Abram said, **"Lord GOD, what wilt thou give me, seeing I go childless**, and the steward of my house is this Eliezer of Damascus? Behold, to me thou hast given no seed: and, lo, one born in my house is mine heir." And, behold, the word of the LORD came unto him, saying, "This shall not be thine heir; but he that shall come forth out of thine own bowels shall be thine heir. And he brought him forth abroad, and said, **Look now toward heaven, and tell the stars, if thou be able to number them: and he said unto him, So shall thy seed be. And he believed in the LORD; and he counted it to him for righteousness. And he said unto him, I am the LORD that brought thee out of Ur of the Chaldees, to give thee this land to inherit it"** (Genesis 15:1-7).

Separate from the Antichrist

Abram came to God and said, "I'm childless, you have not given to me the seed you promised!" God once again confirmed his promise. Yet, Abram and Sarai got tired of waiting on God. So, they **devised their own plan**. When we devise our own plans, it changes to being about me, me, me, and I, I, I. It is no longer God's plan.

"Now Sarai Abram's wife bare him no children: and she had an handmaid, an Egyptian, whose name was Hagar. And **Sarai said unto Abram**, Behold now, the LORD hath restrained me from bearing: **I pray thee, go in unto my maid**; it may be that I may obtain children by her. And Abram hearkened to the voice of Sarai. And Sarai Abram's wife took Hagar her maid the Egyptian, after Abram had dwelt ten years in the land of Canaan, and **gave her to her husband Abram** to be his wife. And he went in unto Hagar, and she conceived: and **when she saw that she had conceived, her mistress was despised in her eyes.** And Sarai said unto Abram, My wrong be upon thee: I have given my maid into thy bosom; and when she saw that she had conceived, I was despised in her eyes: the Lord judge between me and thee. But Abram said unto Sarai, Behold, thy maid is in thy hand; do to her as it pleaseth thee. And when Sarai dealt hardly with her, she fled from her face" (Genesis 16:1-6).

Remember Hagar? Hagar was the handmaiden that Abram picked up in Egypt. Sarai suggested that Hagar produce a child from Abram. Abram bought the idea and lo, and behold, a child was born! **It was a miracle!** Abram was eighty-six years old! (Genesis 16:16)

God worked a miracle for Ishmael to be born. If we want our way bad enough, God may work a miracle. We may hear others say, "Oh, it was a miracle!" But what does it prove that it was a miracle? Does a miracle prove that God ordained it?

The fruit of Abram and Hagar (the bondwoman) produced **a wild ass**. Who cares if it was a miracle? The offspring would be a diversion from God's plan **with major consequences**.

"And he will be **a wild man** [ass]; his hand will be against every man, and every man's hand against him; and he shall dwell in the presence of all his brethren" (Genesis 16:12).

Ishmael is a type of antichrist. Antichrist means "instead of Christ." Ishmael was a good idea, but he is a product of the works of the flesh; it reveals the mark of the beast. Ishmael was a product of Sarah's head, human ideas and wisdom, and Abram's strength. This is a type of the mark in the forehead (wisdom) and right hand (strength).

The last thing Abram needed was a good idea. An idea is often a man-made attempt to bring forth the promises of God.

Ishmael looked like Abram, but he had an Egyptian heart like his mother, Hagar. This type of Ishmael persecutes the Son of Promise. Shepherds are an abomination to Egyptians, and there could be no substitute for the Holy Seed, the Chief Shepherd. This plan of man was a mockery of God's promise.

We have all produced Ishmaels. There are wild asses individually, nationally, and globally. When we take matters into our own hands and end up producing an outcome using our wisdom and strength and not His. We may end up with a miracle of a wild ass! The day comes when we must cast what we produce out. **The relationship with the offspring must be cut off** to stop the mockery of God's plan and his seed.

"And Sarah saw the son of Hagar the Egyptian, which she had born unto Abraham, **mocking**. Wherefore she said unto Abraham, Cast out this bondwoman and her son: for the son of this bondwoman shall not be heir with my son, even with Isaac. And the thing was very grievous in Abraham's sight because of his son. And God said unto Abraham, Let it not be grievous in thy sight because of the lad, and because of thy bondwoman; in all that Sarah hath said unto thee, hearken unto her voice; for in Isaac shall thy seed be called" (Genesis 21:9-12).

The word *mark* means "to stamp or **impress**." The American church is out to **impress**. It has produced a combination of human ideas utilizing man's wisdom and strength. It relies on think tanks (worldly studies providing information, ideas, and advice) and artificial intelligence (computer systems or algorithms which imitate or predict intelligent human behavior) to promote numbers, nickels, and noses. Often churches are run as a business. Intelligent men get together and come up with good ideas. The last thing the church needs are good ideas backed with money and technology.

Forasmuch then as we are the offspring of God, we ought not to think that the Godhead is like unto gold, or silver, or stone, **graven by art and man's device** (Acts 17:29).

Art is **man's device**, man's **knowledge**. Knowledge means *techna* or technology. Technology presents man's knowledge through devices which project a false light. These devices are developed from the inner reasonings of man's head. It starts in a man's mind and comes through **his** hand, by **his** strength. Man's way is **idolatry**. Remember Abram's father's idol shop.

"If any man worship the beast and his image, and **receive his mark** [INDICATOR OF MAN'S WAY] **in his forehead** [MIND], **or in his hand** [STRENGTH], the same shall drink of the wine of the wrath of God, which is poured out without mixture into the cup of his indignation; and he shall be tormented with fire and brimstone in the presence of the holy angels, and in the presence of the Lamb: And the smoke of their torment ascendeth up for ever and ever: and **they have no rest day nor night, who worship the beast and his image, and whosoever receiveth the mark of his name**. Here is the patience of the saints: here are they that keep the commandments of God, and the faith of Jesus" (Revelation 14:9-12).

Ishmael is a type of the carnal mind. He was untamed and wild. We need to separate from the Ishmaels in our life. Separation from Ishmael is to abstain from human ideas, wisdom, and strength in order to bring forth the promise of God.

The promise of God was made to Abram and **his seed**. His seed is Christ. God made those promises to *Jesus*. As joint heirs with Christ, we share in the promises.

When there are human reasoning and human strength involved with a focus on what's good for me, what I want, what is *mine*, or if it is about *me*, then the result will be a fruit of Ishmael (antichrist).

Abram was an instrument of Sarah's human idea and reasoning. God worked a miracle for the eighty-six-year-old Abram to produce Ishmael (Genesis 16:16). We cannot judge if something is a good thing by miracles. The product of the Ishmael miracle was a wild ass. Miracles should not get us excited. We judge miracles by their **source**. The product's source was a human idea and reasoning and human strength.

Abram looked at what *he* did. Abram's choice to lay with Hagar **separated him from God**. For thirteen years, the Lord did not speak to Abram. There is no record in scripture from when Abram was age 86 to 100, for a period of thirteen years, that God spoke to Abram. That's a long time of silence. Thirteen is the number which represents rebellion. Rebellion is as the sin of witchcraft (1 Samuel 15:23). Abram's idea was not God's idea. When we go *our* way instead of *God's* way, it is rebellion against God's Word, and it is idolatry.

Many preachers have produced an "Ishmael." There are over 200 Christian denominations. [407] Every denomination and most non-denominations are Ishmaels. We cannot hear God and know His will until we separate *from* everything and everyone and separate *to* Him.

His kingdom must come first. His kingdom must come before our families. This will put us at the crossroads between our natural families and our spiritual families. We must separate. Separation will bring misunderstanding, but we are required to "seek first the kingdom of God and His righteousness" (Matthew 6:33).

Abram begged God to preserve Ishmael, *his way.* "And Abraham said unto God, O that Ishmael might live before thee!" (Genesis 17:18). We must ask ourselves, "What areas of my life am I putting ahead of what He says and instead of what He wants?"

God honored his request, temporarily. He replied in Genesis 17:20, "And as for Ishmael, I have heard thee: Behold, I have **blessed** him, and will make him **fruitful**, and will multiply him exceedingly; **twelve princes** shall he beget, and I will make him a great nation."

These twelve princes represent the world system. However, Ishmael will eventually have to go. The world system of antichrist must be cast out. Ishmael and the bondwoman must be thrown out of our personal lives. The *"my way,* my ideas, my strength, my wisdom" must go.

Paul said the persecution of those who are born of the spirit is from those who are born of the flesh. Ishmael represents offspring of the flesh.

"Now we, brethren, as Isaac was, are the children of promise. But as then **he that was born after the flesh persecuted him that was born after the Spirit, even so it is now.** Nevertheless, what saith the scripture? **Cast out the bondwoman and her son: for the son of the bondwoman shall not be heir with the son of the**

freewoman. So then, brethren, we are not children of the bondwoman, but of the free" (Galatians 4:28-29).

We must make the separations in order to come into the land of blessing and unlimited provision. There are many affirmations: "For now I know that thou fearest God" (Genesis 22:12). "This is My beloved Son, in whom I am well pleased" (Matthew 3:17). "Well done, good and faithful servant" (Matthew 25:23).

Note this is a spiritual teaching. The actual physical descendants of Ishmael are Gentiles and may accept sonship with Jesus Christ, as many do. There is more discussion on this in the Islam versus Christianity section.

Separate from Who or What You Love the Most

When Abram was ninety years old, God called him to a higher position. Genesis 17:1-7, 15-16 tells us God changed Abram's name to Abraham and Sarai to Sarah and renewed his covenant.

"I am the Almighty God; walk before me, and be thou perfect. And I will make my covenant between me and thee, and will multiply thee exceedingly.

"And Abram fell on his face: and God talked with him, saying, 'As for me, behold, **my covenant is with thee**, and **thou shalt be a father of many nations**. Neither shall thy name any more be called Abram, but **thy name shall be Abraham**; for **a father of many nations have I made thee.**

"And I will make thee exceeding **fruitful**, and I will make **nations** of thee, and **kings shall come out of thee. And I will establish my covenant between me and thee and thy seed after thee** in their generations for **an everlasting covenant**, to **be a God unto thee, and to thy seed** after thee."

"And God said unto Abraham, 'As for Sarai thy wife, thou shalt not call her name Sarai, but **Sarah shall her name be**. And **I will bless her** and give thee a son also of her: yea, I will bless her, and she **shall be a mother of nations; kings of people shall be of her.'"**

After this encounter, Abram received a tall request from God.

"Take now thy son, thine only son Isaac, whom thou lovest, and get thee into the land of Moriah; **and offer him there for a burnt offering"** (Genesis 22:2).

Isaac was the promise, and now God was directing Abram to offer him up. Abram did not question God.

How would you respond if God told you to give up your children?

Can you imagine what went through Abraham's heart? He must have wanted to question God, maybe even cry or proclaim. *"God, You gave me the promise, why are You taking it back?"* Wonder how Sarah would have responded had she known her husband was taking their son to be sacrificed? There is no record that she knew!

Abraham's faith had become his substance! He believed in what he could not see. He trusted God with the promise, Isaac was the seed bearer (Genesis 21:12). He belonged to God.

Do we love God for who He is or what He can do for us, or do we love Him for the promise? Why are we serving God? What is our motive? Is it for healing, salvation, or a home in heaven? Or is it because He gave His seed as a promise?

The glorious church will be a people with the name of God written on their foreheads and they will serve God for *WHO HE IS*, not what He has promised them (Revelation 22:4).

Genesis 22:5-6 says, "And Abraham said unto his young men, Abide ye here with the ass; and I and the lad will go yonder and **worship**, and come again to you. And Abraham took the wood of the burnt offering, and laid it upon Isaac his son; and he took the fire in his hand, and a knife; and they went both of them together."

This is the first time in the Bible the word **worship** is mentioned. Abraham was going up to the mountain to *give* his only son. *Worship* is giving back **all that God has given to us,** including the promises and our children.

Abraham was going up to put a sharp knife to his son, Isaac. The Word is sharp and piercing. Take the most precious thing in your life and let God put his Word on it. Will you trust Him for His outcome? Will you give it all to Him?

Hebrews 4:12, says, "For the word of God is quick, and powerful, and sharper than any two-edged sword, piercing even to the dividing asunder of soul and spirit, and of the joints and marrow, and is a discerner of the thoughts and intents of the heart."

The story continues to show the testing of Abraham. Genesis 22:9-12 says, "And they came to the place which God had told him of; and **Abraham built an altar there, and laid the wood in order,** and bound Isaac his son, and laid him on the altar upon the wood. And Abraham stretched forth his hand, and took the knife to slay his son.

"And the angel of the LORD called unto him out of heaven, and said, 'Abraham, Abraham: and he said, Here am I. And he said, Lay not thine hand upon the lad, neither do thou any thing unto him: **<u>for now I know</u> that thou fearest God, seeing thou hast not withheld thy son, thine only son from me.'"**

Abraham had passed the test. At this point, **God *KNEW* that Abraham feared and would obey Him. God knew that Abraham would not withhold anything from Him,** including his most precious gift, the promise, his son Issac. Abraham had given all that he was, all that he had; he had given *everything* to God. God's name is Jehovah-Jirah, our Provider; He supplied the ram for the burnt offering. The fire of God will burn up the unholy things.

"And Abraham said, My son, God will provide himself a lamb for a burnt offering" (Genesis 22:8).

The Lord Himself became that sacrifice to give us everything. We must keep our minds off of the earthly realm and trust that the Lord will provide the sacrifice. He is Jehovah Jirah, our provider!

The ram provided was caught in the thicket of thorns and thistles, which represents the curse of the earth (Genesis 3:18). The Lord Himself became caught in the curse to become the sacrifice for us.

Abraham named the place, *Jehovah-Jirah*, meaning, "Jehovah sees," "the Lord will provide a substitute." Thanks be unto God for His unspeakable gift. God so loved that "he *GAVE* his only begotten son" (John 3:16).

Genesis 22:13-14 says, "And Abraham lifted up his eyes, and looked, and behold behind him a ram caught in a thicket by his horns: and Abraham went and took the ram, and offered him up for a **burnt offering in the stead of his son. And Abraham called the name of that place Jehovah-Jireh:** as it is said to this day, In the mount of the LORD it shall be seen."

Abraham received the promise of his son, and through faith gave him back to the Lord. God provided a ram for Abraham and a lamb, His Son for us. Jesus was our substitute.

Romans 4:13 says, "For the promise, **that he should be the heir of the world**, was not to Abraham, or to his seed, through the law, but **through the righteousness of faith**."

How much do you love and trust God? Do you love Him enough to give back everything He has promised you? Once you know and understand *who Abraham was* and his walk with God, then you will better understand who his God was. Abraham's God was **not** the God of the so-called "Abrahamic religions."

Who Is Israel?

Who is Israel and how does Israel connect to Abraham?

Abraham was the first Hebrew patriarch. He became the father and ruler of the **Hebrew** family, governing by paternal right. Abraham worshiped God, *Yahweh*, or *Jehovah*. He raised his children to worship Yahweh.

God made a covenant with Abraham. It is called the Abrahamic Covenant. Because of Abraham's obedience and faith, the everlasting covenant with Yahweh and his seed thereafter was established with Isaac.

After Ishmael, Abraham and Sarah had a son, Issac. (Genesis 17:19). Issac had two sons, Jacob and Esau. Esau's story will be discussed later in this book.

Jacob means "**deceiver, swindler.**" After a severe wrestle with God, Jacob's human strength was broken. God said I will not let you go, until you bless me. His heart changed as he submitted to the Father, and Jacob blessed God (Genesis 32:26, 29) After the heart transformation <u>God changed Jacob's name</u> to **Israel**. Israel means, "He will rule as God." It is a reference to the Almighty "El" (God), meaning power, to prevail. [27]

"Thy name shall be called no more Jacob, but Israel: for as a prince hast thou <u>power</u> with God and with men, and hast <u>prevailed</u>" (Genesis 32:28).

Jacob had twelve sons, who became twelve tribes (Genesis 35, 49). The twelve tribes were named after the twelve sons. The descendants of Jacob, the twelve tribes, are the **Israelites**.

Jacob's twelve sons were by four mothers (Genesis 29, 35, 48). The names of the sons and their mothers are below.

- Jacob was tricked into marrying **Leah**. With Leah, he had the following sons:
  o Reuben
  o Simeon
  o Levi
  o Judah
  o Issachar
  o Zebulun

- By Rachel's handmaid, Bilhah, Jacob had the following sons:

  o Dan
  o Naphtali

- By Leah's handmaid, Zilpah, Jacob had the following sons:

  o Gad
  o Asher

- Above all, Jacob loved **Rachel**. With Rachael, he had the following sons.
  o Joseph
    - Manasseh
    - Ephraim
  o Benjamin

Joseph received a double portion of blessing. His two sons replaced him in the tribal leadership of the family, after Reuben lost his birth right because of his transgression with Bilhah (Genesis 25:22; Genesis 48:5). Tribes with notable descendants are as follows:

- **Judah:** Jesus, David, Mary, Solomon, Caleb

- **Levi**: Moses, Aaron, John the Baptist, Barnabas
- **Dan**: Samson
- **Ephraim**: Joshua, Samuel
- **Benjamin**: King Saul, Mordecai, Paul

Judah sold his brother Joseph for twenty pieces of silver to the Ishmaelites (descendants of Ishmael). The Ishmaelites brought Joseph to Egypt (Genesis 37). Joseph had two sons with his Egyptian wife, Asenath - Ephraim and Manasseh (Genesis 41). Read more interesting information about Asenath in the "Church History" section of this book.

Jacob elevated the descendants of Manasseh and Ephraim, **who had an Egyptian mothe**r, to the status of full tribes (Genesis 48).

Joseph rose to power in Egypt. His brothers were driven there by a famine, which Joseph had foretold in a dream. Egypt survived the famine because of Joseph's wisdom in storing food during the good years.

Joseph revealed his identity to his brothers. He forgave them and welcomed them to Egypt.

When **Jacob's family settled in Egypt**, they were well treated and prospered under Joseph's management. Joseph's power was great in Egypt. **The Israelites made Egypt their home**.

"And the children of Israel were fruitful, and increased abundantly, and multiplied, and waxed exceeding mighty; and the land was filled with them" (Exodus 1:7).

However, they knew God had made a covenant with their father to move them to the land of Canaan. God had sworn to give it to their descendants to possess.

Things changed in Egypt after the death of Joseph. The Israelites were made slaves of the Egyptians as had been foretold (Genesis 15:13-16).

This happened because "a new king arose over Egypt who did not know Joseph" (Exodus 1:8).

"Now there arose up **a new king** over Egypt, **which knew not Joseph**. And he said unto his people, Behold, the people of the children of Israel are more and mightier than we: Come on, let us deal wisely with them; lest they multiply, and it come to pass, that, when there falleth out any war, they join also unto our enemies, and fight against us, and **so get them up out of the land. Therefore they did set over them taskmasters to afflict them with their burdens**. And they built for Pharaoh treasure cities, Pithom and Raamses" (Exodus 1:8-11).

The Egyptian Pharoah decreed that all their male children be drowned at birth (Exodus 1:15-22). It is in that circumstance that Moses began his life.

"And Pharaoh charged all his people, saying, Every son that is born ye shall cast into the river, and every daughter ye shall save alive" (Exodus 1:22).

Moses was a descendant of the tribe of **Levi. He became the leader** of the Israelites **out of Egypt**. He was the lawgiver and the **author of the Hebrew Torah** (Genesis, Exodus, Leviticus, Numbers, and Deuteronomy). The Torah is recognized in the Judaism, Islam, Catholic, and Christianity religions.

"And I will take you to me for a people, and I will be to you a God: and ye shall know that I am the LORD your God, which **bringeth you out from under the burdens of the Egyptians**" (Exodus 6:7).

Moses went to the mountain to receive the Ten Commandments. When he descended the mountain, he found all the people **except for the tribe of Levi** (his tribe) worshipping the golden calf. The calf represents the god, Baal (Exodus 32:4).

"Then Moses stood in the gate of the camp, and said, **Who is on the Lord's side**? Let him come unto me. **And all the sons of Levi gathered themselves together unto him**" (Exodus 32:26).

Later on the journey, Moses sent a representative from every tribe to spy out the land of Canaan before they would go in to possess it. When the men returned, only **two**, Joshua, who was from the tribe of Ephraim and Caleb, from the tribe of Judah, had a **positive report**; the other **ten** had an **evil report**. This brought an uprising from the people.

"And all the congregation lifted up their voice, and cried; and the people wept that night. And **all the children of Israel murmured against Moses and against Aaron**: and the whole congregation said unto them, Would God that we had died in the land of Egypt! or **would God we had died in this wilderness**!" (Numbers 14:1-2).

The people got what they spoke! <u>Every Israelite over twenty years of age when they left Egypt under Moses' leadership died in the wilderness,</u> **except for three people**: Moses, Joshua, and Caleb (Numbers 14:38). Forty years of wandering in the wilderness had brought Israel to a standstill on a mountaintop overlooking the land of promise, and death followed.

"And the Lord spoke to Moses and Aaron, saying, 'How long shall I bear with this evil congregation who complain against Me? I have heard the complaints which the children of Israel make against Me. Say to them, "As I live," says the Lord, "just as you have spoken in My hearing, so I will do to you: **The carcasses of you who have complained against Me shall fall in this wilderness**, all of you who were numbered, according to your entire number, from twenty years old and above'" (Numbers 14:26-29).

The murmuring brought death to the original generation. Only the <u>children</u> of the original tribes would move forward. Moses would also die and **not get to see the Promised Land.**

"**And Moses went up** from the plains of Moab unto the mountain of Nebo, to the top of Pisgah, that is over against Jericho. And **the LORD shewed him all the land of Gilead,** unto Dan, And all Naphtali, and the land of Ephraim, and Manasseh, and all the land of Judah, unto the utmost sea, And the south, and the plain of the valley of Jericho, the city of palm trees, unto Zoar. **And the LORD said unto him, This is the land which I sware unto <u>Abraham, unto Isaac, and unto Jacob</u>, saying, I will give it unto thy seed: I** have caused thee to see it with thine eyes, **but thou shalt not go over thither. So Moses the servant of the LORD died there in the**

land of Moab, according to the word of the LORD" (Deuteronomy 34:1-5).

Moses did not get to enter the promised land because God told him in Numbers 20 to *speak* to the rock and the water would come out. Moses *struck* the rock. He disobeyed. Jesus represents the rock. We must be careful not to strike in anger, but to speak with authority.

However, Moses was a **faithful** servant and is listed in the Faithful Hall of Fame in Hebrews 11. He had forsaken Egypt which represents the world to follow the call God had on his life.

"By faith Moses, when he was born, was hid three months of his parents, because they saw he was a proper child; and they were not afraid of the king's commandment. **By faith Moses**, when he was come to years, refused to be called the son of Pharaoh's daughter; **Choosing rather to suffer affliction with the people of God, than to enjoy the pleasures of sin for a season**; Esteeming the reproach of Christ greater riches than the treasures in Egypt: for he had respect unto the recompence of the reward. **By faith he forsook Egypt**, not fearing the wrath of the king: for he endured, as seeing him who is invisible. **Through faith he kept the Passover,** and the sprinkling of blood, lest he that destroyed the firstborn should touch them. **By faith they passed through the Red Sea** as by dry land: which the Egyptians assaying to do were drowned" (Hebrews 11:23-29).

Joshua was a descendant from the tribe of Ephraim. God chose Joshua to lead the Israelites into the promised land, which became a **kingdom of men, ruled by kings** such as Saul and David. The tribes that were given land were:

West of the Jordan: Judah, Benjamin, Ephraim, Issachar, Zebulun, Naphtali, Asher, Simeon, and Dan.

East of the Jordan: Reuben, Gad, and Manasseh

The tribe of **Dan** abandoned the land given to him and moved north. Therefore, from after the conquest of the land by Joshua until the formation of the United Kingdom of Israel, the tribe of Dan was a part of a loose confederacy of Israelite tribes. No central government existed, and in times of crisis the people were led by ad hoc leaders known as **judges**. **The judges came from the tribe of Dan** (Judges 18:1-31). (243) Samson was a judge from the tribe of Dan.

The tribe of **Levi** inherited the responsibility for God's temple and was **in charge of the worship**. Levites were **priests** and they were given offerings from the other tribes.

"To the tribe of Levi, (the priests), Moses had given **no inheritance**; the Lord God of Israel was their inheritance, as He had said to them" (Joshua 13:33; Deuteronomy 18:1-2).

The tribe of **Manasseh** got land on both sides of the Jordan. Moses gave the tribe the west side and Joshua gave the tribe the east side.

The Israelites, descendants of Shem, would displace the Canaanites, who were wicked, idolatrous people. They were descendants of Noah's grandson, Canaan. Giants also lived in the land of Canaan at this time.

"And **there we saw the giants**, the sons of Anak, which come of the giants: and we were in our own sight as grasshoppers, and so we were in their sight" (Numbers 13:33).

Israel is a **national name of twelve tribes**, collectively, excluding the tribe of Judah (Exodus 3:16, 1 Samuel 11:8, 2 Samuel 20:1-2).

The families of the twelve tribes were called the **house of Israel**. (Joshua 7:14,16-18). [199, pg. 887]

When King David became king, he united the twelve tribes **into one kingdom**. He established political and religious control at Jerusalem. King David commissioned the temple of God at Jerusalem. However, he did not get to build the temple, but rather his son, King Solomon, did the construction in 957 BC.

King Solomon's heart turned away from God. Therefore, **God split the kingdom into North and South** due to King Solomon's **sins of idolatry** and **mixed marriages**.

"Wherefore the LORD said unto Solomon, Forasmuch as this is done of thee, and **thou hast not kept my covenant** and my statutes, which I have commanded thee, **I will surely rend the kingdom from thee**, and will give it to thy servant" (1 Kings 11:11).

The **Northern Kingdom of Israel** had ten tribes and the **Southern Kingdom of Judah** had two tribes, Judah and Benjamin.

Israel was the name of the **Northern Kingdom**, in which the tribes of Judah, Benjamin, Levi, Dan, and Simeon **had no share**. [199, pg. 887] The tribe of Simeon disseminated into Judah (Joshua 19:1). The tribe of Dan did not like their territory, so they moved north. The tribe of Levi were given forty-eight cities.

"And the children of Israel gave unto the Levites out of their inheritance, at the commandment of the LORD, these cities and their suburbs.

"All the cities of the Levites within the possession of the children of Israel were forty and eight cities with their suburbs" (Joshua 21:3, 41).

The **northern** kingdom is called **Israel** or sometimes **Ephraim** in Scripture, and the **southern** kingdom is called **Judah**.

The capital of Ephraim was **Samaria,** and the capital of Judah was **Jerusalem**.

The name *Israel* was to denote laymen, as distinguished from priests, Levites, and other ministers (Ezra 6:16).

The **Northern Kingdom** was ruled by Jeroboam. Jeroboam was from the tribe of Ephraim, a servant of King Solomon, and the son of a widow. When he became king, he put two **golden calves** made for the people to worship in the northern kingdom and made priests and celebrations for them (1 Kings 12).

Ephraim or the **Kingdom of Israel, made a covenant with Assyria**. The king of Assyria was **Nimrod,** a type of antichrist (Hosea 4:17; 12:1). Because of this, some of the individuals and families of the northern tribes **moved to the tribe of Judah.**

Assyria conquered and took the **northern kingdom, Israel,** and the Jews in that kingdom were exiled **because of idolatry** (2 Kings 17).

Rehoboam, Solomon's son, ruled the Southern Kingdom, Judah. **The southern kingdom, Judah, fell to the <u>same state</u> as the northern kingdom**. They were exiled by the Babylonians. Babylon means confusion.

"Now Judah did evil in the sight of the Lord, and they provoked Him to jealousy with their sins which they committed, more than all that their fathers had done. For **they also** built for themselves high places, sacred pillars, and wooden images on every high hill and under every green tree. And there were also perverted persons in the land. **They did according to all the abominations of the nations which the Lord had cast out before the children of Israel"** (1 Kings 14:22-24).

The **southern kingdom was in exile** for **seventy years** in Babylon from 606-536 BC (Jeremiah 29:10; 2 Chronicles 36:20-21; Daniel 9:1-2).

The 45th king, Cyrus the Great, allowed the Jews who were exiled to Babylon to return to their homeland for the purpose of rebuilding the temple.

The Jews from the **northern kingdom were exiled** to upper Mesopotamia and Medes, today modern Syria and Iraq. They are known as the Ten Lost Tribes because they were exiled or assimilated into other cultures (2 Kings 17:6). [244] The Bible refers to the tribes as having been scattered (James 1:1).

After the Babylonian captivity, the returned exiles, who were mainly of the tribe of Judah, **resumed the name Israel** for the **nation,** but as **individuals** were called **Jews** (Judahites or Israelites **until the 1500s.** (2 Chronicles 11:3, Ezra 4:12). [367]

For the rebuilding of the new temple, there was instruction **to share the land with strangers, to include the West Bank, specifically the Palestinians as <u>this was always the land of Palestine</u>.** *Palestine* properly means "Philistia" but is used in the **extended** sense, as meaning *"all the land of Israel"* or the *"holy land."* [198, p. 2208] The older Bibles with maps show this land as Palestine.

The order to **share the land** connects the Old Testament with the New Testament in that **the partition-wall between Jew and Gentile was taken down, and both are one in Christ,** in whom there is no difference (Romans 10:12; Acts 17:26). [245]

"Thus saith the Lord GOD; This shall be the border, whereby ye shall inherit the land according to the twelve tribes of Israel: **The west side** also shall be the great sea from the border, till a man come over against Hamath. This is the west side. So shall ye divide this land unto you according to the tribes of Israel. And it shall come to pass, that ye shall divide it by lot for an inheritance unto you, **and to the strangers that sojourn among you,** which shall beget children among you: and they shall be unto you as born in the country among the children of Israel; **they shall have inheritance with you among the tribes of Israel.** And it shall come to pass, that in what tribe the stranger **sojourneth, there shall ye give him his inheritance, saith the Lord GOD"** (Ezekiel 47:13, 20-23).

There were various outside threats during the time of the rebuilding of the temple. It was during this time that Esther saved the Jews. However, the Jews returned to **idolatry** and mixed marriages, just like Solomon had. This became a real threat to the holy seed and the promised birth of Jesus Christ.

So who is Israel? The Old Testament is an example of **physical** Israel and the New Testament an example of **spiritual** Israel. Physical Israel refers to **His people**; His *physical family*; whereas spiritual Israel refers to **all who *know* Him** and are produced as **His children**; His *spiritual family*.

There are more references to **His** *people* in the Old Testament, the shadow, and **His** *children* in the New Testament, with the New and Everlasting Covenant.

The nation of Israel is a **physical** secular country formed in 1948 in **Palestine**. (See the Eschatology chapter in this book for more information.) Most importantly, spiritual Israel **is the Israel of God** (Galatians 6:16). They are those who know their God **through faith** in Jesus Christ, the King of Kings, the Lord of Lords, and the Messiah.

Who Are the Jews?

Let me begin this section by saying that I am not in any way anti-Jewish or antisemitic. Could it be name calling is used to shut up anyone with an opposing view of the politics of national Israel? I am pro-Jesus. Jesus is from the tribe of Judah. He is the King of Kings and Lord of Lords, whom I love. I do not have anything over those who are called Jews, nor do they have anything over me. **We *all* need Jesus!**

"Then Peter opened his mouth, and said, Of a truth I perceive that **God is no respecter of persons"** (Acts 10:34).

The word *Jew* is "a name formed from that of the patriarch Judah and applied in its first use to one belonging to the tribe or the country of Juda, or rather perhaps to a subject of the **separate kingdom of Judah"** (2 Kings 16:6, 25:25). [199]

The source states further, "During the captivity of Babylon the name seems to **have been extended** to include all the people of the Hebrew language and country, without distinction" (Esther 3:6; Daniel 3:8).

Additionally, "This **loose application** of the name was preserved **after the restoration to Palestine,** when it came to denote not only every descendant of Abraham in the largest possible sense, *but even **proselytes** who had **no blood relation** to the Hebrews."* For example, on the day of Pentecost, after the death of Jesus we find the following in the Upper Room.

"And there were dwelling at Jerusalem **Jews**, devout men, **out of every nation under heaven** . . . Phrygia, and Pamphylia, in Egypt, and in the parts of Libya about Cyrene, and strangers of Rome, **Jews and <u>proselytes</u>**" (Acts 2:5, 10).

A *proselyte* is "one who has **converted** from a Gentile **religion** to **Judaism**."

Another example of proselytes is referred to in Esther 8:17. After Haman was hung and Mordecai was promoted, the order went out to slay all the enemies of the Jews. Verse 17 ends with the following, "And many of the people of the land <u>**became Jews**</u> [*to become jews, Judaised*]; for the **fear of the Jews** [*A Jehudite, descendant of Judah*] fell upon them."

At the time of Esther, the world *Jew* meant, "a religious, political, and national entity, **without differentiation** between these categories." In my opinion, this presents an uncanny view of Zionism. *Zionism* is a Jewish **nationalist movement** that has had as its goal the creation and support of a Jewish **national state** in **Palestine**, the ancient homeland of the Jews [199, p. 22, 331]

This explains those today who call themselves Jews but are not Jews. They may take on the *religion of Judaism* but are not a descendant of Judah. Judaism is not associated with one who is of Jesus Christ.

Rabbi D. Philipson explains the meaning of the following: "Hebrew is the linguistic," "Israelite refers to national," "Jew is the **religious** designation." One who speaks the Hebrew language as their primary language is a Hebrew. He says, "Israelites, which was the distinguishing term applied to the people when they inhabited *Palestine* as a nation.

He continues, "Since Hebrew is no longer our spoken language, since further we are not a nation, *our national existence <u>having ceased</u> with the destruction of Jerusalem by the Romans*, it is technically **incorrect** to apply either of these names to the *present day Jew*. There remains, then the word, *Jew*; this is primarily the *religious term, the name of the professor of Judaism.*" [199, p. 953]

The 1905 *Popular and Critical Bible Encyclopaedia* [published **before secular Israel became a nation in 1948]** defines Judaism as follows, "Judaism denotes the Jewish faith in its extravagant form of *blind attachment to rites and traditions and national exclusiveness.* This must have been prevalent in the time of Christ, because of His constant exposure of their formalism and self-assumption, and because in John's Gospel "the Jews" is used as *synonymous with opposers of Christ and His teachings.*" [199, p. 999] Jesus was not of the religion of Judaism. Judaism in Jesus' time was Pharisaism. [409]

Paul tells us that when he was "in the Jews' religion," he persecuted the church and profited from it.

"For ye have heard of my conversation in time past **in the Jews' religion**, how that beyond measure I persecuted the church of God and wasted it: And **profited in the Jews' religion** above many my equals in mine own nation, being more exceedingly zealous of the traditions of my fathers" (Galatians 1:13-14).

One must be from the lineage of Shem or speak the Semitic language in order to be a Semite. [201, 279] It has been established by historians and researchers (more information on this later), that one cannot fully prove a genealogy from the line of Abraham.

God gave the name "Israel," but man gave the names "Jew" and "Gentile." Gentile [GO'-EE] is used first in the current King James Version in Genesis 10:5 and has an interesting meaning in Strong's Concordance. It means, *nation*, 1) usually of non-Hebrew people, 2) of descendants of *Abraham*, and 3) of *Israel*.

The word, *Jews* [YEH-HOO-DEE], is not used until 2 Kings 16:6. Strong's defines it as one who is a Jehudite or descendant of **Judah.**

The 1560 Geneva Bible uses the word *Gentiles* from the beginning but uses the word *Iewes* instead of Jews.

Jesus is referred to as a "Jew" for the first time in the New Testament in the 18th century. The King James Authorized translation of the New Testament into English was first printed in 1611, and the word *Jew* was not in it either. [406]

The 1972 *Encyclopaedia Judacia* states the word *Jew* passed into the English language from the Greek and transformed through several forms: *Iudea, Gyu, Giu, Iuu, Iuw, Iew.*

Hardly anyone today thinks of Jews as being Judeans. Confusion has been brought to the word through the changing of the definition. Christians seem to be the most uneducated on this subject as many believe the Jews of today are the same people as in the time of Jesus.

The term *Jew* gradually replaced the word *Israelite.* After the return from the captivity of Babylon, the tribe of Judah was the most numerous. Foreigners had very little, if any, knowledge of the other tribes.

In the New Testament, the word *Israelite* refers to those belonging to the true spiritual theocracy of Christ. [199, pg. 888]

"For ye are all the children of God **by faith in Christ Jesus**" (Galatians 3:26).

Paul defines spiritual Jews as being separate from physical Jews in Romans, "For he is not a Jew, which is one outwardly; neither is that circumcision, which is outward in the flesh: **But he is a Jew, which is one inwardly; and circumcision is that of the heart, in the spirit, and not in the letter**; whose praise is not of men, but of God" (Romans 2:28-29).

Romans 9:8 says, "They which are the children of the flesh, these are not the children of God: but **the children of the promise are counted for the seed**."

The ruling Jews who opposed Jesus had a physical genealogy tracing back to Abraham and were from the tribe of Judah, the same tribe of Jesus; however, because of disbelief in Jesus as King and Savior, Jesus said that they were actually children of Satan.

"Ye are of your father the devil, and the lusts of your father ye will do. He was a murderer from the beginning, and abode not in the truth, because there is no truth in him. When he speaketh a lie, he speaketh of his own: for he is a liar, and the father of it" (John 8:44).

The **Israelites** came from Abraham's **physical** seed, Isaac. Abraham was chosen by God from among the nations to be the origin of a new nation. **The Jews of Jesus' day and still today look to Abraham, not Jacob/Israel**, as the head of their race.

With Jesus came the **New Covenant** and **a new spiritual nation of Jews**. Paul said in Romans 9:8, "That is, they which are the children of the flesh, these are not the children of God: but the children of the promise are counted for **the seed**." JESUS IS THE SEED OF ABRAHAM! Those who believe on Him are the children of promise!

Circumcision of the heart makes one a true Jew, **the Israel of God**. Romans 2:28-29, says, "For he is not a Jew, which is one outwardly; neither is that circumcision, which is outward in the flesh: But he is a Jew, which is one inwardly; and circumcision is that of the heart, in the spirit, and not in the letter; whose praise is not of men, but of God."

Circumcision of the heart comes from the Word of God. Paul tells us in Hebrews 4:12, "For the word of God is quick, and powerful, and sharper than any two-edged sword, piercing even to the dividing asunder of soul and spirit, and of the joints and marrow, and is a discerner of the thoughts and intents of the heart."

Jesus was **born** in Judah, raised in Galilee, and taught in Jerusalem, the capital of Judah. But Jesus was a rejected Jew because he did not follow the Pharisaical religion of Judaism!

"For it is evident that **our Lord sprang out of Juda**; of which tribe Moses spake nothing concerning priesthood" (Hebrews 7:14).

"He came unto his own, and **his own received him not**" (John 1:11).

It was prophesied in the Old Testament that Jews would betray other Jews as well as the Jewish Messiah. **Jesus** was betrayed by **Judas** for thirty pieces of silver by Judas (Matthew 26). Judas was a Jew who betrayed Jesus the Jew.

"And I said unto them, If ye think good, give me my price; and if not, forbear. **So they weighed for my price thirty pieces of silver.** And the Lord said unto me, Cast it unto the potter: a goodly price that I was prised at of them. And **I took the thirty pieces of silver,** and cast them to the potter in the house of the LORD. Then I cut asunder mine other staff, even Bands, **that I might break the brotherhood between Judah and Israel**" (Zechariah 11:10-14).

After Jesus ascended to heaven, Judah's bloodline was destroyed by Herod following the destruction of Jerusalem in 70 AD. For the past two thousand years no one can prove with 100 percent accuracy they are from the bloodline of Abraham, Isaac, and Jacob. The Romans burned all genealogy records. [251, 252]

The bloodline of the ten tribes of the Northern Kingdom (Israel) was corrupted before Jesus came. The entire human race is now comprised of hybrids. Joseph's two sons, Ephraim and Manasseh, had an Egyptian mother. Jesus came through the line of Ruth, who was a Moabitess. The plan was for the seed to spread throughout the entire world. Psalms 106:26-27 and James 1:1 are just two verses which tells about the tribes being scattered. I believe it was God's plan for them to be scattered so there would be no one who could claim 100% authenticity to physical Jewish ethnicity. Acts 17:26 says, "And hath made of **one blood all nations of men for to dwell on all the face of the earth.**"

During the time of Jesus, the temple was plundered and rededicated a few times and then Herod rebuilt it in 20 BC to 19 AD (1.5 years). He made it magnificent, with gold and elaborate decorations. Interestingly, he erected a golden eagle at the entrance of the temple. From the time Jesus was teaching in Jerusalem, construction continued in the temple complex for another eighty years on out-buildings and courts.

The temple was the meeting place of the **Sanhedrin**, the Jews' **court system that convicted Jesus**. The Jews hated being ruled by the Romans. They were looking for a Messiah to subdue the Romans, but that was not God's plan.

Jesus came to save the Jew first (Romans 1:16) and was rejected. Jesus and His disciples went to the Jews in Jerusalem in person for three and half years, from the time of His baptism to the time of His death.

After Jesus' death, His Holy Spirit was sent to minister through the apostles. There were 120 Hebrews filled with the Spirit in the Upper Room and that same day, 3,000 more were added (Acts 1:15; 2:41). The high priest and the Sanhedrin formally rejected the gospel in Acts 5. Three and a half years after the death of Christ, Stephen was stoned. In Acts 11-15, the center of Christianity moved from a central focus on the Jews in Jerusalem to the Gentiles in Antioch. This is where Paul's ministry began.

"Therefore, say I unto you, **the kingdom of God shall be taken from you, and given to a nation bringing forth the fruits thereof.** And whosoever shall fall on this stone shall be broken: but on whomsoever it shall fall, it will grind him to powder." Matthew 21:43

"Then Paul and Barnabas waxed bold, and said, '**It was necessary that the word of God should first have been spoken to you: but seeing ye put it from you**, and judge yourselves unworthy of everlasting life, **lo, we turn to the Gentiles**'" (Acts 13:46).

"O Jerusalem, Jerusalem, **which killest the prophets, and stonest them that are sent unto thee**; how often would I have gathered thy children together, as a hen doth gather her brood under her wings, and ye would not! **Behold, your house is left unto you desolate**: and verily I say unto you, Ye shall not see me, until the time come when ye shall say, Blessed is he that cometh in the name of the Lord" (Luke 13:34-35).

In 63 BC, the territory of Judea for the first time came under the direct administration of Rome. The Romans ruled with cruelty. The Jews revolted against Rome in 66 BC.

The second temple was destroyed on the 9th day of Av or 30 August 70 AD by the Romans, **spiritual Babylon.**

The 9th day of Av was also the **day** of the destruction of the first temple by the **physical Babylonians**. Both temples were destroyed on the same calendar day.

Jerusalem had turned into the spiritual characteristics of Sodom and Egypt and destruction was forthcoming. Revelation 11:8 says, "And their dead bodies shall lie in the street of the great city, which **spiritually is called Sodom and Egypt, where also our Lord was crucified.**"

According to the historian Flavius Josephus, when the Romans besieged the city in 70 AD, it took about six months to complete the work. The Romans murdered everyone they met. The streets ran with blood, the air was filled with the groans of the dying, the howling of the terrified, and the desperate outcries of the ravished; and the flames of the burning city ascended up to heaven. [(252)]

About six thousand took refuge in the temple. One of the soldiers of Roman Emperor Titus set the temple on fire. Jerusalem was turned into a ruinous heap. The foundations of the temple were ploughed up. Jesus predicted this in Matthew 24:1-2, "And Jesus went out, and departed from the temple: and his disciples came to him for to shew him the buildings of the temple. And Jesus said unto them, See ye not all these things? verily I say unto you, **There shall not be left here one stone upon another,** that shall not be thrown down."

It is said, not only the bellies of the dead but of the living were ripped up for the sake of the gold which they were supposed to have swallowed.

Around 1,100,000 Jews are said to have lost their lives at Jerusalem alone. Titus crucified ringleaders in the rebellion until no more wood for crosses could be had. It is estimated 97,000 were taken prisoner, and many were sent to Egypt to become slaves. About 11,000 died from hunger, some were transported to Syria, to be devoured by wild beasts or sold for slaves.

Not one descendant of David who was left alive could be found.

Those who heeded the words of Jesus and believed upon Him escaped before this judgment came to pass. Jesus gave the directive in Matthew 24:16, "Then let them which be in Judaea flee into the mountains." [252]

The Jews were given a generation, forty years, after Jesus' death to stop the temple sacrifices and accept Him as the ultimate sacrifice, and **they refused**. The destruction of Judea and the temple fulfilled the prophecy in Daniel 9:27: "And he shall confirm the covenant with many for one week: and **in the midst of the week he shall cause the sacrifice and the oblation to cease**, and for the overspreading of abominations **he shall make it desolate,** even until the consummation, and that determined shall be poured upon the desolate."

Jesus became the ultimate sacrifice, and the **New Convent** was confirmed three and half years after His baptism. **The Daniel 9 prophecy ties to Matthew 24.** The ongoing sacrifices after Jesus' ultimate sacrifice were an abomination in the temple. The temple was made desolate as Daniel prophesied. The annihilation of the temple and the city **ended the Sanhedrin Court and the sacrifices. Without a temple, there would be no more sacrifices.** Jesus is the temple; Jesus is the final sacrifice.

Tamuz was the Babylonian god to which sacrifices were made, including human sacrifice. [255] The daily temple sacrifice was abolished on the 17th day of Tammuz in 70 AD. [254] Tammuz is the Hebrew month before the month of Av, the month the temple was destroyed.

After the destruction of the Temple and Jerusalem in 70 AD, **Palestine** was under Roman authority. Emperor Hadrian built a new city and dedicated it to himself and certain Roman gods, in particular Capitoline Jupiter. The buildings in Israel today are not from the time of Jesus. There are only three remanent of buildings in Israel which King Herod built that are standing today. They are in Caesarea Maritime, now owned by the Rothchild's; Masada, an ancient fort; and the Cave of the Patriarchs where Abraham's family was buried *(See Photos)*. [444] The wailing wall *(See Photo)* is not part of the Temple. [445] Jerusalem as it was in Bible times is under ground and some can be access via tunnels. (*See Photo*). [446]

In 130 AD, Emperor Hadrian **renamed the razed city of Jerusalem *Aelia Capitolina.*** Aelia was a family name and Capitolina refers to the **Cult of Jupiter.** On the site that the Romans believed was Calvary, where Jesus died and was buried, **Hadrian built a temple to the god Jupiter.** [273] Circumcision was prohibited, and the Jews were ousted from the city. **Hadrian renamed the province of Judaea to Syria Palaestina.**

Around 312 AD, a Catholic historian and a Catholic bishop began to search for the tomb of Jesus. They found three crosses, one of which was designated as the "True Cross of Jesus." In 326 AD, Emperor Constantine ordered the pagan temple to be torn down. **Under the temple** was found a tomb believed to be the tomb of Jesus. Constantine ordered the building of the **Church of the Holy Sepulcher** to cover Calvary and the tomb. [88, 263] (*See Photo)*

Constantine **merged** Christianity with Catholicism. You will find more about this in the Catholicism versus Christianity section. The Church of the Holy Sepulchre is believed to inhabit both the site where Jesus was crucified at Calvary or Golgotha, and the location of Jesus' empty tomb, where he was buried and resurrected. **It is regarded as the holiest site for Christians.**

Palestine became a center of Christianity, attracting pilgrims, monks, and scholars. It was then conquered by the Muslims, who built the Al-Aqsa Mosque and the **Dome of the Rock**, an Islamic shrine, in 685. **Muslims regard the site as the third holiest in Islam**, after Mecca and Medina.

In 1096, the First Crusaders invaded to recover the Holy Land from Islamic rule. A vast majority of the crusaders were Catholics from France. There they established the Kingdom of Jerusalem with the intention to set up a theocratic state directly under papal control. **A Catholic church hierarchy was established, with rule over the Christian orthodox churches,** including the Syriac Orthodox Church, which was an extension of **the church that Saint Peter had**

instituted at **Antioch** (Acts 11). In 1100, Baldwin I was crowned as the first King of the **Kingdom of Jerusalem.**

In the late 1250s, **Palestine** was invaded again and taken over by **Egypt.** In 1516, Palestine came under the control of the Ottoman Empire from **Turkey.** The religion was predominately **Islamic.** There were no more disruptions until World War I in 1914. [256, 257, 258, 259, 260, 261, 262, 263, 264]

How did most of the Jews who are in national Israel today get there and who are they?

In 2001, Dr. Ariella Oppenheim of **Hebrew University**, a biologist, published the first extensive study of DNA and the origin of the Jews. Her study confirmed that **many claiming to be Jews are not descendants from Abraham** but are descendants from European Khazars (from **Russia** and **Ukraine**) who *converted* to the religion of Judaism in the 8th century. This study can be found online. [249, 251]

It is stated, "Her research found that **virtually all the Jews came from Khazar blood.** Not only that but Oppenheim discovered that the **Palestinians—the very people whom the Jews had been persecuting and ejecting from Israel's land since 1948—had more Israelite blood than did the Jews.**" [250, 251]

Jack Bernstein, Jewish author of *In Racist Marxist Israel: The Life of an American Jew*, wrote, "Isn't it odd that it is not the religious Jews that claim to be God's chosen people; **it is the atheistic non-believing Jews leading the cry 'We are God's chosen people'** when they are the Zionist Marxist Ashkenazi Jews who for political purposes have chosen Judaism and **who do not have a drop of biblical Jewish blood in them.** At one time we Jews were chosen by God to be his messengers but long ago we forfeited that right." This author was killed. [253]

There are many prominent people who are converted Jews. American magazine, *Forward*, the historic voice of American liberal Judaism, ranked Pope Francis among its most prominent Jews, in the *PLUS* category, for the year 2013. [247]

Forbes Magazine listed *The World's Jewish Billionaires*. Most all are connected to the technology industry. [447] They include:

Name	Net Worth (Billion $)	Source of Wealth
Larry Ellison	102.9	Oracle
Larry Page	85.2	Google
Sergey Brin	81.8	Google
Steve Ballmer	78.9	Microsoft
Michael Bloomberg	76.8	Bloomberg LP
Michael Dell	52	Dell Technologies
Mark Zuckerberg	42.7	Facebook

According to the Pew Research Center with figures from 2015, Jews self-identify with one of four subgroups: "Ultra-Orthodox" (9%), "Secular" (49%), "Traditional" (29%), and "Religious" (13%).

The Ultra-Orthodox are the most religiously devout group in Israel, with 96 percent saying religion (**Judaism**) is very important in their lives. Judaism brings conflict to Christianity due to the fact there has been history of a desire to dominate, coupled with the expression of being the "chosen people", when Jesus clearly was not a respecter of persons. In my experience, this group is very unaccepting of outsiders and often disrespectful to others, such as Christians. [217]

The secular Jews are by far **the largest Jewish group in Israel,** making up roughly **half** of national Israeli Jews. Only 18 percent are absolutely certain in their belief in God, and 40 percent do not believe in God at all. [396] In my experience, this group is very friendly to outsiders. They are the most like Americans; many are liberal.

The traditional Jews perceive and define themselves as neither strictly religious nor secular. They value their Jewish traditions like circumcision, holidays, and weddings but are respectful of others.

While 13 percent are considered "religious", it is estimated around only 1 percent are **Messianic Jews,** those who believe in Jesus Christ as Savior.

There is a tremendous need for evangelism to those who claim to be Jews. In my experience, Messianic Jews values their Jewish traditions like holidays, but they love Jesus. They are respectful of others. [438]

Eschatology

I grew up in an ultra-religious home with teaching that the rapture could happen at any minute, and I might be left behind. I read the *Left Behind* books and saw the movies at my church. I lived in terror most of my childhood and adolescent years. Often, I would awaken and go through my house to see if I was left behind. Over the years, nightmares developed, and I was diagnosed with night terrors. It was in my forties that I was set free by coming to know who I was in Christ.

Those who have been taught eschatology are most likely familiar with the topics in this section but may be surprised by things brought to light. For example, do you know how many times the Rapture has been predicted to occur? Have you heard about a seven-year tribulation? Do you believe a red heifer must be sacrificed and a third temple built in order for Jesus to return? Do you believe there is a secret rapture and then Jesus will come again with His saints? (two comings?)

Is what you believe in the Bible? Do you know the historical connection to what you believe?

This chapter will take you through a high-level chronological order of events that have unfolded and given birth to this popular doctrine. I used to believe simply what I was taught without searching the Scriptures and letting the Holy Spirit guide me in all truth.

The fear of missing the rapture and being left behind was exacerbated by watching "rapture" movies and studying charts. I was seeking truth so I could "witness" to others. However, I have since learned that one must know the Word instead of commentaries, movies, hearsay, and charts. The Holy Spirit wrote the **Word**. The Holy Spirit will draw people through His Word. His Word is magnified above His name (Psalm 138:2).

Peter says, "**Be ready always to give an answer** to every man that asketh you a reason of the hope that is in you" (1 Peter 3:15).

"**My people are destroyed for lack of knowledge**: because thou hast rejected knowledge, I will also reject thee" (Hosea 4:6).

"They received the word with all readiness of mind, and **searched the scriptures daily**, whether those things were so" (Acts 17:11).

"But the Comforter, which is the Holy Ghost, whom the Father will send in my name, **he shall teach you all things,** and bring all things to your remembrance, whatsoever I have said unto you" (John 14:26).

No one has all the answers. In this chapter, we are going to examine the Bible and history to obtain a timeline of events to show the connection of how many teachings have become belief systems throughout the church system.

Are the pastors you are listening to preaching the Word or commentaries? Do you know who and what you believe and where it came from?

"*JESUS IS COMING*!" means different things to different people. I do believe that Jesus is physically coming back to earth. The Word is the plumbline, and it supports the return of Christ.

"Ye men of Galilee, why stand ye gazing up into heaven? **This same Jesus, which is taken up from you into heaven, shall so come in like manner** as ye have seen him go into heaven" (Acts 1:11).

Take notice, the Bible focuses on the *coming of the Lord*, instead of the *going of the church.*

Jesus came in the flesh, then in the Spirit on the day of Pentecost. He is here now in the Spirit and will return in the flesh.

"When he shall come to be glorified **in his saints**, and to be admired **in all them** that believe" (2 Thessalonians 1:10).

Currently on Wikipedia, there are fifty-eight rapture predictions that have been made throughout history. These predictions are a mere handful of all the predictions over the centuries. Most of the predictions listed are by prominent people. The prophecy clock fails time and time again but is restated by another "prophet". It seems no matter how many times one makes an inaccurate prediction, they are still respected and command an audience. [280]

Where do the following teachings come from? Have you heard them? Do you know the origin?

- There will be a seven-year tribulation in the future.
- Israel had to be reinstated as a nation for Jesus to return.
- A red heifer must be sacrificed.
- A third temple must be rebuilt.
- The rapture is first and then there is a second coming after the tribulation.
- The antichrist is a single individual.

In 1654, the term, *Christology*, was coined. It refers to the **doctrine of Jesus Christ**. It denotes theology concerned with the Person and work of Jesus Christ. [281]

In 1838, the term, *eschatology*, was coined. It refers to the **doctrine of the last days**. It denotes theology concerned with the final events in the history of the world or of humankind. It is a belief concerning death, the end of the world, or the ultimate destiny of humankind. It refers to any of various Christian doctrines concerning the second coming, the resurrection of the dead, or the last judgment. [282]

Through the centuries, eschatology has replaced Christology. The emphasis on the last day events has superseded the doctrine of Jesus Christ. This, in my opinion, is one of the prominent reasons **many cannot give an answer for what they believe or why they believe it.** Most have been waiting to be taken out rather than spending time knowing Jesus and His Word.

Dispensationalism is an eschatological theological framework of interpreting the Bible, which maintains that history is divided into multiple ages or "dispensations" in which it is projected God acts with His chosen people in different ways at different times.

Dispensationalism is best known for its eschatological doctrines, but at **its heart is the distinction between Israel and the church.** Dispensationalists maintain beliefs in accordance with Christian Zionism. See Christian Zionism section for more information. Dispensationalist doctrine:

- Hinges on Israel and the church being **separate**.
- Stretches Daniel's 70th week to the **future**.
- Teaches that the Jews, and the modern Israeli state, are the **favorite people of God.**
- Teaches Israel's modern statehood status of 1948 is the beginning of a **countdown to the end.**
- Teaches there will be first a **secret rapture** or a snatching away of all true Christians from the earth prior to the great tribulation and then a **second coming** of Christ, prior to the **Millennial Reign.**

"If the foundation is shaky, the whole building will fall" (Matthew 7:26).

Eschatology is different from covenant theology (Christology). These are two competing frameworks of Biblical theology. [283]

Unlike dispensationalists, covenant theologians deny any connection between **ethnic** Israel (Biblical Israel - Israelites) and the current or future land of the **state** of Israel.

"The entitlement of any one **ethnic or religious group** to territory in the Middle East called the 'Holy Land' **cannot be supported by Scripture.** "[284]

Covenant theology is **focused on Jesus**. Who is Jesus? Jesus is the **Seed of Abraham**. The Abrahamic Covenant **gave Jesus the land**, the earth. Jesus is the Seed of David. The Davidic Covenant **gives Jesus the throne.** Jesus is heir to the Land and rules the land from the throne. The Church, true Israel, is **joint heir** with Christ. Covenant theology gives all power and right to Jesus Christ. His **followers** have authority **through Him as they are joint heirs.**

Christian Zionism

In order to understand how the Jews who live in national Israel today ended up there, one must understand Zionism and its connection to Eschatology, doctrine of the last days.

"Christian" and "Zionist" are two different paths. Christian Zionism **advocates the return of the Jewish people to the Holy Land**. It holds that the founding of the State of Israel in 1948 was in accordance with **biblical prophecies** in the Old Testament in that "the re-establishment of Jewish sovereignty, the 'Gathering of Israel,' is a **prerequisite** for the second coming of Jesus Christ."

The term *Christian Zionism* began to be used in the mid-20th century, in place of *Christian Restorationism*, which means restoring the church to biblical form. Proponents rallied behind Zionists in support of a Jewish national homeland. (285)

Christian Zionism was **never** a fundamental component in evangelical thinking. Rather, it was an **outside movement** that grew among some evangelicals during the eighteenth and nineteenth centuries.

Among Zionism's luminaries are Reverend John **Darby** and Cyrus **Scofield**. The publication of the Scofield Bible included commentary that reflected the teachings of Christian Zionism and contributed to popularity among Christians, including evangelicals. (287, 288)

Much of the Zionist plan is outlined in an article entitled, *"Palestinian Evangelicals and Christian Zionism,"* from the Institute of Jerusalem Studies. [288] It states in part, "**This movement** had distinct teachings concerning the end of the world and the 'War of Gog and Magog,' and taught that **certain prophecies will be fulfilled** during the End Times, before the 'second coming' of Jesus. It taught that there will be an 'ingathering of Jews' from all over the world to Palestine at the 'End of Days.'"

It continues, "Obscure references from different books of both the Old and New Testaments were **woven into** an **end-of-the-world drama**. Over the years, different rulers and regimes were labeled 'antichrist' and **woven into** the **different and ever-changing narratives**. Most of these ideas found little currency among Christians **until the creation of Israel in 1948, which was viewed as heralding the start of the End of the World drama prophesized in the Bible.**

The Middle East events created **a great opportunity** for the **secular** Zionist movement to **take advantage** of this **particular Christian interest to garner support for its political program**. They did this by advancing a number of ideas such as the idea that it is **a Christian's duty** to support the State of Israel, which God Himself was supporting, and that **such support would result in speeding up the Second Coming of Jesus**, which true believers were eager to see. **Biblical verses taken out of context and applied to the modern State of Israel** were standard features of this approach. For example, the Bible is quoted as teaching that God "blesses those who bless thee [Israel] and curses those who curse thee." And that "he who touches you [Israel] touches the apple of God's eye." **Also put forward was the assertion that God's promises to Abraham applied to the current State of Israel, and therefore that gave the entire land of Palestine to the Jewish people;** that what is happening today is a mere fulfillment of promises God made and predictions given through his prophets thousands of years ago; **and that these events are clear indicators of the End Times."** [288]

Genesis 12:3 was God speaking to *Abraham*, not to *Israel*. **Jacob was Israel** and Jacob was not born when this verse was spoken.

"Get thee out of thy country, and from thy kindred, and from thy father's house, unto a land that I will shew thee – [**ABRAM**]:

"And I will make of thee [**ABRAM**] a great nation, and I will bless thee [**ABRAM**], and make thy name great; and thou shalt be a blessing:

"And I will bless them that bless thee [**ABRAM**], and curse him that curseth thee [**ABRAM**] and in thee [**ABRAM**] shall all families of the earth be blessed" (Genesis 12:1-3).

The first wave of Protestant leaders, including Martin Luther and John Calvin, **did no**t mention any special eschatological views which included a return of the Jews to Palestine.

Rather, Luther had hoped that the Jews would convert to his brand of Christianity once he had broken with the Catholic church. Luther and Calvin saw the Christian church as being "**spiritual Israel**". They viewed that, since the time of Jesus Christ, the covenant with God was with **faithful** Christians who were exclusively the "**people of God,**" with **no special privileges** or role based on **ancestral** descent. [20, 286]

The 1972 *Encyclopedia Judaica Jerusalem* states, "**From the time of the Reformation**, the belief that the Jews should return to the Holy Land, in accordance with the biblical prophecies became popular.

"This view became particularly strong in the US from the **18th century. The Protestants were flooded with publications.** Sometimes **heads of state** were requested to take **political measures** in order to obtain rights for the Jews to settle in the Holy Land.

"In 1830 the **Plymouth Brethren** (separated from Church of England). [289] It was founded in England by John N. Darby whose doctrine of dispensationalist premillennialism asserted that **all** the

Biblical prophecies relate to the return of the Jewish people to its homeland prior to the "Second Coming."

"Many Protestant Fundamentalist churches adopted this outlook and continue to promote it to this day." [290]

On October 31, **1517**, Martin Luther, a German priest and theologian, sparked the Protestant reformation to separate from the Catholic Church when he nailed his 95 Theses to the door of the Castle Church in Wittenberg, Germany. [291] The Reformation put a lot of heat on the pope, as he was labeled as being the antichrist. [292]

Note that exactly 200 years later, modern Freemasonry began in **1717** and exactly 200 years after that, the Balfour Declaration was written in **1917**. See the section on John Darby under Christian Zionism.

The Counter Reformation began in 1545. In 1585, **Francisco Ribera, a Jesuit theologian** (1537–1591), stretched Daniel's 70 weeks referenced in Daniel 9:24-27 to a **future** time. This began the doctrine of **Futurism**. He also wrote that the antichrist was a **single** future individual; therefore, it could not be the Pope. His writings countered the Protestant Reformation to get the heat off the Pope being the antichrist. [293] The Counter Reformation is said to have ended in 1648, but history shows it is still going on today.

The **Jesuits** were a **secret militant society within** the **Catholic Church, called the Society of Jesus**. You can read more about them in the Judaism versus Christianity section of this book. They were organized by **Crypto-Jews**. This group had adherence to Judaism while **pretending** to be another religion, in this case Catholic. [12, 294] The Jesuit logo is commonly seen on buildings, apparel, and signs in Rome as of this writing. (*See Photo*).

There are many articles touting the objectives of the Jesuits, such as a goal to bring down America and Christianity. The infiltration of the Jesuits via the Illuminati into Freemasonry has been written about in many books. It is said there is a connection to the assassination of Abraham Lincoln and other presidents. [295, 296] The founding of the *Feast Day for Lucifer* on August 15, 1534, is also credited to this group.

Before Ribera, the focus was **on Jesus instead of events**. Before Ribera, the Protestants interpreted Daniel 9:27 and the seventieth week of Daniel as **having been fulfilled by Jesus Christ** and his disciples during the seven years from 27 AD to 34 AD. [292]

The Apostle's creed confirms there was a focus on Jesus. It was written early in the second century and used by both Catholics and Protestants. The telling line was, "He will come again to judge the living and the dead." [297] They believed that His coming was **visible, personal**, and **glorious**.

Looking for that ***BLESSED HOPE***, and the ***GLORIOUS*** appearing of the great God and our Savior ***JESUS CHRIST*** (Titus 2:13).

Reformers were putting heat on the pope, saying *he, the pope,* was the antichrist. Historically, they are correct as **many leaders** have been called antichrist (i.e., Nimrod, Nero, Hitler, Stalin, Gorbachev, Hussein, etc.). [292] The antichrist **spirit** has definitely ruled through **many** (1 John 2:18). The Roman Catholic Church is the **mother** of harlots and Rome the seat of **spiritual Babylon**. All Protestant churches are thus the daughters and granddaughters as the paganism from the Catholic church **is still deeply embedded in these doctrines today**. For example, most Protestant churches still **mix Easter with Passover** and refuse to "come out of her, my people" (Revelation 18:4).

In 1585, Ribera wrote a 500-page commentary on the book of Revelation. He wrote chapters on the Apocalypse and the pre-tribulation. [293] In his commentary, he proposed that the antichrist, a single individual, would:

- Persecute and blaspheme the saints of God
- Rebuild the temple in Jerusalem
- Abolish the Christian religion
- Deny Jesus Christ
- Destroy Rome

- Be received by the Jews
- Pretend to be God
- Kill the two witnesses of God
- Conquer the world

In 1586, Robert Bellarmine (1542-1621), who was a **Jesuit** Cardinal and one of the best-known Jesuit apologists, continued the counter reformation and the "get the heat off the Pope" campaign by writing documents to support Ribera. In his first volume of the *Disputationes*, Bellarmine argued that the Pope is not the temporal ruler of the entire world and that temporal rulers do not derive their authority to rule from God but from the consent of the governed. [298]

In 1605 **King James** I of England declared **Rome as the seat of the antichrist**, the Pope. Of course this caused quite a stir. So much so, that the Jesuits unsuccessfully attempted to **assassinate** him.

Thankfully, he survived the attempt on his life so that we could have the Bible written in English. Building on Wycliff and Tyndale before him, in 1611 King James commanded the translation of the *Authorized Version of 1611* of the Bible. Fifty-four scribes who knew English worked on the translation. As a result of the king's writings, Catholics were converted to the gospel of Jesus Christ.

King James was a Freemason. Almost all political leaders were then and now are either full-fledged, honorary members, or controlled by such. Freemasonry was not officially organized with the infiltration of the **Jesuits** until **1717**. [299]

The Counter Reformation was still ongoing when the **pilgrims** arrived in Massachusetts in 1620. On November 11, 1620, they signed *The Mayflower Compact* with the proclamation to live in accordance with the Christian faith to lay with the purpose of the foundation for American democracy.

The pilgrims were known as Separatists who believed the only way to live according to biblical precepts was to leave the Church of England, which was a combination of Reformed and Catholic doctrine. [300] With this new faith going strong throughout the land, the word *Christology*, the doctrine of Christ, was coined in 1654.

Meanwhile, the gates of hell were raging, and in **1666** Shabbetai Zevi, a Jewish **mystic** and ordained **rabbi** (1626-1676) declared himself to be the **Messiah**. After his death, Jacob Frank (1726-1791), a Polish-Jewish religious leader, rose up as Zevi's reincarnation. Read more about these two in the Judaism versus Christianity chapter. There you will find a description of Frank's connection to Adam Weishaupt (Jesuit) and Meyer Amshel Rothschild in the formation of the *Order of the Illuminati.* [54]

Many of those who claimed to be Messiahs were also labeled, rightfully so, as antichrists. Of course, they were not the true Messiah, as Jesus Christ had already come; therefore, it was the **antichrist spirit** working through **individuals**.

Along comes Issac Newton, a physicist and a **messianic mystic** (1642 – 1727), who some thought may have been the first "Christian" Zionist. [305] Newton held radical reformation views in terms of religion. According to the *Jerusalem Post*, he held a fascination with the Jewish temple. [302] He could not have been a Christian in the very sense of the word as he dabbled in the occult, including the Kabbalah. See Judaism versus Christianity for more information on the Kabbalah. [285]

In 1704, Newton predicted a Jewish return to **Palestine**, with the rebuilding of Jerusalem in the late 19th century and the erection of the third temple in the 20th or 21st century, which he said would lead to the **end of the world** no later than **2060**. [304] His end of the world prediction is listed on Wikipedia as one of the famous predictions and claims of the "Second Coming." [280]

Newton used his discoveries to demonstrate the possibility of a "Natural Religion." He had a passion for alchemy (occult practice) and the foundation to occult philosophies. He was a brilliant scientist as well as a prophet of doom, counting down to the End of Days. He provided mathematical proofs for Enlightenment (magic thinking) and Christian mysticism.

Newton produced manuscripts covering topics such as interpretations of the Bible, theology, the history of ancient cultures, the tabernacle and temple, calculations dealing with the end of time, historical documents, and even **alchemy**. He believed men and women do not possess souls and that eternal life could only be accomplished with the resurrection of the dead.

His denial of the existence of the eternal soul and the Holy Trinity were considered heresy by the Catholic church and the Church of England. These were his employers; therefore, **he was forced to keep his views secret,** managing to avoid the vigilant eye of the Church. [302] Newton also believed that Islam was used by God to punish the corrupt Catholic church, which he likened to "a prostitute." [305]

His manuscripts and his collections of religious writings are located at the *National Library of Israel*. His works are part of the collection of Abraham Shalom Yehuda (1877-1951), an expert in Middle Eastern affairs, and are available to the public in digital format. [303]

Freemasonry was officially founded in **1717**, just two hundred years after the Reformation in **1517**. On **May 1, 1776,** Adam Weishaupt founded the *Order of the Illuminati*, and two months later the *Declaration of Independence* of the United States of America was signed on **July 4, 1776**.

Weishaupt was initiated into the Masonic lodge in 1777 and asked the members of his group, the Illuminati, **to join masonic lodges and infiltrate the Freemasons**. They were directed to move up to **leadership positions** so that they could spread the Illuminati propaganda. Freemasons were and are embedded in political, social, religious, and influential positions. [275]

George Washington was initiated into the Freemasons on November 4, 1752, at the age of 20, in Fredericksburg Lodge No. 4, Virginia. He was also a member of the Alexandria Lodge No. 22 in Alexandria, Virginia, and the Mount Vernon Lodge No. 22 in Mount Vernon, Virginia. Washington's involvement with Freemasonry was significant, and he held various positions within the organization, including Worshipful Master of his lodge.

The *George Washington Masonic National Memorial* is a Masonic building and memorial located in Alexandria, Virginia, outside Washington, D.C. It is dedicated to the memory of George Washington, first President of the United States and charter Master of Alexandria Lodge No. 22, which now is Alexandria-Washington Lodge, No. 22. The tower is fashioned after the ancient Lighthouse of Ostia in **Rome** and is **333** feet tall. The number **three** is a masonic number. [306]

In 1812, Manuel Lacunza, a Jesuit priest (1731-1801), wrote *The Coming of Messiah in Glory and Majesty*. This sounds like something one who knows the Lord might want to read, but rather it supported the works of Francisco Ribera, the Jesuit theologian. Lacunza said since the papacy was timeless, the antichrist had to be a single, identifiable human being, who had yet to arrive. His perceptions formed the basis of Futurist Dispensationalism. Lacunza also stood against Martin Luther, stating that Luther represented 666, the antichrist. [307]

Edward Irving, a Scottish clergyman (1792-1834), not only supported the work of Lacunza, but he translated Lacunza's work into English. Irving was a minister in the Church of Scotland where he focused on unfulfilled prophecy and the apocalypse. The church eventually split, and he founded the Catholic Apostolic Church. [309] His doctrinal emphasis was on the "Second Coming" of Christ. Once he went and stood on a hill waiting for the rapture, and of course it did not occur. [308]

Samuel Maitland, an English historian (1792-1866), was a foundational motivator in spreading the work of Ribera. He was the Librarian to the Archbishop of Canterbury in England. He was the **first Protestant** to accept the Riberan interpretation of antichrist wherein the declaration was made that the Pope was not the antichrist. Additionally, he supported Ribera's interpretation of Daniel 2 in that Rome was not the fourth empire. His 1826 and 1830 writings **helped spread Futurism to the Protestants**. It was during his time in 1838 that the word *Eschatology*, the **doctrine of end time events**, was coined. [310, 311, 317]

John Nelson Darby was an essential player in Dispensationalism, and a person of interest in the chain of Ribera events. He was an Anglo-Irish Bible teacher and a lawyer (1800 – 1882). He built on the work of Lacunza and acquired the title of Father of Futurist Dispensational Theology. This doctrine promoted the idea that **there must be a separation of Israel and the Church.** With the Church and Israel being separate, **the Church must be removed** during the **pre-tribulation before the remnant of Israel could be gathered**. More information on this character will be written later in this chapter. He was also called the Father of the Plymouth Brethren and the Father of Dispensationalism. [312, 318]

During the season of "Darbyism," false religions began to form. The portals opened and major cults were established. They were:

Date	Cult	Leadership
1830	Mormonism	Joseph Smith, "Church of Jesus Christ of Latter-Day Saints
1843	Seventh Day Adventist Church	William Miller's False predictions spurred the "Seventh Day Adventist Church" in 1843, later in 1860 it was led by Ellen G. White.
1847	National Spiritualist Association	Beginning with the Fox sisters, the "National Spiritualist Association" of the USA formed in 1863 with a focus on Necromancy, (talking to the dead)
1875	Christian Science	Mary Baker Eddy published her bible, *Science and Health,* start of the Christian Science religion
1879	Jehovah's Witnesses	Charles Taze Russel published the first issue of The Watchtower – Jehovah's Witnesses.

In 1841, Orson Hyde, the Latter-Day Saints Mormon leader from Utah (1805 – 1878), went to **Jerusalem** and prayed a **Zionist** prayer from the top of the **Mount of Olives**. His purpose was to **dedicate the Promised Land for the return of the Jews**. Later, Brigham Young University, a Mormon University, was built on the Mount of Olives in his honor. [313, 314, 315]

William E. Blackstone, an American Evangelist and Zionist, (1841 – 1935) is known as the Father of Modern Zionism. Blackstone was influenced by Dwight Lyman Moody and John Nelson Darby, the founding fathers of dispensationalism.

Blackstone initially focused on the restoration of the Jews to the Holy Land as a lead up to their conversion to Christianity, as he had a desire to hasten the return of Jesus Christ. He wrote the book, *Jesus Is Coming*.

In 1891, Blackstone gathered the signatures of John D. Rockefeller, J. P. Morgan, Cyrus McCormick, senators, congressmen, religious leaders of all denominations, newspaper editors, the Chief Justice of the U.S. Supreme Court, and others for the Blackstone Memorial. The Blackstone Memorial was a **political** petition **which called upon the United States** to **actively return the Holy Land to the Jewish people**. Blackstone presented the Memorial to U.S. President William Henry Harrison. [316]

C. I. Scofield is the second essential key player of Dispensationalism, a lawyer, an American theologian, and a minister (1843 – 1921). Scofield **wrote a Bible based on Darby's notes** of Futurism and Dispensationalism; many say it was plagiarized. He had two introductory versions, 1909, which is almost impossible to find, and the famous 1917 Scofield Bible. **His Bible was funded by Freemasons.** [367]

It was largely through the influence of Scofield's notes that dispensational premillennialism became influential among fundamentalist Christians **in the United States**, and these notes became a significant source for popular religious writers such as Hal Lindsey. Scoffield's biggest promoter was **Billy Graham**. There will be more to follow on Scoffield in this chapter. [318, 319]

In 1918, Clarence Larkin, a Mechanical Engineer and American Baptist pastor, (1850-1924), wrote the book, *Dispensational Truth: God's Plan and Purpose in the Ages*. This book portrays many of his diagrams, which were made into large wall charts for churches. He called his charts the "Prophetic Truth," for use in the pulpit. His famous charts **opened doors for him to teach throughout many venues.** His charts were prophetic and were **widely circulated** and contributed to articles for the *Sunday School Times*. His charts drew on the major themes found in the works of figures like C. I. Scofield, William Eugene Blackstone, and John Nelson Darby. [320] Larkin credits the basis for his charts, especially those relating to Daniel's seventieth week, as originating with Ribera. [329] Eighty-eight of Larkin's charts are available for download on the Blue Letter Bible website. [330]

The detailed prophetic charts bring many to fear as they present doom of the future. They stir the soul, trigger emotions, but do not move the will or action of man. **Repentance** and **faith** must come from the **Holy Spirit**. John tells us, "No man can come to me, **except the Father which hath sent me draw him**" (John 6:44).

In 1924, Edmond James de Rothschild of the Rothschild banking dynasty (1845-1934) established the Palestine Jewish Colonization Association. From this organization, he gave the first 125 acres for Jewish settlements in the Holy Land. Most of the Jewish settlements were sponsored by the Rothschilds, who had prominent political and economic influence. [324]

Notable financial associations of Edmond James de Rothchild include:

- The **Knesset** was built by his son in his honor.
- His picture is on an Israeli **coin** and **bank note**.
- Rothschild **Boulevard** in Tel Aviv is named after him.
- Funding for and connection to various **landmarks** are credit to him, such as:
  o Holocaust Museum
  o Caesarea by the Sea
  o Various hotels

o   United Nations

The Rothschilds have foundations in England and are connected to the Oppenheimer's. Julius Robert Oppenheimer was the physicist who developed the **atomic bomb**. The Oppenheimer's are identified as being one of the thirteen bloodlines of the Illuminati. [323] The family is said to be **one of the biggest controllers of the world's wealth** and the wealthiest family ever. They have strong connections to the **Vatican** and the **Vatican Bank**. In 1895, they bailed out the US Government with J P Morgan. They established the International Monetary Fund and the World Bank. **Every American bank is now part of the Rothschild-owned Federal Reserve.** Many believe the Rothschilds engineered World War I.

Lord Jacob Rothschild said in a recent interview that his ancestors *"helped pave the way for the creation of Israel,"* forcing the British government to sign the **Balfour Declaration in 1917**. [323, 324, 325, 326, 327, 328] See the section on John Darby under Christian Zionism.

George Dealey, an American businessman (1859-1946) and a long-time publisher *of The Dallas Morning News,* was connected to the promotion of Scofield and his Bible.

A plaza in Dallas, Texas, named in Dealey's honor, became instantly world-famous when it was the site of the **assassination of John F. Kennedy** in 1963. It was also the site of the **first Masonic temple in Dallas.**

Reverend John Torell states research shows Dealey was "heavily involved in the occult, majoring in the Scottish Rite of Masonry with a 33rd degree and active as a Shriner, and was also a member of the Red Cross of Constantine." Note: Red Cross is associated with Red Shield, which is associated with Rothchild. [137, 323]

Dealey used his newspaper influence and contacts within the paper industry to promote Scofield and his teachings and to screen out information that would embarrass him. [321, 322]

In 1897, Theodor Herzl, a Jewish journalist, lawyer, political activist, and playwright (1860-1904), formed the first Zionist

Congress. He is known as the **Father of Political Zionism**. There are **eleven** different types of Zionism, **all dealing with Israel and the return of the Jews to the homeland**. The eleven Zionisms are: political, practical, synthetic, labor, liberal, revisionist, religious, cultural, revolutionary, reform, and Christian. [331]

Herzl is the one who chose the **Star of David** as the symbol for the worldwide Zionist community and later for the broader Jewish community. King David never had a star. The star is a derivation of the seal of Solomon and was used for decorative and mystical purposes by the Muslims and Kabbalistic Jews. Unlike the menorah, the Lion of Judah, and the shofar, the **hexagram** was not originally a uniquely Jewish symbol. It is a six-pointed star resembling a hexagram. The hexagram, like the pentagram, was and is used in practices of the **occult** and ceremonial **magic**. The six-pointed star is frequently used both as a **talisman** and for **conjuring spirits** and **spiritual forces** in diverse forms of **occult magic**. [268, 333, 338]

Herzl is mentioned in the *Israeli Declaration of Independence* and is officially referred to as "the **spiritual father** of the Jewish state," even though it doesn't appear there is any godly spiritual background. [332]

In 1913, Lewis Sperry Chafer, an American theologian (1871-1952), aided Scofield in establishing the Philadelphia School of the Bible. It was at this point **the infiltration of the Scofield doctrine** into the **seminaries** began. **This grew across the United States** with the founding of **Dallas Theological Seminary** (DTS) in 1924. DTS is known as the **center** of modern dispensational teaching.

In 1948, the same year that Israel became a state, Chafer published his theology in a study series called, Systemic Theology. These are **required textbooks** for students at DTS. Systemic Theology differs from biblical theology in that it is framed to interact with and address the contemporary world. Well-known graduates from DTS include: Chuck Swindoll, who was at one time the President of DTS, Hal Lindsay, David Jeremiah, Christy Tebow, and Andy Stanley. [334, 335]

On May 14, 1948, David Ben-Gurion, Israel's Founding Father, Prime Minister, and Zionist (1886-1973), helped draft, sign, and proclaim the State of Israel in the *Israeli Declaration of Independence*. **U.S. President** Harry S. Truman recognized the new nation **on the same day** with Ben-Gurion.

Ben-Gurion was a **pantheist** with a belief that **everything is God.** He named the state of Israel "Israel" **after deliberating on other considerations**, including Zion, Judea, Ivriya, and Herzliya. The name, **Palestine**, was rejected **with the intention of making another state** named **Palestine for the Arabs**. [336, 337]

Since 1948, engraved on steps on First Avenue opposite the new United Nations building in New York, USA, are the words of Isaiah 2:4, "They shall beat their swords into plowshares, and their spears into pruninghooks: nation shall not lift up sword against nation, **neither shall they learn war anymore."** [339]

In 1962, Ben-Gurion was quoted in regard to the Isaiah scripture and his connection to the New World Order in *Look* magazine as stating, "With the exception of the USSR, **all armies will be abolished**, and there **will be no more wars**. With the exception of the USSR, all other continents **will become united** in **a world alliance** (i.e. New World Order) at whose disposal will be an **international police force. In Jerusalem**, <u>the United Nations</u> will build a shrine of the prophets to serve the federated union of all continents; **this will be the seat of the Supreme Court of Mankind, to settle all controversies among the federated continents, <u>as prophesied by Isaiah</u>."** [340] In my opinion, I believe the United Nations may be overtaken by the renewed Sanhedrin Court in an attempt to enforce a global law. Whether God will allow this to go forth, time will tell.

"A man's heart deviseth his way: but the Lord directeth his steps" (Proverbs 16:9).

In 1971, Hal Lindsey (1929-present), graduate of the Dallas Theological Seminary, wrote his famous book, *The Late Great Planet Earth*.

There are thirty-seven books listed as having been authored by Hal Lindsey since 1971. Twenty-five of those books relate to end-time Eschatology. An editorial review of *The Late Great Planet Earth* states, "**The impact of *The Late Great Planet Earth* cannot be overstated.**" The *New York Times* called it the **number one non-fiction bestseller** of the decade. For Christians and non-Christians of the 1970s, Hal Lindsey's blockbuster served as a wake-up call on events soon to come and events already unfolding, all leading up **to the greatest event of all**: the return of Jesus Christ." [398]

However, **none of Hal Lindsey's predictions have ever come to pass, yet he is still very much in business**. It goes on to say, "**the Bible has much to tell you** about the imminent future of this planet. In the midst of an out-of-control generation, **it reveals a grand design that's unfolding exactly according to plan. The rebirth of Israel**." Who's plan? I believe it is man's plan!

One would have to wonder **how much money** has been made from these scare tactic books. His primary life work has been to propagate fear.

"For **God hath not given us the spirit of fear; but of power, and of love, and of a sound mind**" (2 Timothy 1:7).

In 1971, Tim LaHaye, American Baptist evangelical Christian minister, (1926-2016), founded Christian Heritage College.

In the 1980s LaHaye was criticized by the evangelical community for accepting money from Bo Hi Pak, a longtime Sun Myung Moon operative and for joining *Moon's Council for Religious Freedom*. Sun Myung Moon **claimed to be the Messiah** and is said to have a close relationship with **Netanyahu**. Many who claimed to be "the Messiah" were also accused of being "the antichrist."

In 1981, LaHaye went a step further and formed an alliance with participants within the Church of Jesus Christ of Latter-day Saints (LDS). The leader of LDS, Joseph Smith, is connected to Freemasonry. LaHaye and LDS together founded the *Council for National Policy*. This initiative was launched during the **Reagan**

Administration. Ronald Reagan adopted the **Noahide Laws** in United States in 1982. Look for more on this subject later in the Judaism versus Christianity section.

LaHaye's popular apocalyptic fiction *Left Behind* series of books and movies was launched in 1995, spreading fear throughout the church and the world. LaHay died at the age of 90 with the remembrance of being a fundamentalist leader who sold millions of **grisly novels**. [341, 342, 343, 344]

In 1975, Christians United for Israel (CUFI) was established by John Hagee, founder and Chairman. Hagee's one of the most influential Zionist leaders in the Christian arena. CUFI is the largest pro-Israel organization in the United States and surprisingly **it is not comprised of Jews, but of Christian evangelicals**, with a total membership of **10 million**. This is 3 million more members than the total American Jewish community.

CUFI is but one of many organizations throughout American history that have promoted the state of Israel and Zionism on the grounds that a Jewish ethnostate in Palestine **is a requirement for the fulfillment of end-times prophecy** and **necessary for Jesus Christ to return** to earth, an event often referred to as the "Second Coming." [345]

CUFI hosted a summit on July 8, 2019, in Washington, D.C. The summit hosted the founder John Hagee, Israel's Prime Minister Benjamin Netanyahu, and US Vice President Mike Pence as speakers. [346]

Hagee has stated that **he believes the Bible <u>commands</u> Christians to support the <u>State of Israel</u>.** It is also reported he made an outrageous suggestion that the Holocaust was willed by God because most Jews "ignored" Herzl. This is interpreted to mean **most Jews were against returning to Palestine**, refuting **the human effort** to hasten the return of the Messiah. [347] Interestingly, there are reports that Hitler's grandfather was a Jew. [248]

Hagee declares, "The man or nation that lifts a voice or hand against Israel invites the wrath of God." **There is no Bible verse that supports this claim.**

Jesus said, "Therefore, say I unto you, **the kingdom of God shall be taken from you,** and given to a nation bringing forth the fruits thereof. Now when the chief priests and Pharisees heard His parables, they perceived that He was speaking of them. But when they sought to lay hands on Him, they feared the multitudes, because they took Him for a prophet" (Matthew 21:43-45).

In 2023, U.S. Speaker of the United States House of Representatives, **Mike Johnson**, a Zionist and an American lawyer and politician, proposed his first bill. He said, "The **first bill** I'm going to bring to this floor in a little while **will be in support of our dear friend Israel** and we are overdue in getting that done," Johnson said as he accepted the speakership." [348] Supporting Israel over America seems to be the typical political U.S. way of thinking. **Ordinary American Christian Zionists often get caught up in the political drama and confuse the three words: American, Christian, and Zionist.** These all have **totally separate definitions.** Christian defined as a follower of **Jesus Christ** does not fit in this group. Christian does not align with Zionist and vice versa. American does not align with Zionists and vice versa.

The *1972 Encyclopedia Judaica Jerusalem* has information that may help us understand more about the beginning of the journey of the Jews to their homeland. It tells us that Jews were better prepared for a **national movement** than any other ethnic group in Europe; however, **a transformation was needed** for **modern nationalism.** **All nation**s had to undergo important changes in their **attitudes** before they could be **caught up** by a **national movement.**

Jewish society achieved its nationalist **transformation** with the **appearance** of a modern idea, later called **Zionism**. Zionism leaned heavily on the **old messianism** and derived from it much of its ideological and even more its **emotional appeal.**

The era of the Messiah had arrived, and redemption would have to be achieved by *human action*. Jews and non-Jews would need to be **convinced** of the **truth of the mission.**

Most of the Jews from Eastern Europe **were opposed** to the national movement on the grounds that **the coming Messiah should not be urged by human endeavor.**

Propaganda would be needed among **preachers** and **entertainers** and an appeal to **Rothschilds** for a miraculous redemption of **Jerusalem or the temple area.** And so there you have it from the **Jewish view.** This insight provides a somewhat explanation of the roots of this **national movement.** [290]

We are told in Mark 7:13 that we **"make the word of God of no effect through your tradition which you have handed down."** John Darby and Cyrus Scofield have been the two identified people to hand down the eschatological doctrine taught in many churches today. Scofield built on the work of Darby. Darby built on the work of Lacunza and Lacunza built on the work Ribera, a Jesuit. Men who were not filled with the Holy Ghost have projected the dispensationalist teachings, a **different gospel** and **perverted the gospel of Jesus Christ** as described in Galatians 1:7. Below is information on these two foundational teachers.

John Darby

In 1831, John Darby organized the **Plymouth Brethren.** He has structured and promoted dispensational theology and popularized the division of history into several time frames or dispensations. Darby taught **God's plan was a separate plan** in two different programs: one **for Israel** and one **the church.**

Darby promoted **a secret rapture** of all true Christians from the earth prior to the great tribulation and prior to the second coming of Christ. The necessity of the rapture is, with the church and Israel being distinct, **the church must be removed before remnant Israel can be gathered.** [349, 350]

As a result of Darby's travels to **North America,** dispensationalism became **a pillar of the teaching of many**

evangelical and fundamentalist pastors. Darby's view is familiar to many Christians, as it became the **basis** of the well-known and **widely circulated** Scofield's Reference Bibles. Darby's view is **accepted today** by most evangelicals, even though **it was controversial** at the time of release as it lacked historical roots.

Darby's theology, which recognizes the Jews as the rightful heirs to the land of modern Israel, ultimately **led tens of millions of American evangelicals into the Zionist camp**, making the United States the most pro-Israel country in the world. [351, 352]

Cyrus Scofield

Darby's theology began its spread in the United States during the late 19th century through the efforts of evangelists such as James Inglis, James Hall Brookes, **Dwight L. Moody,** the efforts of the Niagara Bible Conference, and the establishment of Bible Institutes.

In March 1886, Cyrus Scofield extensively helped Christian evangelist **Dwight L. Moody** in his revival campaign in Dallas.

In 1893, Scofield headed the Southwestern School of the Bible in Dallas, was President of the Board of Trustees at Lake Charles College and was superintendent of the *American Home Missionary Society* in Colorado. He also founded the Philadelphia School of the Bible.

In 1892, Scofield began calling himself Doctor Scofield without producing any doctorate degree from any seminary or university. [353, 354, 355] In 1909, Scofield introduced the first *Scofield Reference Bible*. The first page shows "D.D." after his name. **This publication solidified dispensationalism in the United States.** Dispensationalism became and continues to be popular within **American evangelicalism**. It is commonly found in nondenominational Bible churches, as well as Baptist, Pentecostal, and charismatic groups. [349]

Scofield's 1909 **Bible notes** stated that the third temple would be rebuilt in Jerusalem in the future and animal sacrifices would be offered. This is a "doctrine of demons," "another gospel," and "another kind of salvation" as **it is not in alignment with scripture**.

Meddling with the blood of Jesus Christ is walking on **dangerous ground**.

"But though we, or an angel from heaven, **preach any other gospel** unto you than that which we have preached unto you, let him be accursed" (Galatians 1:8).

"For **it is not possible that the blood of bulls and of goats should take away sins"** (Hebrews 10:4).

A red heifer sacrifice and a third temple would be an insult to our Savior, and it tramples on His sacrifice.

The 1909 Scofield Reference 'bible' was printed by Oxford University Press just four years after the first International Zionist Congress. The 1909 version is virtually impossible to find today.

The second version was printed in **1917**. The revised edition was hyper-marketed, with limitless advertising, by Oxford University Press, selling millions of copies.

Is it only **coincidence** that 1917 was **also the year of the Balfour Declaration**, in which Britain's government pledged to Lord Walter Rothschild, who was a graduate of Oxford, and the Zionist Federation to establish a **"national home"** for the Jews in Palestine? Oxford University Press was run by staunch Zionists and Fabian Socialists.

The concurrent mass-marketing of Scofield's Bible and the Balfour Declaration **would make it look as if God Himself had cosigned the Declaration**, and "prophecy was being fulfilled" before believers' eyes. [356, 358]

Samual Untermeyer (1858-1940), a wealthy, influential Zionist, promoted and funded Scofield. Professor David W. Lutz, author of *Unjust War Theory: Christian Zionism and the Road to Jerusalem*, wrote, "Untermeyer used Scofield, a Kansas City lawyer with no formal training in theology, **to inject Zionist ideas into American Protestantism**. Untermeyer and other wealthy and influential Zionists whom he introduced to Scofield promoted and funded the latter's career, including travel in Europe." [358]

Untermeyer was also deeply involved in the founding of the **Federal Reserve**. He belonged to the New York City temple of the Hermetic Order of the Golden Dawn, **a secret society** devoted to the study and practice of occult **Hermeticism**. *Hermeticism* is based on the god Hermes, where the **phallus** is the primary symbol. The motto, "As Above, So Below" is well known in **magic, Freemasonry**, and *The Message Bible.* Hermeticism is related to metaphysics, known as **magical order**. [266, 360, 361, 362]

Untermeyer was a speaker for a meeting of Masonic lodges at the Masonic Temple, Yonkers, June 6, 1935. At this time, the powerful, influential Mr. Untermeyer called upon the Masonic lodges to support the boycott against German goods. [359] Many believe this boycott was a connection on a grand scale involving **manipulation to bring the Jews to Palestine.** [399]

Untermeyer is also credited with having carried out **blackmail** against President Woodrow Wilson, who admitted to an affair. The demand was for $40,000, which Untermeyer **is alleged to have paid** in exchange for putting the **first Talmudist Jew on the United States Supreme Court**, Justice Louis Dembitz Brandeis, 1916 – 1939. He was the first Jewish person to be appointed to the Court and is widely regarded as **one of the most influential justices in American history**. [409]

Scofield's Bible passed to the churches from **Bible schools**. Editors of the Bible include the following:

- James M. Gray, president of **Moody Bible Institute**
- William J. Erdman, Presbyterian **minister** and author
- William G. Moorehead, president of Xenia Theological **Seminary**
- Henry G. Weston, president of Crozer Theological **Seminary**
- Elmore Harris, president of Toronto **Bible Training School**

Scofield produced a revolutionary book that radically changed the context of the King James Version.

It was designed to create a subculture around a new worship icon, the modern State of Israel, a state that did not yet exist, but which was already on the drawing boards of the committed, well-funded Jewish authors of World Zionism. [353]

Scofield had a shady past with a few eyebrow raisers. At age 29, he was the youngest U.S. District Attorney for Kansas in the country. The same year he was forced to resign "under a cloud of scandal" because of questionable financial transactions, which allegedly involved accepting bribes from railroads, stealing political contributions, and securing bank promissory notes by falsifying signatures.

Scofield was often described as a shyster. In 1878, he was jailed on charges of check forgery. Additionally, he was a heavy drinker.

In 1879, Scofield was converted while assisting in the St. Louis evangelistic campaign conducted by Dwight L. Moody. [319] However, he continued to have a shady life after becoming a Christian. In October 1883, he was ordained as a Congregationalist minister while his divorce was proceeding. He abandoned his Catholic wife, Leontine Cerrè Scofield, and two daughters. She divorced him on grounds of desertion in 1883, and the same year Scofield married Hettie Hall von Wartz, with whom he was accused of infidelity.

Being a "born again" preacher did not prevent him from becoming a member of an elite New York men's club in 1901 until his death.

The Incredible Scofield and His Book by Joseph M. Canfield suggests, "The admission of Scofield to the Lotus Club, which could not have been sought by Scofield, strengthens the suspicion that has cropped up before, that someone was directing the career of C. I. Scofield." Scofield's admission to the club was approved by Untermeyer.

The club's members were atheists, communists, eugenicists, and people that normally a "Christian theologian and pastor" would never have anything to do with. Many freemasons and Mark Twain, who was also a freemason, and who today is highly touted in Christ's Church in modern Israel, were also members. (*See Photo*).

Scoffield is accused of plagiarizing the works of Darby. Many speculate he was recruited by the Rothschilds in order to infiltrate Protestant Christianity by creating their own "Bible," funded by the powerful Zionist Samuel Untermeyer. [358]

What Darby planted, Scofield watered; what Scofield planted, the church watered. The first big media icon to promote the Scofield Bible was Billy Graham. Graham's formalized theology of the sinner's prayer for salvation was made popular in 1935. No one in the Bible ever prayed for their initial salvation. However, they did believe, repent, confess Jesus, and be immersed in water for the forgiveness of their sins.

Graham's crusades were often funded by Freemason William Hearst (1863-1951), an American newspaper publisher, politician, and owner of the *New York Times*. His father was owner of the *San Francisco Examiner*. He was twice a member of the House of Representatives and ran for President of the U.S. in 1904. He was a book publisher and promoted books both on satanism as well as books about Billy Graham. He was the owner of a Beverly Hills mansion. [366]

Graham is seen in photos meeting with dignitaries, including Pope John Paul wearing a Jesuit logo on his robe. [363, 364, 365]

The 1967 Scofield Bible notes on the infamous Genesis 12:3 verse are questionable. "And I will bless them that bless thee, and curse him that curseth thee: and in thee shall all families of the earth be blessed."

Scofield's notes say, "There was a promise of blessing upon those individuals and nations who bless Abram's <u>descendants</u> and a curse upon those who persecute the Jews." The word *Jew* wasn't a word until the 1500s. [367] Before then, Judahites were specific to the tribe of Judah. [367] The word *Jew* is from man and has several meanings, whereas the word *Israel* is from God.

There were four thousand years from Abraham to Jesus. The big question would be "Why didn't Jesus bless the Israelites based on ethnicity?" There was an apostate church during the time of Jesus as

He addressed them as a "generation of vipers" (Matthew 12:34). Those who pretend to be true Jews but are not, He called the "Synagogue of Satan" (Revelation 2:11).

Scofield notes for this verse continue. "(a) 'I will bless them that bless thee' (Genesis 12:3). Those who honor Abraham will be blessed. (b) "And curse him that curseth thee" (Genesis 12:3). This was a warning literally fulfilled in the history of Israel's persecutions. It has invariably fared ill with the people who have persecuted the Jew–well, with those who have protected him. For a nation to commit the sin of anti-Semitism brings inevitable judgment. The future will still more remarkedly prove this principle."

In my opinion, America has been under a curse ever since they started blessing the nation of Israel instead of blessing the seed of Abraham, Jesus Christ. See the table of events in the Conclusion section of this book.

When God spoke to Abraham, the *MAN,* Israel (Jacob) hadn't been born yet. How did the STATE of Israel, come into the commentary for this verse? When Scofield wrote his Bible, the secular nation of Israel didn't exist. Israel (Jacob) was a *man* with descendants, not a *state*. How was there antisemitism in Abraham's time? It was not even a word then, much less the same definition. How does the commentator know there will be remarkable proof of this in the future? [367]

Scofield died in 1921. Yet his 1967 Bible has more notes than the original 1909 and 1917 versions. In some cases, there are almost three times the notes in the later version. Often the notes supersede the text. Who is updating the Scofield Bible? Could it be the alignment with the Jewish Encyclopedia agenda to advance a nationalist transformation which states, "Jewish society achieved its nationalist transformation with the appearance of a modern idea, later called Zionism." [290]

Oxford Press today continues in step with former publications. A search for the words "study Bible" on their website produces the following Bibles: [368]

- The Old **Scofield** Study Bible
- The Annotated Book of **Mormon**
- The **Catholic** Bible Personal Study Edition
- The **Catholic** Study Bible
- The **New Oxford** Annotated Bible
- The **New Oxford** Annotated Apocrypha
- The **Jewish** Study Bible
- The **Jewish** Annotated New Testament

In the 1907 **Moody Bible Institute Scofield Bible Course**, are the following statements:

- The Antichrist is a person, not a system (Revelation 4-18).
- Satan persecutes Israel, and when she is delivered persecutes the believing remanent of Israel (Revelation 7:13-17).
- The day of the Lord has two phases: His coming into the air *for* his saints; and His subsequent coming to the earth *with* His saints (2 Thessalonians).
- The "last days" **as related to Israel** are **separate** from the "last days" as related to the **church**.
- The last days of **Israel** are synonymous with the millennial reign, and the last days of the **church** begin with the apostasy preceding the second coming of Christ.
- The day of the Lord runs its course from the return of the Lord in glory to the "new heavens and new earth" (Revelation 21:1).
- The day of the Lord includes all unfulfilled prophecy about the earth, beginning with the glorious appearing.
- Israel and the Gentiles are the only ones dwelling on the earth in the day of the Lord as the rapture of the church precedes it.

Responses and clarifications for these statements include:

- The antichrist is **a spirit** that can work through a person or a system.
- Israel and the church are not two separate entities.

- Nowhere in the Bible does it say Christ will come *for* His saints. It says *in* **His saints** and *with* **His saints**.
- These statements bring total confusion to the **kingdom** of Israel, the **land** of Israel, the **people** of Israel, and the current **nation** of Israel.
- The **true church which is Israel** is misrepresented.

A breakdown of these topics can be found in other chapters of this book.

There has been much money made from books publishing predictions relating to the end of the world and catastrophic events. In 1974 there was a book written, *The Jupiter Effect*, predicting the alignment of the planets to produce a major earthquake. **It didn't happen.** The book became a best-seller based on **predicted** catastrophes that did not occur. [369] In 1982, the second book was written, *Beyond the Jupiter Effect*. In this book there was admittance that the predictions didn't occur; however, the method of the prophecies were "**refined**" to **new prophecies, which of course haven't happened either.**

In 1988 there was a book written entitled, *88 Reasons Why the Rapture will be in 1988*. This theory was built on the dispensationalist theory relating to modern Israel, 1948. The idea was forty years for a generation plus 1948 equals 1988. [370] Of course, the rapture did not occur, so in 1989, there was a follow-up book by the same author, *The Final Shout: Rapture Report 1989*. This book's purpose was to explain why the original dating of the rapture to 1988 was a year off. [371]

My uncle, Dr. Kelley Varner, responded to these books by writing the book, *One Reason Why the Rapture Didn't Happen in September, 1988; Another look at Daniel 9:24-27*. His book is an appeal to Dispensationalists to be **teachable** and **to turn from the heresy** while understanding **there are many questions yet to be answered**. The Bible is **covenantal, not dispensational**. There is but **one covenantal people** throughout all the ages, **who come to Christ <u>by faith</u>**. [372]

However, the saga continues. In 2023, Dr. David Jeremiah, a 1967 Dallas Theological Seminary graduate, had an "Instant Wall Street Journal, USA Today, and Publishers Weekly Bestseller" with his book. *The Great Disappearance: 31 Ways to be Rapture Ready.* (373)

At the time of this writing, there are predictions galore on the upcoming rapture(s). Alarms are sounding at the Prophecy Club. **Profits** are being made by the **prophets** as the diversion and distraction is to the end times. It should be more important to **know who you are in Christ** and **how to make Him the Lord of your life. Is he your Savior? Are you doing His will or your will?**

After learning the truth about the Scofield Bible, I dug through my pile of Bibles to find the one that had guided me for years, *Dake's Annotated Reference Bible*. It had been insisted upon me in the mid-1990s that I learn from it when I felt I could not understand the Bible. I was directed to read the **commentary** for understanding by "someone in religious authority" whom I trusted.

Recently, as I opened Dake's, I found a 1995 calendar in the pages proving the 30 years I had had the Bible in my possession. I remember in my younger years skipping the words of the Bible and going straight to the commentary to read what was "interesting."

As I took a look with mature eyes and wisdom, I began to see all kinds of errors in the commentary. [374] The heresy I found includes the following:

- Jesus "became" the Christ or the "Anointed One" 30 years *after* He was born of Mary.
- The reference to the third temple is clear. "The great sacrificial altar, corresponding with the brazen altar of the tabernacle and temples of Israel, will be placed in the very center of the whole sanctuary (when it is built in the future).
- Then there are the thirty reasons for segregation of the races, including:
  - "Even in heaven certain groups will not be allowed to worship together."

- o "Christians and certain other people of a like race are to be segregated."
- o "Jews are recognized as a separate people in all ages because of God's choice and command."
- o "Segregation between Jews and all other nations to remain in all eternity."
- o "All nations will remain segregated from one another in their own parts of the earth forever."

Like Scofield, the author, Finis Jennings Dake, had a shady, unrighteous past, **yet he influenced many through <u>his</u> words, thoughts, and ideas instead of the words of Christ**. The commentary for this Bible is antichrist.

In 1937, Dake was convicted of willfully transporting a 16-year-old girl across the Wisconsin state line "for the purpose of debauchery and other immoral practices." The May 27, 1936, issue of the *Chicago Daily Tribune* reported that Dake registered at hotels in Waukegan, Bloomington, and East St. Louis with the girl under the name "Christian Anderson and wife."

Dake pleaded guilty and served six months in the House of Corrections in Milwaukee, Wisconsin. His ordination with the Assemblies of God was revoked, but he later joined the Church of God, Cleveland, Tennessee, and eventually became independent of any denomination. [375]

It is my understanding that all versions of the Bibles written after King James included **Mormons and Catholics** as editors. Using the Bible Hub application and looking up Romans 8:1 in the parallel view, one will see the total removal of the words, **"who walk not after the flesh, but after the Spirit."** The entire verse in the King James Version is: "There is therefore now no condemnation to them which are in Christ Jesus, who walk not after the flesh, but after the Spirit." Almost all other versions except the New King James have removed the "necessary to walk in the Spirit" in order to receive no condemnation. [376] These are **little things** that make a **big difference**. These are the **little foxes** that spoil the vine (Song of Solomon 2:15).

Do a google search and one can see that **Jesuit control** is still at the forefront. The **Jesuit Pope** is pushing heretical doctrine in the areas of climate change, same sex couples, apocalyptic predictions, and supernatural phenomena as in the appearance of Jesus and angels.

The Protestant reformers identified the papacy as the antichrist, the man of sin.

"Let no man deceive you by any means: for that day shall not come, except there come a falling away first, and **that man of sin** be revealed, the son of perdition;

"Who opposeth and **exalteth himself above all that is called God**, or that is worshipped; so that he as God sitteth in the temple of God, shewing himself that he is God" (2 Thessalonians 2:3-4).

Reformers said figures from the book of Revelation might not only be interpreted as representing figures in the **past** (such as the Emperor Nero) or in the **future** (in the Last Days), but also in the **present**, like the Pope Francis, King Charles, Bill Gates, etc. [5, 293] The Word of God is a *living Word* with a **prophetic overtone**. The Holy Spirit speaks to us in *present truth.* The truth comes together as we learn historical facts and seek Him instead of focusing on **events**.

The purpose for our existence has been distorted. Many of the **Jews**, the **Christians**, the **Catholics** have been blinded and **are being used for by the gods of this world** (money, status, world dominance).

If Jack Van Impe, or someone like him, can quote the scriptures, surely, they must know what they are talking about, or do they? How many people actually study the book of Daniel or Revelation for themselves? Instead, we have hand me down teachings by men **who are not spirit filled. The Holy Ghost wrote the Bible.** It is the *inspired* Word.

"All Scripture is given by inspiration of God, and is profitable for **doctrine**, for **reproof**, for **correction**, for **instruction** in righteousness" (2 Timothy 3:16).

The Bible is **spiritually discerned**. Spiritual things are absolute **foolishness** to the natural man.

"But **the natural man receiveth not the things of the Spirit** of God: for they are foolishness unto him: neither can he know them, because they are **spiritually discerned**" (1 Corinthians 2:14).

Most are not reading the Bible for themselves. Most let preachers do their praying and studying for them and *never study for themselves*. We must ask, "Who is teaching me the Bible?" "Are they spirit-filled?" John 14:26 says, [the Holy Ghost], "he shall teach you all things."

Why do you believe what you believe? Do you know the **roots** of what you believe? Can you give a **reason** for a hope that lies within you? Do you know **scripture** and **history**? Many do not know who they are in Christ or who Christ is. **As He is so are we** (1 John 4:17).

"Antichrist denies he **IS COME** in the flesh" -- not was come or will come (2 John 1:7). **If we do not read, we do not know**. Most people want entertainment. Many love Scofield because it is **the easy way out**. Most read the **commentaries** and don't study for themselves. They are slothful.

Popular thoughts include:

- To "hell" with the world, I want my mansion.
- I'll say the sinner's prayer and soon be raptured.
- I don't need to be filled with the Holy Spirit, discipled, or grow up.
- I can reign without suffering.

Satan's scheme is **to evacuate man from the planet**. However, Luke 19:12-27 says, "**occupy til I come**." The church's vision and destiny have been paralyzed. It's not an "any minute" as in reference to time, but *until* He comes. [311]

How much have you gained by what you have been given? How have you invested your time, talent, treasure since His departure to His return? Jesus' question for all of us will be, "**What have you** produced for me?" Matthew 7:16 says, **"By their fruit ye shall know them."**

The seed is the Word. The Word is Jesus. We must plant and water the seed.

The bottom line is that we must be led by the Holy Spirit and continually go back to the Scriptures as **our only source** for "doing theology." We must **get on our knees** in the secret place and ask the **Holy Spirit to teach us** *all truth*. We must not believe based upon admiration, respect, influence, money, and status. We must be Bereans, checking the conclusions and reasoning of others against the **plumb line of God's Word** and the **leading of the Holy Spirit.**

"They [Bereans] received the word with all readiness of mind, and **searched the scriptures daily, whether those things were so"** (Acts 17:11).

What will **the End** look like? **The End** will look *LIKE HIM*. The End is a PERSON.

"And this gospel of the kingdom shall be preached in all the world for a witness unto all nations; **and then shall <u>the end</u> come"** (Matthew 24:14).

"I am the Alpha and the Omega, the First and the Last, the Beginning **and the End"** (Revelation 1:8).

I encourage you to follow the Doctrine of Jesus Christ, Christology, instead of the Doctrine of Eschatology, end time events.

The "Abrahamic Religions"

Having learned the history of Abraham, we know he worshipped the one true God, Jehovah. Abraham communicated directly with the **Angel of the Lord** who was **JESUS!**

But the **Angel of the LORD** called to him from heaven and said, "**Abraham, Abraham!**" So he said, "Here I am" (Genesis 22:11, 15).

Jesus said unto them, Verily, verily, I say unto you, **Before Abraham was, I am** (John 8:58).

And he [Stephen] said, Men, brethren, and fathers, hearken; **The God of glory appeared unto our father Abraham**, when he was in Mesopotamia, before he dwelt in Charran (Acts 7:2).

He [JESUS] is the image of the invisible God, the firstborn over all creation. (Colossians 1:15).

Abraham had the characteristics of a true Christian.

The 1828 dictionary says that a Christian is a believer in Christ; a real disciple of Christ; one who believes in the truth of the Christian religion, and studies to follow the example, and obey the precepts, of Christ; a believer in Christ who is characterized by real devotion.

There were three major covenants from the time of Abraham to the time of David. All three are directly connected to the **Israel of**

God which have been impactful to all generations, every tribe and nation.

The Abrahamic Covenant

The Abrahamic Covenant was an **unconditional** covenant. It defines **Israel** as **God's people** in <u>all ages</u>, and it proclaims, ***Jesus is the seed*** of **Abraham** (Genesis 17).

"For the promise, that he should be the heir of the world, was not to Abraham, or to **his seed**, through the law, but through the righteousness of faith. **Therefore it is of faith (not race),** that it might be by grace; to the end the promise might be sure to all the seed; not to that only which is of the law, but to that also which is of the **faith of Abraham**; who is **the father of us all**, As it is written, I have made thee a father of many nations, before him whom he believed, even God, who quickeneth the dead, and calleth those things which be not as though they were" (Romans 4:13-17).

Now to **Abraham and <u>his seed</u>** were the promises made. "He saith not, And to seeds, as of many; **but as of one, And to thy seed, <u>which is Christ</u>**" (Galatians 3:16).

God declared all the heirs of the future **before they were born**.

"Esaias also crieth concerning **Israel**, Though the number of the children of Israel be as the sand of the sea, **a remnant shall be saved**" (Romans 9:27).

The Abrahamic Covenant, means there are **<u>no conditions, Jesus is the Seed</u>**! No one can fill this role.

The Mosaic Covenant

The Mosaic Covenant was a **conditional** covenant. It defines the **nation** of Israel in a **particular time** of history when they became a nation **before they turned away from God and rejected** the Messiah (Exodus 19, 24).

"'Now therefore, **if you will indeed obey** My voice and keep My covenant, then you shall be a special treasure to Me above all people; for all the earth is Mine. And you shall be to Me **a kingdom of priests and a holy nation.**' These are the words which you shall speak to the children of Israel" (Exodus 19:6).

Jesus brought the New Covenant and did away with the Old Covenant, which was came through **Moses**.

"Behold, the days come, saith the Lord, when **I will make a new covenant with the house of Israel and with the house of Judah:**

"Not according to the covenant that I made with their fathers in the day when I took them by the hand to lead them out of the land of Egypt; **because they continued not in my covenant, and I regarded them not**, saith the Lord.

"A new covenant, he hath made the first old. Now that which decayeth and waxeth **old is ready to vanish away"** (Hebrews 8:8-9, 13).

The new conditional covenant **still stands** for every kindred, tongue, people, and nation **who choose to comply.**

The New Covenant has **conditions**, one must receive Christ as Lord. **All who receive Jesus** as Messiah are under the promises of the New Covenant. The Old Covenant under Moses has been fulfilled through Christ.

The Davidic Covenant

The Davidic Covenant was an **unconditional** covenant. God promised David and Israel (Jacob) that the Messiah (Jesus Christ) would come from the lineage of David and **the tribe of Judah** and would establish a **kingdom** that would endure forever (2 Samuel 7; 1 Chronicles 17).

"And it shall come to pass, when thy days be expired that thou must go to be with thy fathers, that **I will raise up thy seed** after thee, which shall be of thy sons; and **I will establish <u>his kingdom</u>. He shall build me an house, and I will stablish his throne forever.** I will be his father, and he shall be my son" (1 Chronicles 17:11-13).

"And, behold, thou shalt conceive in thy womb, and bring forth a son, and shalt call his name *Jesus* [**the seed**]. He shall be great, and shall be called the Son of the Highest: and the Lord God shall give unto him the **throne** of his father David: And **he shall <u>reign</u> over the house of Jacob for ever; and of <u>his kingdom there shall be no end</u>**" (Luke 1:31-33).

"But ye are **a chosen generation, a royal priesthood**, an holy nation, a peculiar people; that ye should shew forth the praises of him **who hath called you out of darkness into his marvellous light:** Which in time past were not a people, but are now the people of God: which had not obtained mercy, but now have obtained mercy" (1 Peter 2:9-10).

"And they sung a new song, saying, Thou art worthy to take the book, and to open the seals thereof: for thou wast slain, and hast redeemed us to God by thy blood out of **every kindred, and tongue, and people, and nation; And hast made us unto our God kings and priests**: and we shall reign on the earth" (Revelation 5:9-10).

Under the Davidic Covenant, there are **no conditions, Jesus is the King forever**! Those who know Christ are in the Kingdom and reign with him.

Covenant Summary

These three covenants are all about Jesus!

- Abrahamic Covenant - **Jesus** is the **Seed**
- Mosaic Covenant - **Jesus** is the **New Covenant**
- David Covenant - **Jesus** is the **King**

The world system is pushing in many forms to merge all religions into a one world religion. The three largest religions, Judaism, Islam, and Catholicism are touted as the "Abrahamic religions." None of the "Abrahamic religions" recognize **Jesus** as the **authority** of these **covenants**.

The next sections of this book will show a comparison of the three religions, the similarities and differences, to Christianity.

Judaism versus Christianity

The plane was packed. The smiling twenty-six-year-old Jewish boy from Israel slid into the seat beside me. The flight was an eight-hour trip from Washington, DC, to Paris, France. Once I learned R_E was on his way to Israel, I was intrigued to chat and ask him questions. It was June 2024, just eight months after the war started in Israel, October 2023.

We both were respectful as we chatted. We were interested in each other's viewpoint of the ongoing war and how it started. I asked him what his generation's view was regarding Netanyahu's leadership and the questions surrounding the purpose of the war.

R_E was quick to say his generation wanted Netanyahu **out of office**. He was too controlling and not open to hearing the citizens' point of view. He said there are many questions surrounding how the war got started and the justification of the ongoing turmoil. On the other hand, he stood for his country's right to defend itself, of which I agreed. I told him I thought Netanyahu wanted to control the world. His eyes widened at that idea.

He was interested to hear about my having been to Israel three times and the unscheduled blood moon experience. He sat listening intently. I asked him if he knew the history of how Israel became a nation in 1948. He did not. I asked him his origin of nationality. He said he was a Khazar. Remember, Jewish research shows that

Khazar Jews *converted* to Judaism, rather than having been of Abraham descent. I relayed this information to him.

He said, "Are you calling me a fake Jew?"

I answered by saying, "I'm a Jew." His eyes beheld disbelief.

I said, "**<u>Anyone</u> who believes in <u>Jesus Christ</u> as Savior, <u>is a Jew</u>**. I'm no better than you and you are no better than me as a human being. God is no respecter of persons."

He said, "I agree that we are the same."

I said, "Do you know that the Jewish Bible says non-Jews are less human than those who proclaim to be Jews?" [441]

Disturbed, he said, "No, I didn't know that."

I told him about my concerns with the war, in that I had personally taken a tour of the high wire fence surrounding Israel and was told a cockroach could not go under without the Israel Defense Force being aware. I was instructed not to touch the wire fence, or all forces would come and arrest me. He agreed that he had the same understanding. (*See Photo*).

I proceeded to tell him that I knew of those who had helped develop the Iron Dome software, and they could not believe the technology did not detect those who parachuted into Israel and killed Israelis. He agreed there are many unanswered questions. Additionally, reports say for eight hours Israel was attacked **with no adequate response**. Israel is touted as the **most highly sophisticated technical country in the world**. Being the size of New Jersey, they are second only to the United States in science and technology. [439] Remember those who are Jewish billionaires were leaders of technology: Google, Oracle, Facebook, etc. (See chart in Who are the Jews?)

R_E agreed, as he was involved in the technology field himself, having just been to Boston on a **technical assignment**.

We talked about the killings of the Palestinians as well as the Israelis. I asked him if he knew the history of Palestine. He did not. I explained that the entire region has always been Palestine, and that the Old Testament **ordered the Israelites to share the land with the Palestinians**. He sat quietly, listening.

Finally, he said, "Are you accusing my nation of genocide?"

I said, "Not you personally, but one must ask what is the purpose behind clearing out Gaza?" I told him about a recent article and a prediction in a 1954 book I had read. The **November 2023** article states, "Recently, **thanks to the war,** the idea of **the Ben Gurion Canal project** has been revived in the media. The canal would connect the Gulf of Aqaba (Eilat) in the Red Sea with the Mediterranean Sea and would pass through Israel **and end in or near the Gaza Strip** (Ashkelon). **It is an Israeli alternative to the Suez Canal.**" [442]

The 1954 book states, "The Rothschilds commenced their final stage by building the present oil pipeline from Ashkelon (Gaza) on the Mediterranean to Aqaba (Eilat), **along the route of their future modern long-planned steel and concrete two-lane canal.** The Middle East situation is the result of the **Rothschild efforts to secure permanent and secure access to the Far East.**

This nonsense about the "repatriation" of "God's chosen people" to "promised land" has been revealed **the greatest hoax ever perpetrated on mankind.** The single purpose of the Rothschilds was to secure permanent and **secure access to their vast natural resources in the Far East.**" [406]

R_E sat there quietly with widened eyes. I implored him to do his own research and find the truth. I explained that all governments around the world have secrets from the people.

I switched the subject and showed R_E some photos of my home. He spotted a menorah in my house.

"Yes!" I exclaimed, "And I have a few shofars, as well, but **no Star of David.**"

His eyes showed he was beginning to trust me. It was then I told him about Jesus.

He quietly listened as I explained that Jesus came with a **New Covenant** to replace the sacrifice of animals for sin, and that He is the temple. He died for our sins, was buried, and resurrected in Jerusalem with the Jews. He was rejected by His own people (John 1:11). I explained that Isaiah 53 is missing or often just not taught from the Hebrew Bible, and that the chapter was a prophecy foretelling the Messiah. [440] I told him about the love of Jesus for **all people**, regardless of ethnicity, and that **all families of the earth** have the opportunity for **the blessings of Christ**. Afterall, **Jesus inherited ALL THINGS!**

He sat and absorbed it like a sponge. The seed was planted.

As the plane landed, R_E and I exchanged fond goodbyes. He said, "We may have different views, but I have enjoyed talking with you." I warmly exchanged the farewell and wished him God's blessings. Now that, my friend, was a divine appointment for seed planting!

Judaism is of the Jewish faith. It is defined as an excessive form of **blind attachment** to rites and traditions and **national exclusiveness**. The Bible concurs with this definition as Jesus often exposed formalism and arrogance in His teachings. In John's Gospel, "the Jews" are viewed as **the opposers of Christ** and His teachings. [199, p. 999]

Types of Judaism

Levi was one of Jacob's sons.-(Genesis 29:34). Moses appointed the Levis as priests per the Lord's instruction. The priests followed the law found in Leviticus.

But **thou shalt appoint the Levites over the tabernacle of testimony,** and over all the vessels thereof, and over all things that belong to it: **they shall bear the tabernacle,** and all the vessels thereof; and they **shall minister** unto it, and shall **encamp round about the tabernacle** (Numbers 1:50).

Abraham is recorded in the Torah (Genesis, Exodus, Leviticus, Numbers, and Deuteronomy) as the ancestor of the Israelites through his son Isaac, born to Sarah through the promise made in Genesis (Genesis 17:16).

Christians affirm the ancestral origin of the Israelites in Abraham. Jesus descended from Abraham through the tribe of Judah. The tribe of Judah is the lineage of Jacob (**Israel**) (Matthew 1:1–17).

Judaism has changed since Abraham's time. The faiths are different in that Abraham followed **Levitical Judaism** as outlined in the Old Testament. Today, many Jews are not physical descendants of Abraham and they follow **Talmudic Judaism,** which is **not in alignment** with the teachings of Moses or the New Testament.

Talmudic Judaism's origin is traced **to the Pharisees** in the time of the return from Babylonian captivity. This is a marked time of dividing **the older and <u>purer</u> age** of Judaism from the **later and more <u>corrupt</u> times**. (199, p. 1331)

In order to be blessed and to gain favor with God, the children of Israel were given the commandments, the **written law** of Moses. This is reiterated time and again throughout the Old and New Testaments (Joshua 8:31; 23:6; 1 Kings 2:3; 2 Kings 14:6, 2 Chronicles 23:18, 25:4, 35:12; Ezra 3:2; 6:18, Nehemiah 8:14; 13:1, Daniel 9:11, 13; Luke 24:44; 1 Corinthians 9:9). Yet the Pharisees delivered to the people many **oral observances** by succession from their fathers which **were not written in the law of Moses.** (199, p. 1331)

Today's Jews believe in the Old Testament prophets and have a special respect for Moses as the prophet to whom God gave the law. **They recognize Moses as their forerunner instead of Jesus.** However, Jesus brought in the New Covenant which replaced the Old Covenant under Moses. Most Jews did not then nor do not today accept Jesus or the New Covenant.

Judaism **does not** teach **salvation** or that Jesus will return. The Jews rejected Jesus and are still waiting for the first coming of their Messiah, one who will promote their beliefs in Judaism. There are some resemblances between Judaism and Christianity which may bring confusion to some.

For example, Judaism teaches about eternal life in "the world to come." This phrase is referenced **five times** in the **New Testament** referring to a world of eternal or everlasting life.

The 1828 Webster's Dictionary states that Judaism was to be a **temporary** dispensation **until Christ came to fulfill the law.**

Judaism is monotheistic and recognizes Jesus as a "good teacher" and a "prophet of God," but **strongly denies** that **Jesus was God, the Messiah**, divine, or that Jesus was the **sacrifice for salvation**.

Christians, however, believe that Jesus **was God in the flesh** (John 1:14). Jesus said, "If you believed Moses, you would believe me, **for he wrote of me**" (John 5:46). Jesus brought attention to the **written** word instead of the **oral** word.

Instead of calling God, Jehovah, the Jews call God, *HaShem*, which is Hebrew for "The Name," or *Adonai* meaning, "The Lord."

Currently only **one percent** of the Jews are Messianic, meaning they recognize the **New Covenant** and **Jesus Christ** of Nazareth as **Messiah**, Savior.

The popular symbol of Judaism is the **star of David**, a **hexagram**. The symbol has occultic connections. The hexagram is a six-pointed star and is commonly used as an **amulet** as well as for conjuring spirits and spiritual forces in varied forms of **occult magic**. (See Christian Zionism section.) In the book *The History and Practice of Magic*, Vol. 2, the six-pointed star is called the **talisman** of Saturn, and it is also referred to as the **Seal of Solomon**. [45, 265, 266, 268]

Elsewhere in this book we have shown the connection of Judaism to Freemasonry. Albert Pike, author of the book, *Morals and Dogma of the Ancient and Accepted Scottish Rite of Freemasonry,* shows the connection of the star to Freemasonry. states, "For the master, the Compass of Faith is **ABOVE** the Square of Reason, but BOTH rest **upon** the Holy Scriptures and combine to form the **Blazing Star of Truth**" (p. 336). Freemasons put the compass and square **on top** of the Word of God symbolizing their teachings take precedence over God's law.. The compass and the square together form the hexagram, the star, representing **their** truth which is **in contradiction** to the Word of God.

Some researchers have theorized that the hexagram represents the astrological chart at the time of David's birth or anointment as king. The **hexagram** is also known as the "King's Star" in **astrological** circles. There are numerous occultic associations with the hexagram, some of which are covered in this book. [46]

Astrology is connected to the Roman Emperor Constantine via the horoscope, and Constantine is connected to the church (Morals and Dogma, pg. 118). (See Catholicism versus Christianity).

Bibles of Judaism

Judaism does not recognize the New Testament or the New Covenant. The doctrine of Judaism comes from several sources, primarily the **Tanakh** (the Hebrew Bible), the **Talmud** (the Oral Law), and the **Zohar** (mysticism).

The Tanakh includes the Torah, the first five books of Moses, which is the **scriptural Jewish law.** [47, 48] There are 24 books in Judaism. It was written during the Second Temple Period. [121, 267]

There was oral law at the time of Moses. The **Talmud** is the oral law and traditions **written down**; it includes a **commentary** on the **Torah**. The written document has been **handed down over time** and **changed with tradition. The Talmud is Judaism's holiest book.** It is a collection of explanations of **duties imposed on the people**, either from scripture, by tradition or custom, or by those in authority. The Jewish **legal law** of the Talmud is called the **Halakha**. It supplements the Torah's **scriptural law.** It's a very complicated doctrine, and I believe that is the intent. The Rabbis can change, add, or delete laws at any time.

The Talmud's authority takes precedence over the Old Testament. Evidence of this is found in the Talmud itself, Erubin 21b (Soncino edition): "My son, be more careful in the observance of the words of the Scribes **than in the words of the Torah** (Old Testament)."

The Talmud consists of two parts, the **Mishna**, and the **Gemara**. The Mishna is the **written "oral" law** which was written in **190 AD**. It covers topics relating to traditions regarding seeds, holidays, women, damages, holy things, and pure things. There are **two sources** of **rabbinical authority**. One for the **Jerusalem Talmud**, which was actually written in Tiberias, and one for the **Babylonian Talmud**, written in 500 AD. [422] **The Babylonian Talmud is the most common today**.

Remember to the Jews, the **Talmud supersedes the Torah** (the **Bible**). There are many disturbing and shocking texts reported to be in the **Talmud**. Research on the online Torah library https://www.sefaria.org/texts shows a sampling of the Talmudic doctrine. [49, 50, 424] One must wonder if this is likened to the foundation of **wickedness** in our world.

- Yebamoth 63a. States that Adam had sexual intercourse with all the animals in the Garden of Eden.
- Kethuboth 11b. "When a grown-up man has intercourse with a little girl it is nothing."
- Menahoth 43b-44a. A Jewish man is obligated to say the following prayer every day: Thank you God for not making me a gentile, a woman, or a slave.
- Sanhedrin 58b. If a heathen (Gentile) hits a Jew, the Gentile must be killed. Hitting a Jew is the same as hitting God.
- Sanhedrin 57a. A Jew need not pay a Gentile the wages owed him for work.
- Baba Mezia 24a. If a Jew finds an object lost by a Gentile ("heathen") it does not have to be returned.
- Baba Kamma 113a. Jews may use lies ("subterfuges") to circumvent a Gentile.
- Yebamoth 98a. All Gentile children are animals.

All gentiles are considered as non-Jews, heathen, pagan people. This group includes the descendants of **Ishamel**. See the Islam versus Christianity section of this book.

In the thirteenth century, a Jewish convert to Christianity, pressed 35 charges against the Talmud to Pope Gregory IX in France. This trial of the Talmud was called the *Disputation of Paris*. Many **blasphemous passages** about **Jesus**, **Mary**, and **Christianity** were presented. There is a quoted Talmudic passage, for example, where a person named Yeshu, who some people have claimed is **Jesus** of Nazareth, is **sent to hell to be boiled in excrement for eternity** (BT Gittin 57a).

BT Sanhedrin 43a of the Talmud states, "On Passover Eve they hung the corpse of **Jesus** the Nazarene after they killed him by way of **stoning**. And a crier went out before him for forty days, publicly proclaiming: **Jesus the Nazarene is going out to be stoned** because he practiced **sorcery**, incited people to **idol worship**, and led the Jewish people astray. Anyone who knows of a reason to acquit him should come forward and teach it on his behalf. And the court did not find a reason to acquit him, and **so they stoned him** and **hung his corpse on Passover** eve." [411]

Jesus said, "**He that shall blaspheme against the Holy Ghost hath never forgiveness, but is in danger of eternal damnation**" (Mark 3:29).

The blaspheme continues in other passages. Sanhedrin 107b states, "Jesus performed **sorcery**, incited Jews to engage in **idolatry**, and led **Israel astray**." [411, 412]

Among the obscene folklore included in the Talmud is a story that Adam copulated with each of the animals before finding Eve, and Noah was castrated by his son Ham.

A segment of the Talmud permits Jews to kill non-Jews.

In 1240, the *Disputation of Paris* set in place a series of events which finished in a burning of the Talmud. It is estimated that due to the outcome of the trial 24 wagonloads of 10,000 volumes of Hebrew handwritten manuscripts were burned. [120, 121]

Kabbalah and Connection to Freemasonry

If the **Talmud** is found offensive, one can only surmise what is found in the belief ideology of the **Kabbalah**. The Kabbalah is connected to the Jewish oral teachings **believed to be** a revelation from God received by Jews. These teachings have been **passed down** through the generations by **oral tradition**.

Kabbalah is a **mystical** occult form of Judaism. It is "the teaching of the **secret."** **The power of sin is in secrecy**. We see this doctrine demonstrated in and transferred to secret societies such as **Freemasonry**.

It is believed that **King Solomon** brought the Kabbalist teaching to Israel. The **hexagram** is one of the connections to Solomon. (See Christian Zionism section). It is taught in the Kabbalah that when Moses went to the mountaintop, he did not receive the real message from God. **Instead**, it was given to the **70 elders** at the base of the mountain. Many claim the Old Testament was written in a code, and only men **initiated into the Kabbalist secrets** could access the code and understand its message. [137]

Rabbis and students of the Kabbalah have been trying for thousands of years to find the **Bible code** to predict the future. This Bible code is based on a **mathematical computation**, called Gemara. [422]

The **Zohar**, another scriptural text in the Jewish portfolio, is the **primary source** of the beliefs of **Kabbalah**. It is a foundational work in the literature of Kabbalah. [36, 37] The Zohar was written in the 1200s AD. It is **mysticism**. According to the Zohar, God's message in the Torah is meant to be understood at four levels:

- Literal (lowest level)
- Allegorical (symbolic)
- Rabbinic
- Secretive (highest level)

Traditional practitioners believe the Kabbalah's earliest origins pre-date most world religions and form the primordial blueprint for

Creation's philosophies, religions, sciences, arts, and political systems.

According to the Kabbalah, the more powerful and truthful purpose of the Torah is **only accessible to those with special knowledge** and insight. This places the **Zohar** and **Kabbalah** firmly in the sphere of **Gnosticism** and **Mysticism**. [53]

Gnosticism is a belief in acquiring special, mystical knowledge as the means for salvation. *Mysticism* is a belief that **one can hold immediate intercourse with the divine Spirit**. These beliefs are clearly **satanic. The Jewish authority lies with the** <u>rabbis for all these texts</u>. **The rabbis interpret** and disseminate the information to those who are of the Jewish faith. [51, 52]

The **Zohar** played a major role in the lives of at least two false Messiahs in Judaism, Shabbetai **Zvei** (1626-1676) and Jacob **Frank** (1726-1791).

In 1666, Zevi declared himself to be the Messiah. He began to sign his letters **"I am the Lord your God Shabbetai Tzvi."** He proclaimed redemption was available through **acts of sin**, he amassed a following of over **one million** passionate believers, about **half the world's Jewish** population during the seventeenth century. His teachings encouraged and practiced **sexual promiscuity, adultery, incest, and religious orgies**. [54]

After Zevi's death, Jacob **Frank** claimed to be the **reincarnation** of Zevi. He, like Zevi, would perform **"strange acts"** that violated traditional religious taboos, such as, **ritual sacrifice**, and promoting orgies and **sexual immorality**. He often slept with his followers, as well as <u>his own daughter</u>, while preaching a doctrine that **the best way to imitate God was to cross every boundary, transgress every taboo, and mix the sacred with the profane.**

Frank eventually **entered into an alliance** formed by Jesuit and former **Catholic** priest Adam **Weishaupt** and Meyer Amshel **Rothschild** called the **Order of the Illuminati.** The objectives of the Illuminati were to **undermine the world's religions** and **power structures**, in an effort to usher in a utopian era of global communism, which they would covertly rule by their hidden hand: **the New World Order**.

Weishaupt used **Freemasonry** to **recruit** for his own quasi-masonic society, with the goal of "perfecting human nature" through **re-education** to achieve a **communal** state with nature, free of government and organized religion. [57] **Re-education** methodology is still being used today in many facets to usher in the New World Order. **Some** of Weishaupt's books include:

- *Christianity: The Devil's Greatest Trick*
- *Hypersex*
- *Jehovah: The First Nazi*
- *High Priests of Hell*
- *Jesus: Prince of Hell*
- *The Secret School of Wisdom: The Authentic Rituals and Doctrines of the Illuminati*
- *The Triune Brain, Hypnosis and the Evolution of Consciousness*
- *Sex for Salvation*
- *Resurrection: The Origin of a Religious Fallacy*

Using secret societies, such as the **Freemasons**, to infiltrate every area of influence (i.e., home, church, education, legal, government, medical, entertainment, media, etc.), their agenda has played itself out over the centuries and now our generation is reaping what has been sown. **Pope Francis** is the first **Jesuit pope** and a player portraying the **antichrist spirit** behind the plans of the New World Order. [54]

Weishaupt's plan would be rolled out to deceive the masses with four primary objectives: [55]

- Do not advocate a Satanic kingdom.
- Gently steer by questioning the existence of God.
- Demand "sexual liberation," "independence" for women, "inclusiveness," "internationalism," "diversity," and "religious tolerance."
- Promote a hidden agenda: to undermine **"all collective forces except our own."** [54, 55]

Freemasonry's Connection to America

In November **1620**, the individuals we know as the **Pilgrims** created the first **social contract** in the New World. That short document, the *Mayflower Compact*, set a precedent for **religious freedom** and ordered **liberty** that became a foundation for later charters of self-government in North America. [56] However, their efforts are little known or taught.

I made a trip to Boston to visit the Mayflower and to examine the history behind the pilgrimage. To my amazement, *The Mayflower Compact* was hidden from view. It appears what started out as a **foundational covenant** was **purposely** being diminished. **Very few people are educated** about the Pilgrims coming to America for religious freedom. However, what is celebrated is the Declaration of Independence, established by our **masonic** fathers. Yes, the **document itself holds power**, but one cannot ignore the **spiritual impact** of these men who, knowingly or not, had a **spiritual covenant with Lucifer** through **Freemasonry**. Through Freemasonry, they **aligned** themselves with Adam **Weishaupt**, often called a **human devil** [85], and the **Illuminati**, the inner core of **Freemasonry**.

The first Grand Lodge of Freemasonry in the United States was founded in 1733 in Massachusetts. It was St. John's Lodge of Boston, Massachusetts. In 1736, Benjamin Franklin charted a lodge in Philadelphia, Pennsylvania. [450]

The Illuminati was founded on **May 1, 1776**, and the *Declaration of Independence* was signed on **July 4, 1776**. Among our country's early masonic leaders were founding fathers George Washington, Benjamin Franklin, Paul Revere, and John Hancock.[58] The spiritual impact of deception with which these men were entangled is still being unveiled over America today.

How did we get from **Judaism** to the **Illuminati** to **Freemasonry** to **America**? **We followed the path of religion**. It doesn't stop there. The path leads to the **church**. The **pagan** portion of religion can be traced from **America to Israel**, and its infiltration has had a **Luciferian** effect on the **church** and the **home**. Israel cites itself as the "**symbolic cradle of Freemasonry.**" [(212)] (See Photo) Jesus said in 1 John 2:18, "Little children, it is the last time: and as ye have heard that antichrist shall come, **even now are there many antichrists;** whereby we know that it is the last time."

Red Heifer Sacrifice

The Jews are looking to usher in their Messiah to rule in the New World Order. Christian Zionists support this initiative. (See Christian Zionism section). God hates religion and many are **blinded by religion**. The Jews plan to build a third temple. One goal is to have a place to reinstitute animal sacrifices. The Temple Institute touted plans to hold the first red heifer sacrifice in over 2,000 years. This is an insult to our Lord and Savior! **I do not believe God will allow it to happen.**

"Of how much worse punishment, do you suppose, will he be thought worthy **who has trampled the Son of God underfoot, counted the blood of the covenant by which he was sanctified a common thing, and insulted the Spirit of grace?** For we know Him who said, 'Vengeance is Mine, I will repay,' says the Lord. And again, 'The Lord will judge His people.' It is **a fearful thing to fall into the hands of the living God**'" (Hebrews 10:29-31).

I had the opportunity to hold a short interview with Byron Stinson, the farmer from Texas from whom the red heifers were acquired. He said, "We believe that it's very likely that the ceremony would happen somewhere in the area of Passover, 2024, out to the possibility of Shavuot, 2024," God clearly did not allow this to happen as was planned.

Stinson believes this would be the first possibility for such a ceremony in 2,000 years, and that the process toward building a third Jewish temple began when the Jewish people started their return to the Promised Land from the four corners of the world, culminating with Israel becoming a nation. [(59)] (See Christian Zionism section).

The Jews believe the red heifer sacrifice is needed for the purification of the priests for the third temple. [(60)] However, *Jesus* has already made the sacrifice. <u>We do not need another sacrifice</u>. Man's plans cannot supersede God's plans. Through the New Covenant, Jesus abolished Judaism. We, his church, are now the temple that Jesus dwells in.

Know ye not that **your body is the temple of the Holy Ghost** which is **in you, which ye have of God**, and **ye are not your own**? (1 Corinthians 6:19).

"For it is not possible that the blood of bulls and of goats should take away sins" (Hebrews 10:4).

"For had they known it, they would not have crucified the Lord of glory" (1 Corinthians 2:8).

Noahide Law

Many Jewish people, both ancient and modern, **regard the worship of Jesus as God as idolatry.** Idolatry is among the most **serious sins** in Judaism. In rabbinic sources, idolatry is referred to as "foreign worship." [62]

According to the *Foundations of the Torah* 5:2, **idolatry, murder** and **illicit sex**, are the three carnal sins which warrant the death penalty. [62]

On a visit to Israel in 2017, I was handed a card by a Jewish man. I threw the card in my purse with my other Israeli memorabilia. I found the card a few days prior to writing this chapter. The card said, "**Want Divine Protection**? Simply say this **biblical verse** every morning and evening with the intent of fulfilling God's will and you will be divinely protected all your life!" The verse was "Hear oh Israel, God is our Lord, God is only One!"

Those who are true to Judaism quote the **daily Jewish prayer** called *Shema*. The *Shema* is an affirmation of Judaism and a declaration of faith in one God. The obligation to recite the Shema is **separate from the obligation to pray.** Jews are obligated to say Shema in the morning and at night (Deuteronomy 6:7). The first line of the Shema is the same verse, "Hear O Israel, the Lord is our God, the Lord is One." [61] This was the second scripture the Lord gave me pertaining to the blood moon warning.

Judaism does not declare Yeshua (**Jesus**) as the Savior or Messiah for either Jew or non-Jew (Gentiles). The rabbis have a doctrine for the **salvation of non-Jews**. They call it the **Noahide Laws** or Noahide Covenant. A **ban on idolatry** is one of the Noahide commandments. The Noahide laws are the seven laws that Judaism teaches are incumbent **on all of humanity**. These laws are projected as **universal**, moral, natural laws (remember this when reading the section on Catholicism). [10, 62, 63] They say these laws are connected to the rainbow, and that God gave them to Noah. Again, resemblances to the ten commandments may cause confusion.

The back of the card given to me by the Jewish man stated the following: "The **Laws of Noah** were given by G-d to Moses on Mt. Sinai for **all the people of the world**." The seven laws are listed:

1. Belief in G-d. Do not worship idols.
2. Respect G-d and Praise Him – Do not blaspheme His Name.
3. Respect Human Life – Do not murder.
4. Respect the Family – Do not commit immoral sexual acts.
5. Respect other's property – Do not steal.
6. Respect All Creatures – Do not be cruel to animals.
7. Create of Judicial System – Pursue justice.

The motto on the card is, "I love everyone and thereby fulfill G-d's will."

This all sounds good until you understand the **meaning of each law** and the **consequences** when broken. There are over 200 sub laws which can be changed by the Rabbis. It is **disturbing** when one understands **the infiltration of these laws <u>into the United States law</u>**. These laws come from the **Babylonian Talmud** and **apply <u>mandatorily</u> to non-Jews**. The laws **prohibit freedom of religion, freedom of speech, and freedom of sexuality or <u>death by decapitation</u>**. [276]

Law Number Seven is to bring about the court system to enforce laws one through six and all the sub laws which are connected. It is my belief that the court system mostly run by the Freemasons will be used to carry out this enforcement.

It was a week before I had the blood moon experience, February 14, 2023, when with great anticipation I asked my kind Jewish tour guide, who had been my guide on a prior visit, to take me to the **Cave of Machpelah**, also known as the **Cave of the Patriarchs**. He was hesitant due to the uprising protests and on-going conflicts. He had not been there in over three years. Our van was searched, and we were questioned when we entered Hebron.

The Cave of the Patriarchs is where **Abraham, Sarah, Isaac, Rebekah, Jacob, and Leah are buried** (Genesis 25:9-10; 49:29-32). It is located near the ancient city of **Hebron. Abraham** purchased the property **when his wife Sarah died**, around 2,000 years before Christ was born (Genesis 23:17-18).

Even though I had visited Israel twice before, I had never been to Hebron. It was a **special place**, as all the elders of Israel had come to **Hebron** to **anoint David king over Israel** (2 Samuel 5:3-5). **King Herod was the builder** of the building covering the cave of the Patriarchs. **This is the only fully surviving Herodian structure from the period of Hellenistic Judaism**. [2] Hebron is an area under Palestinian control and there are many insurrections that take place there. [3] Hebron was not a safe place to visit; however, I felt a draw to go and encouraged my nervous guide to lead the way. (*See Photo*).

Upon entry, I saw both **Palestinians** (Arabs), some who were **Muslim**, and **Jews**, and of course we were **Christians**; thus, three religions were represented in this very important historical site. Many were in prayer, and some were reading; others were giving alms at the monuments of "our father, Abraham" and to his family members. (*See Photo*).

Once inside, my guide chatted with the Jewish attendant. Then he demonstrated putting on the **tefillin**. I may have seen this demonstrated by the Jewish men in my previous trips, but it didn't register with me the significance and meaning. **Tefillin** are a pair of black leather boxes containing Hebrew parchment scrolls. A set includes two—one for the head and one for the arm. Each consists of three main components: the **scrolls**, the **box**, and the **strap**. (*See Photo*). One of the boxes is placed on the arm to rest against the heart, the **seat of the emotions,** and the leather strap is wound around the left arm and hand. The other box is placed on the **head**, above the **forehead**. It is a reminder to dedicate oneself to the service of God in all **thought, feelings**, and **action**. [11]

"If any man worship the beast and his image, and receive his mark in his **forehead**, or in his **hand**, The same shall drink of the wine of the wrath of God" (Revelation 14:9-10).

The Jews base this ritual on the following verse: **"Hear, O Israel: The Lord our God is one Lord**: And thou shalt love the Lord thy God with all thine heart, and with all thy soul, and with all thy might. And these words, which I command thee this day, shall be in thine heart: And thou shalt teach them diligently unto thy children, and shalt talk of them when thou sittest in thine house, and when thou walkest by the way, and when thou liest down, and when thou risest up. **And thou shalt bind them for a sign upon thine hand, and they shall be as frontlets between thine eyes.** And thou shalt write them upon the posts of thy house, and on thy gates" (Deuteronomy 6:4-9).

Jesus Christ is God to the Christians. Proclaiming this ideology in this "holy place", the Cave of Machpelah, where Abraham is buried, **would have been forbidden**. The administration at the site was ran by Jews. Praying aloud to Jesus would have most likely caused an offense (Romans 9:33).

The young Jewish attendant was very friendly. I mentioned to him the fact that Hebron and specifically this site was an area of much religious conflict. He surprised me and said, **"But we have an answer! <u>Soon</u>** it will be resolved."

I replied, "Oh yeah?"

He said, **"We will soon** have the **universal** laws in place, the **Noahide** laws." I was floored that he proclaimed this to an American woman.

I said, "**I am well aware** of the Noahide laws and **the plan**."

It was his turn to be surprised. He said, "**You are**??"

What surprised me most was the acceptance by the younger generation and the agreement with **the plan to propose these laws globally.** A written conversation in the Sanhedrin, also called the *New Jewish Congress*, [64] assumes that Jewish courts should enforce the Noahide laws. This push can be traced back to Moses ben Maimon.

Moses ben Maimon (1138–1204), commonly known as **Maimonides**, or Moses, son of Maimon, or Rambam, was one of the most prolific and influential **Torah scholars** of the Middle Ages. In his time, he was also a preeminent **astronomer** and **physician** (note these important connections and remember the pandemic), posthumously acknowledged as one of the foremost **rabbinic decisors**. He **decided law** where there was **no clear oral** or **written** Jewish law. He was a philosopher in Jewish history, and his copious work comprises a cornerstone of Jewish scholarship. He **wrote the Mishnah Torah** or the Halakha, Jewish Talmud **legal law**. [65]

According to Maimonides, it is **unacceptable** for **non-Jews** living under a Jewish authority **not to accept the Noahide laws**. [66] He bases this belief on the following Torah and Talmud scriptures:

If someone from the other nations wants to convert [they may] as it says '[the law is the same] for you, for a stranger' (Numbers 15:15). But if they do not want to, we do not compel them to accept the Torah and the commandments. Moses did, however, command in the name of God **to compel all people** to accept the Noahide laws. . . ." (Laws of Kings 8:10).

There are some **rabbis** who are calling for **anyone regardless of where they live to be killed who does not believe as they do**, specifically in the **Noahide laws**, and especially **those who believe on Jesus Christ**. Romans 9:30-33 tells us that **the gospel of Jesus Christ is an offense!**

Rabbi Yosef Mizrachi recently stated that **six billion people** are **idol worshipers** and **do not deserve to live**. [68] He says that **two**

billion of these are **idol worshipers** of J. C. (**Jesus Christ**). He cannot bring himself to say the name of **Jesus**. We know that **Jesus**, Himself, was **accused of blasphemy** (John 10:33). While there is strong disagreement in certain sects against Mizrachi, **tens of thousands of Jews worldwide** have **embraced** Judaism due to his teachings, and **many are unaware that <u>the United States has embraced the Noahide laws.</u>** [69]

In 1978, **the U.S. Congress** asked **President Jimmy Carter** to designate Menachem Mendel Schneerson's birthday as the national **Education Day U.S.A.** Remember the plan to **re-educate**? <u>**This was the initiation of the Noahide laws in the United States.**</u> Schneerson was the leader of the Chabad-Lubavitch movement, one of the most influential movements in religious Jewry, bringing **infiltration of Noahide theology.** Many supporters believed he was the **Messiah.** Education Day U.S.A. has been since commemorated as **Education and Sharing Day**. In 1994, Schneerson was posthumously awarded the Congressional Gold Medal for his "outstanding and lasting contributions toward improvements in **world education**, morality, and acts of charity." [70] It has been reported that Rabbi Schneerson said **<u>non-Jews have satanic souls</u>, yet in the United States, the Noahide laws are stated to be <u>the foundation upon which America</u> (non-Jews) <u>was founded.</u>** [276] Astounding!

In 1982, then **President Ronald Reagan** signed Proclamation 4921 in which he stated that the Noahide Laws are the **<u>moral foundation of America's character,</u>** and the Noahide Laws are a **<u>moral code</u> for all <u>regardless of faith</u>**. He also **praised** the Lubavitch movement and Rabbi Schneerson for their **example in educating the world** about the **Jewish Noahide Laws.** He then requested Congress to sign **Joint Resolution 477,** which celebrates Rabbi Schneerson's birthday as a "National Day of Reflection." [69]

In 1983, Schneerson launched a global campaign to promote awareness of the Supreme Being and observance of the Noahide Laws **among all people,** arguing that this was the **<u>basis for human rights for all civilization</u>**. Several times each year, his addresses were broadcast on **national television in the United States.** On these occasions, Schneerson would address the public on general communal affairs and issues relating to **world peace, such as a moment of silence in U.S. public schools** (promotion of **universalism** in religion) increased government funding for **solar energy** research, U.S. foreign aid to developing countries, and nuclear disarmament. [69] The increase in solar fields in Israel from 2017 to 2023 is unbelievable. (*See Photo*).

In 1991, **both houses of Congress** passed a bill, signed into law by **President George H. W. Bush**, that declared the **Noahide Laws** to be "<u>**the bedrock of society from the dawn of civilization**</u>" and the "**ethical values** and principles . . . **upon which our great Nation was founded**" (H.J.RES.104.ENR). [71, 76]

Donald Trump is known as the **Noahide Champion**. One misguided person stated, "An often-ignored aspect of **his administration** has been its **promotion of Noahide Law** and values. During his almost four years in office, **Donald Trump has been the <u>greatest supporter of Noahide law in US history</u>** and he must be reelected if only for that reason. By saying that the President supports Noahide law, I do not mean to say that he has imposed these laws on the general population, but rather that he has contributed to **dismantle the liberal agenda to impose their secularist dogma** on the entire population and has defended the rights of American who want to live by **God's law**." [72]

The Trump reviewer confused **Noahide law** with **God's law!** One **cannot follow Jesus Christ under Noahide laws without the threat of being <u>put to death</u>**. Be warned, there are **two wings** of the same bird in Washington, DC, and the agenda is to **control the opposition** to accomplish <u>**one plan.**</u>

I had the opportunity to tour the new, recently open to the public **Sanhedrin Synagogue** in Israel. (*See Photo*). The *Sanhedrin* was the high court and legislative authority for Jews made up of both **Pharisees** and **Sadducees**. This was **the court that condemned Jesus to death.**

As of June 2023, there has been an ongoing official effort supported mainly by the Temple Institute to **revive the Sanhedrin**.

[269] Many believe that the hidden agenda is for the **Sanhedrin to replace the United Nations** in order to **legislate the Noahide laws worldwide**. It has been reported that plans for the third temple were established in the Sanhedrin Synagogue. [270]

In 2020, **United States Secretary of State Mike Pompeo** joined the leadership of the nation of Israel to sign historic documents in this synagogue (Ezekiel 8:8-12).

This visit was historic as it is the **first time** *ever* senior **US** officials and senior **Israeli** Government officials have **joined together** to visit the old city. [67] Additionally, Pompeo visited a museum in Jerusalem that honors **Christian Zionists**. The Israeli Museum was founded **by a prominent evangelical adviser to the Trump administration, Mike Evans, an American Christian evangelist.** [400, 401]

In interesting contrast, **Pompey** the Great, **Roman** Politician, was one of the greatest generals of his age. His conquest of Jerusalem in 63 BC spelled the end of Jewish independence and the incorporation of Judea as a client kingdom of the Roman Republic. [73] Could the **Pompeo** visit also be a signal of **an end of Israel** as we know it? It sure seems possible with the talks of an imminent civil war and the current aggression of war. [86]

Evidence shows the **Noahide** push is becoming more integrated on a **global scale**. More recently, *The Institute of Noahide Code INC* has proposed a strategic alliance with the **United Nations** post 2030 agenda to promote the codification into **national legislation** of the United Nations resolutions on the culture of peace, environmental ethics, and social justice. [74]

Janna Benuun, a reporter and researcher for Israeli News Live, wrote,

"One very important fact that American Christians need to remember is that **whatever Israel does is affecting the United States** as a country. Many states in USA are proposing bills to make **any criticism of Israel and the Jews** or Jewish religion **a felony**. This constant redefinition of who is to be labeled as anti-Semite is a

desperate attempt by the ruling powers **to silence** any brave souls who would dare to speak out against the **extreme religious** tyranny that could potentially affect **American** lives.

Many Chabad rabbis, who are influencers of our politicians, are proselyting for the Noahide Laws **for the gentiles** (a.k.a. Americans). The Noahide Laws **are already a part of the public laws in the United States** and especially **promoted in our public-school education system**." [75]

What is the penalty for not following the Noahide laws? Bill Dannemeyer, <u>US Congressman</u>, 1979-1992, posted on his website, **"Your U.S. government can now legally kill Christians for the 'crime' of worshipping Jesus Christ!** A diabolic deception has been perpetrated on the American people by their *own* **leaders, Senators,** and **Congressmen,** who **have sold their soul to the devil**. On March 5, 1991, in the House of Representatives, and March 7, 1991, in the U.S. Senate, **without any knowledge of, or input by, the people of the United States,** U.S. Senators and Congressmen **passed a law** that is so outrageous, and frankly unconstitutional, **that it <u>forces the American people</u> to be bound by a set of monstrous rules, called the <u>Noahide Laws,</u>** rules that make **the belief in Jesus Christ a crime punishable by <u>death</u>!**" On March 20, 1991, **President George H. W. Bush**, a supposed Christian, <u>**signed the bill into law**</u>." [402]

We know that ultimately, this is a **spiritual battle**, and the **seed of Satan** is against the **seed of Christ**. It goes back to the garden of Eden when the Lord God said to the serpent, "And I will put **enmity** between **thee** and the **woman**, and between thy **seed** [*devil*] and her **seed** [*Jesus*]; it shall bruise thy **head**, and thou shalt bruise his **heel**" (Genesis 3:14). These seeds have produced the **children of God** and the **children of the devil** as outlined in 1 John 3.

Anti-Semitic, Anti-Christian, Anti-Palestinian

The United States Department of State 2016 website, "Defining Antisemitism", lists a definition and examples of antisemitism. [408] The definition given states:

"Antisemitism is a certain **perception of Jews**, which may be expressed as hatred toward Jews. Rhetorical and physical manifestations of antisemitism are directed toward Jewish or non-Jewish individuals and/or their property, toward Jewish community institutions and religious facilities."

You can check out all the examples on the site at https://www.state.gov/defining-antisemitism. The example that stands out the most to Christians is "**Using the symbols and images associated with classic antisemitism (e.g., claims of Jews killing Jesus or blood libel) to characterize Israel or Israelis.**"

Jews are the **only group of people** that I am aware of who have **worldwide protection**. Christians have been **martyred** and **slaughtered** since **Cain killed Abel, and yet are without protection**. As of this writing, **innocent Palestinians**, women, and children **are being killed in Gaza**. I have seen the tall walls around this small area. I have been personally told by a friendly Jew (most Jews do not hold the beliefs of the elite Jews), that the Palestinians are only able to come in and out of the tall prison walls under **strict restrictions**.

Gaza has been the largest open-air prison in the world. For example, they have not had the freedom to **drive to work** in Israel, and the jobs available to them have been **limited**. There has been **no effort** to remove the innocent from the terrorist. It has been reported that even the **relief workers** and those bringing humanitarian aid have been put in danger. **Any word standing against the slaughter is shot down with the accusation of antisemitism**. Not being able to seek and find the truth is a **blow to free speech**.

The Noahide laws have been promoted by the elite Jewish leaders and **infiltrated to the United States against the knowledge of the American people**, yet many are **afraid to stand** and ask for details. These decisions affect the majority, yet the **majority are not educated**, nor do they understand the **future ramifications**. If they do understand, they are belittled and **forced into silence**.

I have visited Israel three times and have personally witnessed the increase of **persecution of Christians** while there. Shortly after my last visit in February 2023, videos circulated of **children spitting on Christians.** Spitting on Christians in disrespect has been occurring in Israel for years. [409] While there are many wonderful, nice tour guides in Israel, one **will not find a Christian tour guide.** They are trained to speak the **history of the Bible** and often to give **propaganda** to the tourists. One **cannot** be a citizen of Israel and **publicly proclaim Jesus is Lord,** only the historical relation to the area.

One of the most obnoxious tour guides on my last visit continually talked about stories from the **Talmud**, which are not biblical, such as Mary and Jesus sleeping together, Solomon's hot sex night with Bathsheba, and the child that came as a result. **Incorrect data was given about Jesus**, such as His age not being 33 when he died, and that He **died by stoning**. When asked about Freemasonry (in which 33 is a prominent number, 33 degrees), he ignored the questions. Some on the team asked him to stop quoting the Talmud as it was in opposition to the Bible. Many in the group were offended. His actions caused negativity in the group and made time with him unenjoyable.

Many Jews believe **trusting in Christ is antisemitic**. However, the original definition of antisemitism states one **must be from the lineage of Shem** or **speak the Semitic language** in order to be a Semite. [201, 279] Information has already been given in this book that **no one can** absolutely **prove** they are from the lineage of Shem, which includes the twelve tribes as they were scattered (Psalms 106:27; James 1:1).

The church has been viewed as being responsible for forcing the Jewish people to face contempt, persecution, forced conversion, and genocide–all at the hands of those who called themselves Christians. [77] I love the Jews enough to tell them **Jesus is the only way**. I consider myself to be a true Jew according to Romans 2:29. **Anyone** who follows Jesus can be a **true Jew** as stated by Paul.

We are warned in Hebrews 12:14 about the effects of a **root of bitterness**. It says, "lest any root of bitterness [*wickedness, hatred*] springing up trouble you, and thereby many be defiled [*polluted, contaminated*].

We know that the Bible speaks of the **spirit of antichrist** from the beginning. However, many injustices in more recent times have fanned the flame and these wrongs are partially to blame for the **root of bitterness**. Examples include:

The **Catholic Crusades** (1095-1291) were launched for the specific reason of reclaiming the Holy Land from those deemed unworthy (i.e., Muslims and Jews). There are even reports about how the Crusaders lit the Great Synagogue of Jerusalem on fire with its congregants inside, and as it burned, marched around it singing *"Christ, We Adore Thee."* **Many church leaders during the Crusades** supported these sentiments.

The **Spanish and Portuguese Inquisitions** (1536) especially focused on **Jewish Christians** who continued practicing Shabbat, Jewish holidays, and other rituals. As a result, the Spanish and Portuguese Inquisitions targeted **Messianic Jews**, whether they were sincere in their faith or not. Those found "guilty" were usually **burned at the stake.**

During the **Holocaust** (1933-1945), even though Nazism was opposed to the true tenets of Christian faith, the *Confessing Church* (German Protestants) was the **only official Christian sect** that took a public stand against the Nazis. The rest of the church **did very little** to combat or decry this evil at the time (arguably due to Luther's influence on German ideology). Most of the Nazis were self-proclaimed Christians, and while we know that the horrendous acts committed were not at all aligned with the teachings of the New Testament, as expected, that was not clear to the Jewish community.

To this day, many Jewish people consider much of the responsibility for the Holocaust to fall on the **Christian church,** even though many **individual Christians** risked and **even sacrificed** their lives to hide Jewish families and smuggle countless Jewish children out of Nazi-occupied areas. [77] We must remember that during this time, **communication and travel were not as prevalent**

as today. Many who were concerned most likely **were not aware** of how **to find truth** or **how to respond.**

So, yes, many mean and hateful actions can be viewed as the responsibility of the "Christian" community, but we know Ephesians 6:12 says, "For we wrestle not against flesh and blood, but against **principalities**, against **powers**, against the **rulers** of the **darkness** of this **world**, against **spiritual wickedness** in **high places**."

The Jews are not attacked because they are Jews but rather due to the ideology being imposed on others. In the previous section you have been presented with documentation from the Talmud and the Zohar teachings **that are antichrist. Many are being labeled antisemitic because they are bringing issues to the table where Jewish influences have spilled across lines in <u>domination of others</u>**. [433] Also, if **antisemitism** is an issue, **then we must bring antichristian issues** to the table, such as spitting on Christians.

The Talmud is the legal code which forms the basis of Jewish religious law and it is **the textbook used in the training of rabbis**. Benjamin Freedman, a wealthy Jewish man, who dedicated himself and his considerable fortune to exposing the Zionist tyranny, wrote in his book, *Facts are Facts*, that **the Talmud is being indoctrinated into the minds of children <u>in the United States</u> from the time they are able to read and write**. [406]

I brought the Holocaust issue to the Lord in prayer and asked for revelation. There is a difference in **knowledge** and **revelation**. **Knowledge** is what we know from **studying**, but **revelation** is what the **Holy Spirit** can give us as He **guides** us in all **truth** and shows us things **we did not know** (John 16:13).

I began looking back on the research regarding the **Zohar**, which is the foundational work in the literature of Jewish mystical thought known as **Kabbalah.** It is based on **mysticism, occult** sciences, and **divination**. It is ritual **magic**. [78] **Kabbalah** forms the foundation of **mystical religious interpretations within Judaism**. It is a part of Jewish tradition that deals with the essence of God. [79]

The Lord prompted me to research **Nazism**. I found the book, *Occult Roots of Nazism Secret Aryan Cults and Their Influence on Nazi Ideology* by Nicholas Goodrick-Clarke. [443] It states: "**Occultism was invoked** to endorse the enduring validity of an obsolescent and precarious **social order**. The ideas and symbols of **ancient theocracies, secret societies, and the mystical gnosis of Rosicrucianism, Cabbalism**, and **Freemasonry** were **woven** into the volkisch **theology**, to prove that **the modern world** was based on **false and evil principles** and to describe the values and institutions **of the ideal world**."

Wow, this blew me away. Whatever we come into agreement within the spiritual world becomes a <u>**binding legal contract**</u>. This is what got Adam and Eve into trouble. They bonded with evil. That is why it is important to **not agree** with **thoughts and ideologies** that are <u>**against the Word of God**</u>. The **physical contracts** you make are the result of those **spiritual contracts** made **in your heart** and there is no freedom **until you can sever the bonds** of those self-serving **spiritual contracts** with the ways of evil. Unless there is **spiritual repentance**, there will be no freedom from the **physical contracts**. [80] Could it be the Holocaust was **a physical manifestation of a spiritual contract**?

We see the Lord God spoke through Samuel to Saul in 1 Samuel 15:23 that rebellion is the spirit of witchcraft. "For <u>**rebellion**</u> [BITTERNESS] is as **the sin of <u>witchcraft</u>, and stubbornness is as iniquity** and <u>**idolatry**</u>. **Because thou hast rejected the word of the Lord**, he hath also rejected thee from being king." Interesting that the word *rebellion* here means *BITTERNESS*!

The word *rebellion* means bitterness, disobedience, generally translated "**against God**" or "**against the Word of God**."

Jesus reminded us that Jesus Himself through the Word of God was spoken **from Moses and the prophets to the people of Israel, and yet they refused to listen.** After Jesus' resurrection He was on the road to Emmaus, talking to the two walking with Him, who did not know who He was until He vanished. (*See Photo*). "Then [Jesus] said unto them, O fools, and **slow of heart to believe all that the**

prophets have spoken. And beginning at Moses and all the prophets, he expounded unto them in all the scriptures the things **concerning himself**" (Luke 24:25, 27).

Rebellion is first found in Deuteronomy 31:27. "For I know thy **rebellion**, and thy **stiff neck**: behold, while I am yet alive with you this day, ye have been **rebellious against the Lord**; and how much more after my death?" He continues on in verse 29, "For **I know that after my death ye will utterly corrupt yourselves, and turn aside** from the way which I have commanded you; and <u>evil will befall you in the latter days</u>; because **ye will do evil in the sight of the Lord, to provoke him to anger** through the work of your hands."

At the time of this writing in Deuteronomy, the official life of Moses was coming to a close. Moses returned from the tabernacle, **finished writing the laws,** and then **gave the book of the law to the Levites, with a command to put it by the side of the ark of the covenant,** that it might be there for **a witness against the people**, as **He knew their rebellion** and stiff-neckedness [stubbornness, hardness].

Zephaniah gave a vivid image of the nature of the rebellious spirit, "Woe to her that is filthy and polluted, to the oppressing city! **She obeyed not the voice**; she **received not correction**; she **trusted not in the Lord; she drew not** near to her God" (Zephaniah 3:1-2).

Bitterness is first found in reference to **Esau's bitter cry** when he was begging his father to bless him (Genesis 27:34). Has the bitterness of **Esau,** which is **Edom,** which is **Rome,** crept into the line of **Judaism**? Remember the **Jews** hated the **Romans**. It appears that somewhere along the line **bitterness has paved the way for witchcraft** [DIVINATION, PRACTICE MAGIC].

Paul expounds more about what happens when one gets caught up in the **gods of this world** and **refuses to accept Jesus as Lord.**

"In whom **the god of this world** hath **blinded the minds** of them **which believe not**, lest the light of the glorious gospel of

Christ, who is the image of God, should shine unto them" (2 Corinthians 4:4).

"**But their minds were blinded**. For until this day the same veil remains unlifted **in the reading of the Old Testament [Torah]**, because the veil is taken away **in Christ [New Covenant].** But even to this day, <u>when Moses is read</u>, a veil lies on their hearts. Nevertheless, **when one turns to the Lord, the veil is taken away.** Now the Lord is the Spirit; and where the Spirit of the Lord is, there is liberty" (2 Corinthians 3:14-16).

Does this mean we are not to read Moses or the Old Testament? No, the **Old Testament** is revealed in the **New Testament**. It is a **shadow** of Christ who would come and fulfil the law. **When we understand the Old Testament, the New Testament comes to life.**

Evangelism

We know for three and a half years Jesus specifically told his disciples to focus on ministering to the Jews. Jesus' ministry to the Jews was all through the book of Matthew, Mark, Luke, John, and the first part of Acts, and through the Upper Room experience.

In Matthew we are told that, "These twelve Jesus sent forth, and commanded them, saying, Go not into the way of the Gentiles, and into any city of the Samaritans enter ye not: **But go rather to the lost sheep of the house of Israel**. And as ye go, preach, saying, The kingdom of heaven is at hand" (Matthew 10:5-7).

The Gentiles were the non-Jewish, heathen, pagans and the Samaritans were half-Jews who were "Romanized." **Samaria** was the **capital of Israel** until it fell to the **Assyrians**. The **Samaritans** lived in "ivory" houses, with luxury, and worshiped pagan gods. [81]

Yet, Joel 2:32 prophesies, **"For in mount Zion and in Jerusalem shall be deliverance, as the Lord hath said, and in the remnant whom the Lord shall call."** So how will the remnant come out of this blind, unbelieving, and perverse people? (Matthew 15:14; 17:17)

The **true *CHURCH*** (spiritual Israel) has been sent forth **as the Deliverer** to the house of Jacob (physical Israel).

How then shall they call on him in whom they have not believed? and **how shall they believe in him of whom they have not heard?** and **how shall they hear without a preacher**? (Romans 10:14).

"And so all Israel shall be saved: as it is written, There shall come out of **Sion** [the church] the **Deliverer** [the Man Child], and shall turn away ungodliness from Jacob" (Romans 11:26).

God has magnified **his Word above his Name** (Psalm 138:2). He works in the confines of what He, Himself has declared. He seeks for a *man*! The church is His incarnation. We are the man He seeks.

The church must evangelize to the <u>Jews</u> and the <u>Muslims</u>, the descendants of **Jacob** and **Ishmael**. Ishmael's descendants are considered Gentile and **would most likely be the group to most provoke the Jews to jealousy**. Paul says, "Through their fall salvation is come unto the Gentiles, for to provoke them to jealousy" (Romans 11:11).

Another possibility, if it is to come about, is that through the preparations to open the third temple, singing the Psalms, might soften the hearts of the Jews as they speak the Word of God. [82] What the enemy means for evil, God will use it for good (Genesis 50:20).

Jews traveling to Jerusalem for one of the three main annual Jewish festivals traditionally sang the Psalms on the "ascent" or the uphill road to the city. The *Songs of Ascent* are found in Psalm 120-134. According to some traditions, the Jewish priests also sang some of the Songs of Ascent as they walked up the steps to the temple in Jerusalem.

The Pool of Siloam, where Jesus is said to have healed a blind man, is slated to be opened to the public for the first time after approximately two thousand years. [83] It is the on the path of ascent.

I believe one day many of **His people** will become **His children**. I'm reminded of when Jesus said to Simon, "Of those who have been forgiven much, they will love Him much" (Luke 7:4). It is so true, the more we realize that we have been **forgiven** much, **of all our sins**, the more we will **love** the Lord Jesus!

This analogy is expressed in the story of the woman who washed the feet of Jesus. "And he [Jesus] turned to the woman, and said unto Simon, 'Seest thou this woman? I entered into thine house, thou gavest me no water for my feet: but she hath washed my feet with tears, and wiped them with the hairs of her head. Wherefore I say unto thee, **Her sins, which are many, are forgiven; for she loved much: but to whom little is forgiven, the same loveth little**.' And he said unto her, 'Thy sins are forgiven'" (Luke 7:44, 47-48).

I'm sure the thought of **His people** becoming **His children** must make the heart of Jesus beam! At this time, the full realization of the scripture given to me as a second warning and the scripture so prominent in the Jewish prayers will be realized. "Jesus answered [one of the scribes], The first of all the commandments is: '**Hear, O Israel, the Lord our God, the Lord is one**'" (Mark 12:29).

Because of the Jews' stubbornness and stiff-necked ways, **the gospel was taken to the Gentiles.** Romans says that the Jews are the root and some of the branches from the root **will be broken off** and the **Gentiles will be grafted in**. "And if some of the branches be broken off, and thou, being a wild olive tree, wert graffed in among them, and with them partakest of the root and fatness of the olive tree; Boast not against the branches. But if thou boast, **thou bearest not the root, but the root thee** (Romans 11:17-18).

Jesus is the rod out of Jesse, and all must be grated into and abide in him. The root of the physical Israel had an axe put to it when Jesus came.

And there shall come forth a **rod out of the stem of Jesse**, and a Branch shall grow out of his roots (Isaiah 11:1).

Abide in me, and I in you. As **the branch cannot bear fruit of itself, except it abide in the vin**e; no more can ye, **except ye abide in me** (John 15:4).

And now also **the axe is laid unto the root of the trees**: therefore **every tree which bringeth not forth good fruit is hewn down**, and cast into the fire (Matthew 3:10).

Romans 2:28-29 says, "For **he is not a Jew, which is one outwardly**; neither is that circumcision, which is outward in the flesh: **But he is a Jew, which is one inwardly**; and circumcision is that of the **heart**, in the **spirit**, and not in the letter; whose praise is not of men, but of God."

Christians worship one God, a *Messiah* from the tribe of *Judah*, the God of Abraham, Isaac, and Jacob, the God of promise and fulfillment. Jesus Christ is the fulfillment of the Hebrew prophecies of a coming Messiah. This was foretold in Isaiah fifty-three. Most Jews never hear about this chapter because they depend upon their rabbi to teach it, and many leave it out. [43]

One Jewish lady from the *Jews for Jesus* organization said, "**The subject was never discussed** in my pre-war-Poland Hebrew school. In the rabbinical training I had received, the fifty-third chapter of **the book of Isaiah had been continually avoided** in favor of other "weightier" matters to be learned. Yet, when I first read this passage, my mind was filled with questions."

When many Jews hear for the first time Isaiah 53:5, **they cannot deny that it is *Jesus* to whom Isaiah is referring.** "But he was **wounded for our transgressions,** he was **bruised for our iniquities**: the chastisement of our **peace** was upon him; and with his stripes **we are healed.** "[44]

Rashi (Rabbi Shlomo Itzchaki, 1040-1105) and some of the later rabbis, though, interpreted the passage as referring **to Israel rather than to Jesus.** They knew that the older interpretations referred to **Messiah.** However, Rashi lived at a time when a degenerate medieval distortion of Christianity was practiced. [43] **Because of**

bitterness and rebellion, the Old Testament has not been taught in its truth and entirety.

Jesus Christ as the Son of God is the one primary issue that Christianity and Judaism cannot agree upon. Therefore **"Judeo"** and **"Christian"** are <u>two separate paths</u>. Mark 14:61-65 tells how the high priests **accused Jesus of blasphemy** and they beat Him and sought to kill Him for saying He was the Son of God. **They didn't believe His words or accept Him as the Messiah.** [33]

"Again, the high priest asked him, and said unto him, Art thou the Christ, the Son of the Blessed? And **Jesus said, I am**: and ye shall see the Son of man sitting on the **right hand of power**, and coming in the clouds of heaven. Then the high priest rent his clothes, and saith, What need we any further witnesses? **Ye have heard the blasphemy**: what think ye? **And they all condemned him to be guilty of death**. And **some began to spit on him**, and to cover his face, and to buffet him, and to say unto him, Prophesy: and the servants did strike him with the palms of their hands" (Mark 14:60-65).

The government of Israel and the Jews in charge still have this view today. The Israeli government welcomes **Christian tourists** to Israel. **Christian conventions** are welcomed in Israel. **Christian funds** for the exploration of archaeological sites and investments for the development of natural resources are welcomed in Israel. **But the Christian missionary to the Jew is not welcomed.** [34]

Many "Christian" Zionist ministries in the United States **make a deal** with the **Israeli government to not mention Jesus** in order to **gain partnership** with Israel. [97]

However! God is opening the eyes of the Jewish people to Jesus Christ more than any time in 2,000 years! **There is an increase** in the internet searches by the Jewish for **Messiah, Yeshua, Jesus, New Testament**, with an estimated 175,000 hits per week. There are an estimated 200 Messianic synagogues in Israel at the time of this writing. [84] Praise God!

In conclusion, this section has shown that **Judaism does not equal Christianity.** In Judaism, Abraham is the **founding** father of the special relationship between the Jews and God. In Christianity, Abraham is the **spiritual forerunner of <u>all believers</u>**, whether Jewish or non-Jewish.

When one accepts Jesus Christ as their Savior, they are grafted into the root and **thus anyone, no matter their physical descent, can become a spiritual Jew and a joint-heir with the Seed of Abraham, Jesus Christ**. (Romans 11) Praise God!

Catholicism versus Christianity

The worldview is held that Catholicism is synonymous with Christianity. This is deceptive. The Catholic church **claims** to have descended from Jesus Christ; however, there should be enough verification in this chapter to show doubts to this claim and the evident connection to **paganism**. The association of Catholicism to Christianity has deceived many and lured them away from the true doctrine of Christ.

This section deals mostly with the **pre-reformation** era. Not every detail is covered about Catholicism or the Roman Empire. However, it but will give a brief overview to help the reader understand how and where Christianity was corrupted and why many have lost sight of the doctrine of Christ.

The word *Catholic* is defined in the Webster's Dictionary as:

- "**Universal** or general. **Originally** this epithet was given to the Christian church in general but **is now** appropriated to the Romanish church.
- **Liberal**, not narrow-minded.
- A **papist**."

A *papist* is defined as a Roman Catholic; one who adheres to the church **of Rome** and who is under the <u>authority of the **pope**</u>.

The *Pope* is defined as the **bishop of Rome**; the **head** of the Catholic church; as in **authority**. [13, 28]

The *Holy See* is the governing body, which consists of the pope and his administration. The Holy See means the Church is the "**seat of government**." It is a monarchy in which **the pope is the "king."** The pope is in control of executive, legislative, and judicial power over the city **and the church**. [134]

The *Vatican* or *vaticinium* is the celebrated church of Saint Peter is in **Rome**. Although as you will see, **Saint Peter** had nothing to do with this association. *Vaticinium* is synonymous with the word Oracle. [177] *Oracle* is a person **through whom** a deity is believed to speak. [19, 176]

The **Vatican** became a country in **1929**. It is the smallest country in the world. The Vatican is a magnificent palace of the pope, situated at the foot of one of the **seven hills** on which Rome was built. Many believe this is a fulfillment of the prophecy in Revelation 17:9, "The seven heads are **seven mountains** on which the **woman** [Vatican] sits." Interestingly, **Washington, DC**, was originally named **Rome**, Maryland. It also has **seven hills** with **Capitol Hill** being the most famous. [277]

In the valley between two of the seven hills in Rome are the hills of Aventine and Palatine. This is where the famous **Circus Maximus** was located. The *Circus Maximus* was the model for circuses throughout the Roman Empire. It could accommodate 150,000 spectators. Temples to several deities overlooked the track. **Emperor Nero** held chariot racing, gladiator shows with wild beasts, festivals, and theatres at the Circus Maximus. An Egyptian obelisk was erected in the middle of the track. It is said Saint Peter was **beheaded** near the **obelisk**.

The sacred obelisk towered over the Circus Maximus arena, located in the center, close to Sol's temple and the finishing line for the races.

During this time, *Sol* was the honored **male sun god**, the divine patron of the Circus and its games. Sol was the ultimate, victorious charioteer, driving his four-horse chariot through the **heavenly circuit** from sunrise to sunset.

Sol's partner *Luna* was the **female moon god** who drove a two-horse chariot. Together, these two gods represented the predictable, orderly movement of the cosmos and the circuit of time, which found similarity in the Circus track.

It is believed that the majority of Christian martyrdom in Rome took place at the Maximus. [278] **The obelisk from the Circus Maximus where Saint Peter was beheaded now stands in Vatican Square.**

Vatican City and Rome's Churches

Vatican City is in Rome. It is the city-state **governed** by the **Holy See** in Rome. Much of Vatican City is hidden by walls and impossible to enter as a non-citizen or invited guest. [134]

There is a forty-foot wall around part of Vatican City and the courtyard. It is an independent country with 44 towers covering 121 acres. The population is about 825. (*See Photo*).

The city is marbleized and blooming with **statutes** and **paganism**. For example, there is a statute of Laocoon, a trojan priest with a depiction of him and his two young sons being attacked by **giant serpents** sent by the gods. There is also a statute of the goddess Diana (Artemis), with many breasts. These gods play an important role in the history of the **church's deviation from truth**.

There are rooms celebrating the **Circus**, displaying the **animal** sculptures portraying those which would have been used to martyr the Christians at the Circus Maximus. (*See Photo*). Creepy hollow **faces** and **gods** are **high above**, positioned on the top of buildings **overlooking** the throngs of visitors. (*See Photo*). **Every inch** of **the ceiling tells a story**. It would be impossible to decipher the many hidden tales. (*See Photo*).

Michelangelo was the main designer. The artist's **homosexuality** was an open secret among his contemporaries and integral to understanding much of his artistic production. [386] His most famous painting and the magnet for many is the **Sistine Chapel**, Judgment Day. The *Sistine Chapel* is a chapel in the Apostolic Palace in Vatican City.

His famous ceiling painting is sacrilegious called, *The Separation of Light from Darkness*. The painting displays organs on the face of God. The human spinal cord and brain stem are on God's chest and throat.

At the age of 17, Michelangelo began **dissecting corpses** from the **church graveyard**. Most likely, some of these were Christian martyrs. Five hundred years after his famous painting, the hidden anatomical illustrations were found, painted on the ceiling of the Sistine Chapel, cleverly concealed from the eyes of Pope Julius II and countless religious worshipers, historians, and art lovers for centuries. **He had put man inside the body of God.**

What was Michelangelo saying by his construction of the **voice box** of **God out of** the brain stem of **man**? I believe it is sacrilegious, depicting **humanism** projecting that the **thoughts of man are from God.**

The painted panel is supposed to depict God separating light from darkness. **Yet he has mixed man with God as God.** Researchers report that Michelangelo **hid** the human brain stem, eyes and optic nerve of man **inside the figure of God** directly **above the altar.** [387]

Moving on through the large facility, I was surprised to see a Catholic pharmacy with medications made and sold by supporters. Signs of paganism and a plea for money were plentiful. "For by thy sorceries **[pharmakia] were all nations deceived"** (Revelation 18:23).

The *Vatican Square* consists of St. Peter's Basilica, the Sistine Chapel, the Pope's official residence, the Vatican Museums, and the famous Egyptian **obelisk** from the Circus Maximus, marking the death of Peter. (*See Photo*).

St. Peter's Basilica as a work of architecture is regarded as the greatest building of its age. It has one of the largest domes in the world. The dome covers 5.7 acres and is 448 feet high. **It is the most prominent building in Vatican City.** (*See Photo*).

The Basilica is the largest church in the world by interior measure. Catholic tradition **claims** that the basilica is the **burial site of Saint Peter**, chief among Jesus's apostles. The Catholics say he was the **first Bishop of Rome** (Pope); however, **there is no biblical reference to this belief.**

St. Peter's tomb is said to be **directly below the high altar** of the basilica, also known as the **Altar of the Confession**. Many popes, cardinals, and bishops have been buried at St. Peter's where there are more than a hundred interior tombs. Vatican City is a place where **many dead Christians have become "holy relics" for profit.**

The **Basilica** was a **burial ground** for the numerous **executions** in the circus and contained many **Christian burials**. For many years after the burial of Saint Peter, many Christians chose to be buried where they **believed** Peter's grave was located.

Outside the Vatican complex there are other significant churches. *Saint Peter in Chains Church*, supposedly holds the chains of Peter. A **Jesuit logo** is prominent on the door of the church. (*See Photo*).

St. John Lateran is called the **mother of all churches**. This church is the **official seat of the pope**. The original church was commissioned by **Emperor Constantine**. Constantine built the baptistery in 315 AD.

The faithful believe the **heads of St. Peter and Paul** are **under the altar** in St. John's, but wait, I thought Peter was buried under the St. Peter's Basilica! **Like the nation of Israel**, tourists are told many questionable details that are **conflicting** or **just not the truth**.

St. Paul's Cathedral, representing the Apostle Paul, is also outside of Vatican City. The church is called *St. Paul's Outside the Walls*. It is the third largest church in the world. St. Paul was beheaded in Rome.

Above the proclaimed tomb of St. Paul, there are 1285 decorated ceiling tiles with skillfully **combined pagan and Christian** motifs. Only the pope can have Mass at St. Paul's Cathedral. [390]

Faces of the popes line the border of the high ceilings. Confession booths are set up in the church. An offertory box sits at the entrance of the restrooms for monetary donations. (*See Photo*).

Paul's Ministry in Rome

Paul arrived in **Rome** in 59 AD. **Jerusalem** was destroyed by the **Romans** in 70 AD. God had set Paul on a course to go to Rome.

"Paul purposed in the spirit, when he had passed through Macedonia and Achaia, to go to Jerusalem, saying, After I have been there, **I must also see Rome**" (Acts 19:21).

[In the Roman army barracks] "And the night following the Lord stood by him, and said, 'Be of good cheer, Paul: for as thou hast testified of me in Jerusalem, **so must thou bear witness also at Rome**. When it was day, certain of the Jews banded together, and bound themselves under a curse, saying that they would **neither eat nor drink till they had killed Paul**. And they were more than forty which had made this conspiracy'" (Acts 23:11-13).

"But after two years Porcius Festus came into Felix' room: and Felix [Roman procurator], **willing to shew the Jews a pleasure, left Paul bound**" (Acts 24:27).

Paul said, "I appeal unto Caesar" (Romans 25:11). Caesar was the **evil Roman emperor, Nero**, who many called the **antichrist**.

Paul **spoke about Jesus to the high government officials**. God's elect servants **will have access to the evil kingdom**. Daniel, Joseph, and Paul were examples of this. In 59 AD, Paul had an important conversation with **King Agrippa**.

"When Agrippa was come, and Bernice, with great pomp, and was entered into the place of hearing, with the chief captains, and principal men of the city, at Festus' commandment Paul was brought forth. Then Agrippa said unto Paul, '**Almost thou persuadest me to be a Christian**'" (Acts 26:28).

"Then said Agrippa unto Festus, This man might have been set at liberty, **if he had not appealed unto Caesar**" (Acts 26:32).

In 61 AD, on the **Appian Way road in Rome**, Paul was met by Roman Christians who heard he was coming. They joined him and walked with him into the city of Rome. (*See Photo*).

"It was determined that **we should sail into Italy.** Where we found brethren, and were desired to tarry with them seven days: and so we **went toward Rome**. And from thence, when the brethren heard of us, they came to **meet us as far as Appii forum, and The three taverns**: whom when Paul saw, he thanked God, and took courage. And when we came to Rome, the centurion delivered the prisoners to the captain of the guard: but Paul was suffered to dwell by himself with a soldier that kept him" (Acts 27:1; 28:14-16).

God will give his elect servants a **place to stay** and **access to the evil kingdom** and **evil leaders**. Paul had **God's favor** and **protection**. God allowed Paul to live in his own *hired house* for two years to preach the Word.

"And Paul **dwelt two whole years in his own hired house**, and received all that came in unto him, **preaching the kingdom of God**, and teaching those things which concern the Lord Jesus Christ, **with all confidence, no man forbidding him**" (Acts 28:30).

Paul became famous even in the emperor's court. Many of the **emperor's employees became Christians**.

"All the saints salute you, **chiefly they that are of Caesar's household**" (Philippians 4:22).

It appears Paul was liberated in 63 AD. [199, p. 1230] Shortly thereafter he was beheaded, somewhere between the years of 64-68 AD.

Baroque Architecture

The new St. Peters Basilica was constructed from April 1506 to November 1626. It took 120 years to complete. [194] The basilica features **baroque architecture**.

Baroque architecture is a highly decorative and theatrical style, which appeared in Italy in the early 17th century and gradually spread across Europe.

Baroque architecture was originally **introduced by the Catholic church, particularly by the Jesuits, to combat the Reformation and the Protestant church**. (See Reformation section). *Geomancy* was the style of the architecture. Its purpose was to inspire surprise and awe when one was in the temple.

Geomancy is "science of the sand." The geomantic figure was created by making lines of random numbers of dots in the sand.

" . . . a **foolish** man, which **built his house upon the sand**" (Matthew 7:26).

Geomancy is an **ancient magic concept**. It is one of the most widespread **DIVINATION** systems in the world. It is a means of **communicating with the mind**.

When geomancy construction is done, buildings are placed in accordance with the **energy flow** of the universe. Architects who follow the laws of geomancy are able to come into contact with the **underlying magic order**.

Freemasons are the builders of these "magically correct" buildings. This power put those who came into the building **under the influence** of the impulses of nature.

Art of geomancy is considered **magic** and **prophecy** using **shapes** and **numbers**. It consists of **abstract** ideas, which are transformed into **visual**, tactile **formations**, such as the epicycles of the cosmos, **the sexual mystique surrounding the cube**, and the imperfections of heavenly bodies.

Geomancy symbols include: **the cube**, geometric shapes, arches, rotundas, obelisks, circus animals, **Phoenician birds**, sexuality, fertility, trees, and stars. Interestingly, **the cube** is of importance to both the **Jew** and the **Muslim** as referenced in this book. Additionally, the **black and white square (cube) is the geomancy symbol of Freemasonry.** [389]

The builders are **architects of deception. How shapes are placed in relation to each other** is important. **Magic geometry** is used to **balance buildings** with **earth's radiation energy lines**. [435]

Geometric calculations are the **methodology** used to **create magic**. The **parallel is the human body**. It is believed that geomantic principles are built into the human genetic code, the DNA double helix, the solar system, and the spiral galaxy.

The Freemasons knew the ancient Greek secret of how to **heighten the level of human consciousness** using **perfect forms** to **stimulate spirituality,** which is not from God.

Harmony can be acquired through music, buildings, clothes, or the appearance of everyday articles. The effort is to **balance energies** and **affect organs** in the body. These techniques are still very much in place today in society and in the church.

For example, **color affects the mind** in an inexplicable way. Infrared light and ultraviolet light are invisible to the eye but can affect the body. Have you noticed the color of the lights on the stages of the modern church?

If one looks at the **black and white chequered floor, the Freemason symbol for the relationship between good and evil,** for a long time, one experiences certain **psychological** phenomena, producing **lethargy** and **lack of stimulus**. Some people can feel **sick** and **irritated**. [435]

Building design can have a destructive or positive effect on the human psyche. For example, an operating room contrasted with a music hall is presented in different colors and design.

Freemasons held the **secrets of the city** as they were the designers of the buildings. These **secrets** gave them tremendous **power** over the regions. It granted them **privileges** from popes, princes, and high leaders.

The defiled and unholy temples, physically and spiritually, are coming down. Jesus foretold the destruction of the man-made temple, and it happened in 70 AD. Paul tells about **the fire that will reveal** the foundation of the **spiritual temples**.

All will have to make a choice, Christ or antichrist in their physical temples, (churches), and their spiritual temples, (lives).

"And as some spake of the temple, how it was adorned with goodly stones and gifts, he said, As for these things which ye behold, the days will come, in the which **there shall not be left one stone upon another,** that shall not be thrown down" (Luke 21:5).

"Now if any man build upon this foundation gold, silver, precious stones, wood, hay, stubble; every man's work shall be made manifest: for the day shall declare it, because it shall be revealed by fire; and the fire **shall try every man's work of what sort it is"** (1 Corinthians 3:12-14).

Many churches today have a **Babylonian** atmosphere. Charles Spurgeon said, "A time will come when instead of Shepherds **feeding the sheep**, the church will have clowns **entertaining** the **goats**." We are there.

Today's churches **seek** to provide an overall **aesthetic** effect of a work of art, setting the **tone**, **effect**, and/or **appeal** of the air of a locality. There is an **attempt to influence** the environment **to entice** rather than to let the Holy Spirit do the work. It is a **DECIVING ATMOSPHERE.**

The true church is a spiritual temple, **tabernacled with Christ.**

"But the hour cometh, and now is, when the true worshippers **shall worship the Father in spirit and in truth**: for the Father seeketh such to worship him" (John 4:23).

Jesus is the temple. We must be in *awe* of Him, not of man-made buildings and colorful atmospheres!

"Let all the inhabitants of the world stand in **awe [ABIDE, DWELL] of him**" (Psalm 33:8).

Church History

The **true Church** is the church that **Jesus Christ** died for, the church that was established and built by the apostles.

"Having been built on the foundation of the apostles and **prophets, Jesus Christ Himself being the chief cornerstone**, in whom the whole building, being fitted together, grows into a holy temple in the Lord, in whom you also are being built together for a dwelling place of God in the Spirit" (Ephesians 2:20-22).

From my observation, the Catholic Church has been built on the **martyrdom of the apostles**.

Before the Catholic church was organized, during the first 280 years after Jesus, Christianity was banned by the Roman Empire, and Christians were terribly persecuted.

Early Christianity arose following the teachings of Jesus of Nazareth. The gospel of Christ was to **both Jews and Gentiles** (non-Jews). The history of the Gentiles was pagan and with the acceptance of the teachings of Jesus, Gentiles were grafted into the family of **spiritual Jews.**

The Gentiles who accepted the **doctrine of Christ** clashed with those who follow **Judaism**. Christ taught that **circumcision** is of the **heart**. This is opposed to a **physical circumcision**, which is practiced by the Jews. The **covenantal seal changed from circumcision to water baptism with the new covenant.** The Jewish religious leaders **did not accept the new covenant** or those who followed Jesus Christ.

The death of Christ was approximately in 31 AD and the stoning of Stephen was three and half years later around 34 AD. From this point on, **Christian persecution increased.**

After the death of Christ, the book of Acts tells of how the church grew and spread throughout the **Roman Empire**, and how **many of the apostles** took the message **even further into other countries**. As Christianity rapidly moved into the greater Roman empire, there was another clash. This time it was with the **pagan religions of Rome**. [87]

Saint Luke recounts an incident of the apostle Paul in Acts 19. A riot occurred in Ephesus, instigated by silversmiths who crafted images of the goddess Diana. Just as the Jews were afraid that Jesus might take away their positions of **power**, craftsmen were concerned that Paul's success in ministry was cutting into their trade and causing them to lose **money**.

Any religion that **threatened** the **Roman empire** was open to retaliation by the Romans. Christianity fell into this category. Therefore, **persecution and martyrdom** were great.

The first documented case of imperially supervised persecution of the Christians in the Roman Empire begins with **Nero** in 37 to 68. He began his persecution against the Christian church in 64 AD. He was recognized as **the most cruel**, wicked, depraved, and savage of all men. In his time of reign, Nero inflicted the most exquisite **tortures** and **persecution on the Christians ever recorded**. The Christians suffered **horrible persecution** for **over three hundred years**. [102]

Under **Nero, Paul was beheaded**, and **Peter was crucified upside down**. It is believed many of the other apostles were also martyred during this time. [101]

Catholic tradition holds that **Peter**, after a ministry of thirty-four years, travelled to Rome and **met his martyrdom** there along with Paul. It is believed that Peter died October 13, 64 AD while festivities were being held to recognize the power of the wicked Emperor Nero. [448]

According to Jerome, a Christian scholar (345-420), Peter was crucified head downwards, by his own request because **he considered himself unworthy to die in the same manner as Jesus.**

The crucifixion took place in the **Circus Maximus** under **Nero** near the ancient obelisk brought from the **Egyptian** city of **Heliopolis.**

"The word of the Lord came to Jeremiah warning of judgment. 'He will also smash to pieces **the obelisks of Heliopolis**, which is **in the land of Egypt**; and the temples of the gods of Egypt he will burn with fire'" (Jeremiah 43:13).

About two hours northeast of Cairo, Egypt, is the city of Heliopolis. It is one of the oldest cities in the world, and it is signified as the **"city of the sun."** In the Bible, this city is also called **On.** It was the **chief seat of sun worship.** [199, p. 1618] **Religious festivals** were held in Heliopolis or On. These festivals were attended by religious processions to pay **homage to the gods in honor of the sun.**

The *Temple of the Sun* is located in Heliopolis, Egypt. **Pharoah** gave a wife to **Joseph.** Her name was **Asenath.** She was the **daughter** of Potipherah, **who was the priest of Temple of the Sun** (Genesis 43:45). [199, p. 1260] This marriage connected the **Egyptians** to the **Israelites.**

Asenath bore two children to Joseph: **Manasseh** and **Ephraim.** They were named as two of the tribes of Israel (Jacob). Hosea 4:17 says, **"Ephraim is joined to idols"**. [203]

Near the Egyptian Temple of the Sun, where Joseph's father-in-law was the priest, was a **solitary obelisk. This obelisk** was the one later taken to Rome to the Circus Maximus **where Peter was martyred** and then moved to St. Peter's Square <u>where it now stands</u>. It is revered as a "witness" to Peter's death. (*See Photo*).

The *obelisk* means "sacred stone" or idolatrous "pillar" [187, p. 2177, 2398] "to pierce." It **is a symbol of the <u>sexual male organ, the phallic</u>.** The **Christmas tree** and the **church steeple** are representations of the obelisk.

The **obelisk** is a rectangular stone pillar with a tapered top forming a pyramidion. It is set on a base, **erected** to commemorate an individual or event and to honor the gods. The pillar is raised and carefully positioned so that the first and last light of day would touch the peak in order **to honor the sun god**. Obelisks were frequently positioned in the courtyards of temples to honor the god **within** as well as the sun god, who would pass by **above**. [204]

"And **ye shall overthrow their altars, and break their pillars**, and burn their groves with fire; and ye shall **hew down the graven images of their gods**, and destroy the names of them out of that place" (Deuteronomy 12:3).

On July 18, 64 AD, a great fire broke out in Rome, destroying portions of the city and economically devastating the Roman population. [87] Many saw the economic decline and the fire as a curse which had come upon the Empire. The gods had been provoked! And it was surmised it was the Christians who had brought this bad luck! [102] A **rumor** circulated that **Nero** had been the one who had actually set the fire.

To stop the rumor, Nero turned even more on the Christians and falsely charged them as the "fire starters." He brought punishment with the **most fearful tortures to the Christians**, who were already generally hated. They were mostly hated because they were a **separate people**, **living a separate lifestyle**. They **refused to participate in the Roman system of festivities and the worship of pagan gods.**

The Apostle Peter wrote about "The church that is at Babylon," referring to Rome as spiritual Babylon (1 Peter 5:13). The Strong's Concordance defines *Babylon* as **the most corrupt seat of idolatry and an enemy to Christianity.**

The Christians **at this time** were **following the Bible**, which **separated** them from **paganism**. Revelation 18:4 says, "And I heard another voice from heaven, saying, 'Come out of **her [Babylon],** my people, that ye be not partakers of her sins, and that ye receive not of her plagues.'"

With this charge of arson against them, it became **a patriotic service to slay a Christian**. [102] Christians were given a chance to **renounce their faith by denying Christ**. To prove their sincerity,

they were required to **offer a sacrifice** to the **Roman gods** and swear by the emperor's genius. Those **who refused** to do **so were executed**. Christian churches and texts **were destroyed**, and meeting for Christian worship **was forbidden. Countless were martyred.**
(100)

There is evidence that there were Christian soldiers in the Roman army (Matthew 8:5-10; John 4:46-54). These soldiers would have been commanded to bring retribution to their brothers and sisters. One must wonder what horrific persecution would happen if they were to be found out having supported Christianity. [60]

Christians were often rounded up and killed in the most horrific manner for the amusement of the citizens of Rome. The ghastly way in which the victims were put to death aroused sympathy among many Romans, although **most felt their execution was justified**. [91]

In their deaths they were made the subjects of sport. Some were covered with the hides of wild beasts and **tortured to death** by dogs; others were **nailed to crosses** or **set on fire**, and when night fell, many were burned, serving as evening lights in the darkness. Nero offered his own garden players for the spectacle, and exhibited a Circensian game (such as Chariot races, horse races, acrobatic performances and theatrical shows, and/or parades), indiscriminately mingling with the common people in the dress of a charioteer. He would stand observing the "games" from the comfort of his chariot.
(91)

Many Christians believed **Nero was the antichrist** or that one day he would return as the antichrist. This was founded on 2 Thessalonians 2:1–11, "For the mystery of iniquity doth already work." Many believed this alluded to Nero, whose deeds seemed to be as the deeds of antichrist. **Anti means "against" or "instead place of."**

Some modern biblical scholars, such as Delbert Hillers *of Johns Hopkins University of the American Schools of Oriental Research,* and the editors of the *Oxford Study Bible* and *HarperCollins Study Bible,* contend that the number 666 in the book of Revelation is a code for Nero. This view is also supported in Roman Catholic biblical commentaries.

Revelation 17:1-18, is the explanatory passage which predicts the destruction of Rome as one of the most powerful empires ever known in human history. This passage identifies Babylon the Great with Rome, which has poured the blood of saints and martyrs and subsequently become the seat of the Vatican State, reigning over all the kings existing on earth. [90] Verse six says, "And I saw the woman **drunken with the blood of the saints, and with the blood of the martyrs of Jesus**: and when I saw her, I wondered with great admiration."

In 284 AD, **Diocletian** was the Roman emperor, and he may have been **even worse** than Nero. Diocletian associated himself with the god **Jupiter**; his co-emperor, **Maximian**, associated himself with the god **Hercules**, the son of Jupiter. **In ten years**, Diocletian **almost wiped out the entire church**. He **killed all the pastors** he could and **burned church buildings** and **Bibles**. <u>In order to preserve what Bibles were left, Christians tore the Bibles apart and distributed single pages</u>. There are no complete Bibles dating earlier than 313; **there are only remnants**. [123]

Even **through the persecution**, Christianity had infiltrated the **elite class a**nd a multitude of people who were **rich** and in **honorable positions came to the faith**. This gave cause for **Christian leaders** to be targeted for **severe persecution**. There was a demand to an open show of support for the pagan faith, **and all inhabitants of the empire were required** to **sacrifice to the gods,** eat sacrificial meat, and testify to these acts. **Those who did not were arrested, tried, and executed.**

Christians were also deprived of many rights, **including the right to petition the courts.** Nor could they respond to actions brought against them in court. Christian senators, horsemen, officers, veterans, and soldiers **were deprived of their ranks**; and Christians who were **honorable citizens were enslaved**. Many were **burned alive** [124] Horrors abounded **until the reign of Constantine.**

Sun Worship

Graven images and other gods have infiltrated every area of our lives. The **sun** and the **moon** are historically prominent gods of the past.

Then God said, "Let there be lights in the firmament of the heavens to divide the day from the night; and let them be for signs and seasons, and for days and years; and **let them be for lights** in the firmament of the heavens to give light on the earth"; and it was so. Then **God made two great lights**: the greater light to rule the day, and the lesser light to rule the night" (Genesis 1:14-16).

From the earliest of times, the **obelisk** was connected with sun worship. [199, p. 1260] When the children of Israel **were brought out of Egypt where the Temple of the Sun (Heliopolis or On) was located** (the city from where the obelisk came from and now stands in St. Peter's Square), they must have been aware of **sun worship** and it being a form of **idolatry**. Once they entered Canaan, they encountered many forms of **idolatry** once again connected with **sun worship**. [199, p. 1618]

The word *sun* means "to be brilliant." It is the great **luminary God created** to govern the day. The **sunrise** and **sunset** give us the hour of the day. *They* define time. The sun also serves to fix the four quarters of the hemisphere: east, west, north, and south. The sun helps us tell **direction** and **navigate**, giving us **position**, such as in front of us, behind, or to the left or right.

The sun was signified as a **"reproductive force." The most sacred animal at the Temple of the Sun <u>was the bull</u>**. The *bull* represents power and force. [199, p. 1260] <u>The god of **Baal** was often worshiped in the form of a bull, and the god, **Moloch** had the head of a calf.</u> [199, p. 313]

The *Phoenicians* were a people in Canaan when the Israelites arrived. The Phoenicians worshipped **the sun,** and they also called the sun god, **Baal**. The Phoenicians' most important bird was the heron or **phoenix**. Check your American money for these symbols.

Baal had other names. The **Moabites** worshipped Baal, but they had another name for Baal. They called Baal, **Chemosh**. The Ammonites worshipped Baal, and they called Baal, **Moloch**. Moloch is associated with **child sacrifice**. Moses **warned** the Israelites against the participation in sun worship. It was **idolatry** to do such, and the **punishment was to stone those who were perverted to worship other gods.** (199, p. 1618)

"And take heed, lest you lift your eyes to heaven, and when you see the **sun, the moon, and the stars**, all the host of heaven, **you feel driven to worship them and serve them**, which the Lord your God has given to all the peoples under the whole heaven as a heritage" (Deuteronomy 4:19).

In Jeremiah 43:13, God calls Nebuchadrezzar the king of Babylon "my servant" and says, "He shall break also the images of Bethshemesh [House of the Sun], that is in the land of Egypt; and the **houses of the gods of the Egyptians shall he burn with fire."**

There were many warnings in the Old Testament against sun worship and unfortunately it **infiltrated into Judah and temple worship**. The Lord showed Ezekiel a vision that **one of the abominations** in the temple were **those who worshipped the sun**.

"So He brought me into the **inner court of the Lord's house**; and there, at the door of the temple of the Lord, between the porch and the altar, were about twenty-five men with their backs toward the temple of the Lord and their faces toward the east, and **they were worshiping the sun toward the east"** (Ezekiel 8:16).

King Josiah sought to restore true worship **and to rid the temple in Jerusalem from idol worship**. We read in 2 Kings where the horses were **dedicated to the sun** and kept in the **precincts of the temple**. Josiah in his great reformation took them away and burned the chariots with fire.

"Then he **removed the horses** that the kings of Judah had **dedicated to the sun**, at the **entrance to the house of the Lord**, by the chamber of Nathan-Melech, the officer who was in the court; and he **burned the chariots of the sun with fire"** (2 Kings 23:11).

Baal is a sun god, recognized as a male, <u>thus the meaning of the obelisk!</u> Baal means lord, master, possessor of the sun. The principal seat of Baal worship was Tyre, a city in Lebanon, next to **Palestine (now national Israel)**. It was the idol of the Moabites (Numbers 25:1-9) and Midianites (Numbers 31:16).

Altars, images, and temples were erected to Baal (1 Kings 16:31-32). The altars were on the summits of hills or roofs of houses (Jeremiah 19:5). Incense was offered (2 Kings 23:4-5), bullocks were sacrificed (1 Kings 18:26), and **children were sacrificed to Moloch** (Jeremiah 19:5). When prayers were not answered they cut themselves. Worshippers **bowed the knee** and **kissed the image of Baal** (1 Kings 19:18) and swore by his name using **obscene rites**.

The **Israelites** received this idolatry from women who were **Moabites**; they ate the sacrifices and were infiltrated through **sexual seduction. We are seeing the sacrifice of our children and the connection to sexual seduction now in America.**

Not all Moabites worshipped Baal. *Ruth*, the wife of *Boaz*, a type of Jesus, was a Moabitess (Ruth 1:22). Ruth was not an idol worshipper. **She was in the line of Jesus!** This shows that Jesus came to save **all who turn from idol worship, regardless of ethnicity.**

The **female** counterpart to Baal is **Ashtoreth**, a **Moon god**. Remember **Abraham's father** in the city of Ur was a moon worshipper. The **idolatrous Israelites** adopted the worship of these gods (Judges 2:13, 2 Chronicles 28:2, 2 Kings 21:3).

The planet, **Jupiter,** represents the male god of **Baal** and the planet, **Venus,** represents the female god of Baal, **Ashtoreth,** who is **a sexual goddess**. The planets are recognized as having the same powers as the gods. This is how astrology is connected to idolatry.

Emperor Constantine

Relief came in 306 AD when **Constantine** became the emperor of Rome and the **founder of Catholicism**. [87, 138] While persecution subsided, **paganism infiltrated the true Christian church**. There became a **blending** with **paganism** and **idolatry** in **rituals** and **traditions**. [123] Constantine grew up and lived most of his life **as a pagan**. His paganist teachings can be traced to **Isis**, the mother-goddess religion of **Egypt**. [99] In 312 AD, Constantine made a profession of Christianity. But there is speculation and evidence that it was for **political purposes** and not a true heart change.

The Bible tells us Abraham's father Terah worshipped many gods, as he lived in the physical **Babylonian city of Ur** of the Chaldeans (Joshua 24:2). Research shows Terah's primary god was Nanna, the **moon** god. Similarly, **Constantine** lived in the spiritual **Babylonian city of Rome** and he was a **sun** worshipper. His primary god was Sol or *Sol Invictus,* meaning "Unconquered Sun." Sol is the personification of the sun and one of the **many** gods in ancient Roman religion. [108, 230]

Constantine **did not abandon this paganism** after conversion. His god was seen as his companion, and he used frequent references to his god. Constantine's official **coinage** continued to **bear images** of Sol until 326 AD. His **triumphal arch** was carefully positioned to align with the colossal statue of Sol by the Roman Colosseum, so that Sol formed the dominant backdrop when seen from the direction of the main approach towards the arch. [103] (*See Photo*). The solar or **radiate crown** was worn by Constantine. It was reinterpreted as representing the "holy nails," the nails that crucified Jesus. Much later, the radiate crown became associated with **Liberty** personified, usually in the form of a **circular disc** with radiating rays in different directions. [140] **This is the representative in the crown on the Statute of Liberty.**

The word *Sunday* means the "day of the Sun." It is derived from Hellenistic astrology. In pagan theology, the sun was the source of life, giving **warmth** and **illumination** to mankind. **Winter solstice** celebration was part of the **Roman cult of the sun**. The members of this cult stood at dawn to catch the first rays of sunshine as they prayed. **This is the origin of the Easter sunrise service.**

The Bible instructs the Sabbath (**seventh**) day is the day to keep holy and the Sabbath is to be a **day of rest**.

However, on March 7, 321, Constantine, Rome's first "Christian Emperor," decreed that Sunday, the **first** day of the week, would be observed as the **Roman day of rest**. [94]

The modern seven-day week can be traced back to the **Babylonians**, who used it within their calendar. The seven days were **named by the Romans** for the planets and the Greek and Roman gods were associated with the planets. [109]

	Sunday	Monday	Tuesday	Wednesday	Thursday	Friday	Saturday
Planet	Sun	Moon	Mars	Mercury	Jupiter	Venis	Saturn
god	Sol	Luna	Mars	Mercury	Jupiter	Venus	Saturn

During the time of the Israelites, the sabbath originally was **dependent** upon the lunar cycle, the **moon**. This is why the Jews' day begins at sunset. The Romans followed the Julian calendar, which is a solar calendar, honoring the sun, to be in alignment with their sun god.

The Julian calendar was named after **Julius Caesar**, and was established **by pagans, for pagans**. The Julian calendar was the officially adopted calendar for religious use at the Council of Nicaea. The *Council of Nicaea* was Constantine's board to address theological issues. Later the **Gregorian solar calendar replaced the Julian calendar** to incorporate the leap years. The only difference in the calendars is the length of the year.

The **Sunday law** decree of Constantine stated, "**On the venerable (reverend) Day of the Sun** let the magistrates and people residing in cities **rest**, and let all workshops be **closed**. In the country, however, persons engaged in agriculture may freely and lawfully continue their pursuits; because it often happens that another day is not so suitable for grain-sowing or vine-planting; lest by neglecting the proper moment for such operations the bounty of heaven should be lost."

The Sunday law of Constantine forbade the public desecration of Sunday. The day was not under the name of Sabbatum (Sabbath) or **dies Domini (Lord's day),** but under its old astrological and heathen title, **dies Solis (Sunday),** familiar to all his subjects, so that the law was as applicable **to the worshipers** of Hercules, Apollo, and **Mithras,** as to the **Christians.**

Mithraism was a Roman mystery religion linked to **imagery.** It has long been recognized that there are very many **similarities** between the initiatory **rituals** and the **symbolism** of the ancient **Mithraic** mysteries and those of modern **Freemasonry.** The unity of all religions is promoted. [141]

The Catholic Encyclopedia states: ". . . many of the emperors yielded to the delusion that they could **unite all their subjects in the adoration of the one sun-god** who combined in himself the **Father-God of the Christians** and the **much-worshipped Mithras;** thus the empire could be founded anew on **unity of religion."** [95] The center of the cult of Mithras, a mystery religion, was in Rome. Mithras is a rival of Christianity.

The observance of the **Sunday law would unite pagan religions and "Christianity" across the board.** <u>Even then there was a push for a one world religion.</u> Constantine's Sunday law **did not** have a reference to the **biblical** fourth commandment from Exodus 20:8, "Remember the sabbath day, to keep it holy" or to the resurrection of Christ.

Constantine's Sunday law **was successful** in uniting those who were **pagans,** and unfortunately, many of those who were **Christians.** [98]

So while religious **toleration** was restored in 313 AD, Constantine refused to fully embrace the Christian faith. He continued many of his pagan beliefs and practices; therefore, **the Christian church that Constantine and his successors promoted became <u>a mixture of Christian practices and Roman paganism.</u>**

Constantine's **success** in blending the **Christian** faith with the **pagan** traditions of Rome **is still in practice today** in the Protestant churches. He blended the belief systems through several avenues. He won over many of the Christians by being influential in proclaiming the *Edict of Milan* in 313 AD, which declared **tolerance** for Christianity in the Roman Empire. **Tolerance** is the word of the current hour! Churches were **free of taxation** and **legal actions** against them. (See Church Doctrine section). Bishops had more authority **based on their relationship with Constantine** (nepotism). There was a **blurring** of where **religious authority** started and where **secular authority** began. Increasingly, one needed to be a "**Christian**" to hold a **government office**. [123] **Circumcision of the heart was not a requirement**. While many true Christians did move to powerful positions, **Christianity was fast becoming an outward form of religion**.

The umbrella for Constantine's official infiltration came through the organization of the first Council of Nicaea in 325 AD. This group would deal with "false" teaching within the church. It would develop the **Roman doctrine** to rule the church, and this doctrine would supersede the **doctrine of Christ.**

This council was the first **ecumenical** board of Christian bishops. The consensus of beliefs was decided upon **for all of Christendom**, including the Trinity as the three-fold nature of the persona of God. [105] *Ecumenism* is the concept that all religions and denominations should **work together** to develop closer relationships among their churches and promote Christian **unity**. [106] This concept is in alignment with the present-day **Abraham Accords**, mediated by the **United States** in 2020, and signed in **Rome**. Its initiative is to bring together the "**Abrahamic religions**" toward a one-world control, peace, and religion. [271]

The Council of Nicaea produced the statement of Christian belief known as the **Nicene Creed**. It was a document that sounded good; however, it is deceptive.

The *Nicene Creed* meaning, "I believe" is a confession of faith and is still used in most of the major Christian denominations, including the Roman Catholic, Eastern Orthodox, and Protestant churches. However, there have been several controversies pertaining to the nature of the Godhead in the prayer. The first version omitted the Holy Spirit.

The second version of the Creed was revised by the second board called the *Council of Constantinople* (now modern day Turkey) in 381 AD by Emperor Theodosius. It declared the Trinitarian doctrine of the equality of the Holy Spirit with the Father and the Son. It is the nature of God as one in three persons [104]; however, the recognition that Jesus is God is ambiguous in the proclamation.

Constantine made **Christianity the official state religion** of the Roman Empire. He supposedly **transferred authority** over Rome and the western part of the Roman Empire **to the Pope**. The transfer was made in a document called the *Donation of Constantine*. In 1929, the Catholic church admitted this document was forged, but by this time **much power had already been obtained by the church over the state.** [89]

It was at the Council of Nicaea where it was decided that **Easter** should be celebrated **independent of the Torah** and Jewish custom. It was determined it should take place on the **same date** throughout the Roman Empire and <u>always fall on a Sun</u>day. The Bible says, "In the **fourteenth day of the first month at even is the Lord's Passover**" (Leviticus 23:5). **Most Christians do not know the difference between Easter and Passover.** Passover on the Hebrew calendar is in the first month of Nisan. **The fourteenth day may or may not fall on a Sunday.** The word *Easter* is not found in the Geneva Bible, meaning that it was given by King James of England in alignment with the Roman teachings. **Easter is not synonymous with Passover.** The Church of England had broken away from the Roman Catholic church but kept many of the Catholic traditions and customs.

Easter is a **pagan holiday** intermingled with **Passover**. According to the *World History Encyclopedia*, the word *Easter* is from the word *Eostre*, an Anglo-Saxon and German **fertility goddess**. It was the local term for the month of April. Eostre celebrated the renewal of fertility each spring, with symbols that included eggs and rabbits (both ancient concepts of fertility and renewal of the cycles of life). [93] **Easter is the celebration of the god, Ishtar. Ishtar is transgender**. Bunnies and eggs are symbols of fertility. [272] **The kingdom of darkness builds power from all who celebrate Ishtar, Easter.**

The result of Constantine's ecumenism was swiftly felt. All who **refused to give up the use of the biblical calendar for calculating Passover, felt the heavy hand of oppression fall on them**. The remembrance of persecution compared to the new "**freedom of religion**" became more dominant as time went on. The masses **preferred to just get along** and **not have to suffer persecution** for **believing in the true teachings of Jesus.**

The Jews had always used the biblical Hebrew calendar for calculating the date of the Passover. Constantine's son, Constantius, took his father's act one step further and **outlawed the use of the biblical calendar for Jews as well.** Historian David Sidersky observed: "It was no more possible under Constance to apply the old calendar." [98]

The pagan holiday, Easter, is still celebrated on the first Sunday after the first full moon after the spring equinox and sometimes Easter coincides with the Jewish Passover and sometimes it does not. [93]

Other pagan holidays were introduced at the Council of Nicaea, including Mardi Gras, Lent, Christmas, and New Year's.

Mardi Gras or *Carnival* is believed to have originated when early Christians **melded their celebrations with Roman pagan holidays**, such as Saturnalia. [96] *Mardi Gras* precedes the Lenten season. It is a day that includes **parades** with **masked characters**, singing, and dancing. The revelry is understood as one last extreme before the next 40 days of self-denial. [93]

Lent consists of prayer, penance, charity, and self-denial. Shrove Tuesday is the day before Ash Wednesday (the first day of Lent). It is a time of confession and formal remission of sin imparted **by a priest,** as in the sacrament of penance. *Shrove* comes from the word *absolve* and one should be shriven of past sins before Lent begins.

There is **no biblical alignment** for this concept of rituals. Hebrews 4:16 says, "Let us therefore come **boldly unto the throne of grace**, that we may **obtain mercy**, and find grace to help in time of need."

Peter preached, "Repent, and let every one of you be baptized in the name of Jesus Christ for the **remission of sins**; and you shall receive the gift of the Holy Spirit" (Acts 2:38).

In 336 AD, Constantine officially converted the "Christian" holiday of Christmas. The **pagan celebration** of the god Saturn and the rebirth of the sun god during the winter solstice period **became what we know as Christmas**. The winter holiday known as *Saturnalia* began the week prior to December 25th. The festival was characterized by gift-giving, feasting, singing, and downright debauchery, as the priests of Saturn carried **wreaths of evergreen boughs** in procession throughout the **Roman temples**. [92]

Furthermore, the **Mithraic New Year** began on December 25, **the birthday of Rome's invincible god, Sol**, the heavenly goddess. **It is the birthday of the Sun god!** This day is when the new light appears from the vault of heaven. [65] It is the **Nativity of the Sun**.

It is said that **Christians borrowed the Christmas, Sol, holiday directly from the heathen.** Christmas **was not celebrated by Christians until after the "conversion" of the Roman emperor Constantine.** [93] The Gospels say nothing about **Christ's day of birth** and the **early church** did **not celebrate it.** Additionally, December 25th is believed to be the **birthday of Nimrod**, the Babylonian god of the sun, the founder of physical Babylon and the **first prominent antichrist**. [125]

Many other celebrations have pagan roots. For example, the Romans derived the name for the month of January from their god **Janus**, who had **two faces**, one looking **backward** and the other forward. The practice of making resolutions to rid oneself of bad habits and to adopt better ones also dates to ancient times. The *Feast of All Souls* in November is a continuation of an old heathen feast of the dead, celebrating **death; known as Halloween**. [126]

In addition to the pagan holidays, relics such as bones, blood, items of clothing, crosses, even skulls of saints and martyrs were worshiped. Symbolism such as the obelisk, statutes, bent crucifix, rosary, and the upside cross, **became a part of worship**.

The rosary beads are used to pray with vain repetitions. Matthew 6:7 says, "And when you pray, do not use vain repetitions as the heathen do. For they think that they will be heard for their many words." The full rosary consists of nearly 270 memorized prayers with over 200 of those **being to Mary**.

The most prominent prayer to Mary "**Hail Mary** full of grace, the Lord is with thee. Blessed art thou among women and blessed is the fruit of thy womb, Jesus. Holy Mary, mother of God, pray for us sinners, now and at the hour of our death. Amen." Why is Mary being prayed to? Is she God? Where does the Bible direct us to pray to Mary? [138] Jesus says in Matthew 6:8 we are to pray to God our Father. [132] **Nowhere in the Word are we instructed to pray to Mary.**

The **crucifix** is a **graven image** of a naked, longhaired man hanging on a cross in the shameful position of defeat. **Jesus is not dead. He is alive!** The angel said, "He is not here: for he is risen!" Matthew 28:6. **He lives within us, the church!**

Catholics do a superstitious maneuver of touching their forehead, then the left breast, and then the right breast. Some say it is a representation of an upside down cross. This ritualistic movement is supposed to identify the Trinity and save one from trouble or show devotion. A *superstition* is a belief that an action, object, or circumstance can affect a situation even if they are in no way related. In 1 Kings 18, Elijah went to great lengths to show the foolishness of superstitious beliefs. He challenged the priests of Baal to a showdown, their god against the God of Israel. Of course, they could not do it.

A Roman Catholic ritual for selling a home is to put a statue of St. Joseph in a bottle or mason jar and bury it in the front headfirst. They believe this guarantees a quick sale of the home. After the sale, the seller is to dig up St. Joseph, put him in a prominent place in the new residence, and pray to him (Mother Angelica, EWTN Catholic TV, 10/95). [138]

The use of **incense** was a practice of **pagan** worship. Many Christians died during the persecution years **because they refused** to **burn incense to the Roman gods** or emperors. Many chose death instead of disobeying God's commandments.

The Catholic mass requires attendees to believe in *transubstantiation*, meaning the communion bread is transformed into the **actual flesh of Christ** and the wine is transformed into the **actual blood of Christ**. Transubstantiation is a doctrine of the Roman Catholic Church. The Scriptures declare that the Lord's Supper is **a memorial** to the body and blood of Christ (Luke 22:19; 1 Corinthians 11:24-25), not the actual consumption of His physical body and blood. Catholics believe that transubstantiation is a **re-sacrifice** for sins. This is not biblical. Jesus died "once for all" and does not need to be sacrificed again (Hebrews 10:10; 1 Peter 3:18, Hebrews 7:27). [133]

God hates the worship of idols, images, statues, icons, prayers to Mary, and images, relics, orders of priests, hierarchy of bishops, cardinals, and popes. These are examples of paganism.

Important dates in Catholicism include:

(Important dates in Catholicism include: *Tammuz*, who is the god of fertility (Ezekiel 8:14) was born on December 25; **Stephen** was martyred on December 26; and the *Feast of the Holy Innocents* is on December 28, honoring the memory of the **babies killed by Herod**.

*The Feast of St. John **the Baptist*** is an important holiday for Catholics and Freemasonry. The holiday falls on June 24, the day of St. John birth. The **first Freemasonry Grand Lodge** of England was formed on June 24, 1717. The date of St. John the Baptist's martyrdom was August 29. It is also celebrated with a feast.

John the **Evangelist** or **Apostle** died on December 27. Both June 24 and December 27 are important dates in Freemasonry. These two dates are the **markers** for **summer** and **winter solstice** and to install new members. These are also popular days for Freemasonry cornerstone laying ceremonies. [403, 404, 405] We know that **Jesus Christ** must be the foundation of **our temple** (our lives).

"According to the grace of God which is given unto me, as a wise masterbuilder, **I have laid the foundation**, and another buildeth thereon. But let every man take heed how he buildeth thereupon. For **other foundation can no man lay than that is laid, which is Jesus Christ**" (1 Corinthians 3:10-11).

In summary, **Catholic Church doctrine does not align with the doctrine of Christ.** Constantine has historically been referred to as the "First Christian Emperor." A tremendous change happened after the "conversion" of the Roman Emperor Constantine, and it was not all for the good of Christianity. There are many questions about his conversion, but one indisputable fact is evident: he did much to push the church into the mainstream of Roman culture, which spread throughout America and the world. **Today we are reaping fruits of destruction due to the acceptance of a church infiltrated with paganism.**

Rome is spiritual Babylon. Babylon means [spiritual] confusion, corruption, idolatry, and enemy of Jesus Christ. Other countries fit the Babylonian description and many are called "Christian."

Who is Rome?

Rome is called the **Eternal City**. Tibullus, a first century poet, was responsible for starting the trend among Romans of thinking of their city as the **pinnacle of society**. The thought of Rome as an eternal city created a **mindset** among the world. If Rome fell, so would the rest of the world.

In Roman mythology, **Romulus** and **Remus** were twin brothers. Their story led Romulus to **founding the city of Rome** and the Roman Kingdom on April 21, 753 BC. Romulus became the **first King of Rome.**

The image of a she-wolf suckling the twins in their infancy is a symbol of the city of Rome. The legend says their mother was a virgin impregnated by the god Mars, the god of War. The twins were thrown into the Tiber River by a wicked uncle and ended up on **Palatine Hill** suckled by a she-wolf. The boys quarreled and Romulus killed Remus.

In order to expand the population, Romulus staged games to attract virgins and then upon signal, the men would grab the women and fight off men and take them for their wives. It was known as the *Rape of the Sabine Women*. Rome is older than the myth. [391]

Rome was founded on Palatine Hill. (*See Photo*). It rises 230 feet above the city and offers some of the more spectacular views of Rome. Palatine stands for Palace. It was a hill of royalty, the **most famous** of the seven hills of Rome. The first Emperor of Rome was Caesar Augustus, 27 BC to 14 AD. He was born on Palatine hill in 63 BC. He was known as **Octavian** and **ruled during the time of Jesus.**

As mentioned earlier Washington, DC, was originally named Rome, Maryland. The visionary behind the American Rome was **Francis Pope**, who acquired the Maryland land on June 5th, 1663. **Francis Pope was the original landowner of Washington, DC.**

Is it a coincidence that **Pope Francis**, the first **American Jesuit** pope, shares his name? Francis Pope renamed Goose Creek, a tributary of the Potomac River in Washington, DC, to Tiber Creek. Presently, Tiber Creek flows under the city in tunnels, including under Constitution Avenue.

The city of Rome was built on **seven hills**, and likewise, Washington, DC was also built on seven hills. **Capitol Hill** in Washington, DC, and **Palatine Hill** in Rome are the most famous hills. [392]

In Rome, the Catholic Church's influence on Palatine Hill really began to take hold. Churches and convents began to populate the area. Around 1550, a Roman Catholic Cardinal by the name of Allesandro Farnese acquired most of the area on Palatine Hill.

Palatine is a **high mountain** looking out over the Roman Forum, the public square.

"And the devil, taking him [Jesus] up into an **high mountain**, shewed unto him all the kingdoms [royal, power, dominion, to rule] of the world in **a moment of time**. And the devil said unto him, **All this power will I give thee**, and the glory of them: for that is delivered unto me; and to whomsoever I will I give it. If thou therefore wilt worship me, all shall be thine. And Jesus answered and said unto him, **Get thee behind me, Satan:** for it is written, Thou shalt worship the Lord thy God, and him only shalt thou serve" (Matthew 4:8-10).

Palatine Hill is where the Circus Maximus was located. As previously mentioned, it is believed that the majority of Christian martyrdom in Rome took place at the Maximus. The apostle Paul may have referred to this large circus venue when he wrote the following in 1 Corinthians 16:9, "For a great door and effectual is opened unto me, and there are many adversaries."

Paul may be alluding to "the throwing open of the great doors of the Circus Maximus before the chariot races began" and the phrase "many adversaries" could also indicate the numerous competitors in such races. [278]

The prime ministry of Jesus was from around 27 AD to 31 AD. In 40 BC, the Roman senate proclaimed Herod **"King of the Jews"** (Matthew 2). At this time, **Judea**, where the tribe of Judah was from, was put under the immediate **government of Rome**. [199, p. 1479]

Caeser Augustus was in power when Jesus was born. Augustus worshipped **pagan gods** and **allowed himself to be worshipped "as a god."** [26]

We hear that "all roads lead to Rome." Roads were built all through the Roman Empire for commerce and trade. **Caeser** was one of the **greatest world leaders in history**. His great-uncle was **Julius Caesar,** who adopted him. Caesar was an heir to his uncle's estate and position. In addition to Judea, he successfully took over many countries. His resume included:

- Reforming the system of taxation
- Building a network of roads with a courier system (communication system)
- Establishing career soldiers (military)
- Positioning political bodyguards for high-ranking officials, intelligence agents
- Forming the office of police
- Hiring the first firefighters

"And it came to pass in those days, that there went out **a decree from Caesar Augustus, that all the world should be taxed**" (Luke 2:1).

His image was on the Denarii coin. The coin included a **crescent moon**. <u>Jesus refers to Caesar</u> in Mark 12:16-17 when the Pharisees of the Herodians brought a coin to Jesus and tried to trip Him in His words. [129]

"**Whose is this image and superscription?** And they said unto him, **Caesar's**. And **Jesus answering** said unto them, **Render to Caesar the things that are Caesar's,** and to God the things that are God's. And they marvelled at him" (Mark 12:16-17).

Tiberius Julius Caesar Augustus succeeded his stepfather Caesar Agustus. He ruled from 14 - 37 AD. **He was in power when Jesus was crucified.** Caesar Augustus ordered Tiberius to marry his stepsister.

Tiberius was a skilled **soldier** and **commander**, leading many victories. He was also a man of **perversion** and **abused power**. His palace walls were filled with **pornographic imagery**. He practiced **homosexuality** and **sexual perversity** with **young boys and babies** with **inhumane cruelt**y.

Tiberius Leap is a cliff located on the Island of Capri, Italy, is where Tiberius hurled discarded sexual conquests into the sea for orgasmic pleasure. It has been said, "It was for **pedophilia** that Tiberius was most notorious."

During the time of Jesus, Tiberius ordered the Jews to join the Roman Army in 19 AD. In 33 AD, he founded the **first credit bank in Rome**. He was a political **master** of **both** Herod the Great and Pilate. [393, 394] **Remember the rare crescent blood moon was seen over the Sea of Galilee in Tiberias. This is the place where Jesus called His disciples!** (Matthew 4:18-22) [198, p. 1765] [14] The city was named after wicked Tiberius Julius Caesar Augustus.

During the Roman Imperial period. Rome was the world kingdom, and it was the **time of Jesus**. It was the height of the expansion of **political** and **cultural** influence of the Roman Empire.

Jewish literature refers to the Roman Empire as the **Kingdom of Edom, Esau's descendants**. [15.110], Herod took over the Jewish monarchy and began the **horrible persecutions of Christians** that the Roman Empire began. **Herod was an Edomite**. [111] Herod Agrippa appears in the Acts of the Apostles, where **he killed James**, the brother of John, and **arrested Peter** (Acts 12:1-11).

In 1 Peter 5:13, Babylon's Greek definition describes Rome as spiritual Babylon. Both temples in Jerusalem were destroyed on the **same day**, the first by **physical** Babylon; the second by **spiritual** Babylon, Rome. Strong's Concordance describes *Babylon* as **"the symbolic seat of idolatry."**

On the tenth of the Hebrew month, Tevet (corresponds to the months December or January, depending on the yearly calculations), 425 BC, the Babylonian King Nebuchadnezzar began the siege of Jerusalem. On the seventh day of Av (corresponds to the months of July or August), the chief of Nebuchadnezzar's army, Nebuzaradan, **began the destruction** of **Jerusalem**. The walls of the city were **torn down**, and the royal palace and other structures in the city were **set on fire. On the ninth day of Av**, toward evening, **the First Temple was set on fire and destroyed**. The fire burned for 24 hours.

In 66 AD, the Jewish population rebelled against the Roman Empire. Four years later, on August 4, 70 AD or **the ninth day of Av (the same day** as the first temple destruction), Roman legions under Titus retook and **destroyed** much of Jerusalem and the **second**

temple. The Arch of Titus was built in Rome to commemorate Titus's victory in Judea. (*See Photo*). It depicts a Roman victory procession with soldiers carrying spoils from the temple, **including the Menorah.** According to an inscription on the Colosseum, Emperor Vespasian **built the Colosseum with war spoils** in 79 AD and possibly **from the spoils** of the **second temple**. [112]

The Colosseum was where many Christians were martyred. (*See Photo*). **The first Christian martyred in the Colosseum** is said to have been St. Ignatius of Antioch, who was thrown to the lions. [113] He was believed to be a **disciple of the Apostle John**. He was **appointed by St. Peter** as the overseer of the **first Gentile Christian community**. Tradition says that he was one of the children whom Jesus Christ took in his arms and blessed. [114]

The Romans loved power, had many pagan gods, and **Ceasar was their Lord**. The Christians were humble, their God died on a cross, and **Jesus Christ was their Lord.**

We have discussed Emperors Caesar, Nero and Hadrian. Constantine was the last emperor to rule over a unified Rome. While there are several reasons cited as to why the Roman empire failed, **some believe the rise of Christianity** may have played a part. During this time, **Christianity somewhat displaced the paganistic Roman religion**, which viewed the emperor as having a divine status and switched the focus to church leaders. The increased role in political affairs by the religious leaders further confused state governance. [122]

A notable Roman emperor after Constantine was Theodosius the Great. He was instrumental in establishing the Creed of Nicaea as the orthodox doctrine for Christianity. In 380 AD, Theodosius issued the *Edict of Thessalonica*, which made **Nicene Christianity** the state church of the Roman Empire. The Edict applied only to Christians. Theodosius pronounced a decree to the city of Constantinople, stating that **only Christians who believed in the Godhead as the Father, Son, and Holy Spirit could style themselves as "Catholic"** and have their own places of worship officially recognized as "churches." Those who opposed this view were

labeled as heretics and described as "out of their minds and insane."
(119)

Canon Law

In the **first** three **centuries**, rules and norms for Christianity came from the **Gospels** and sacred **scripture**. The most important windows into the structures and customs of Christian communities are the "Pastoral Epistles," 1 Timothy and Titus. These letters were viewed as **guidance to establish rules for early Christian communities**. Titus 1:5 says, "For this cause left I thee in Crete, **that thou shouldest set in order** the things that are wanting, and **ordain elders** in every city, as I had appointed thee."

Timothy gives more detail about the governance of early Christian communities. In 1 Timothy 3:15, "But if I tarry long, that **thou mayest know how thou <u>oughtest to behave thyself in the house of God</u>, <u>which is the church of the living God</u>**, the pillar and ground of the truth."

Timothy established a **procedural model** in cases when **accusations** were leveled **against the clergy**. These rules would remain a part of the canonical tradition for centuries. Christians could accuse elders only when two or three witnesses could substantiate the charges" (1 Timothy 5:19).

As time went on and society developed, **the New Testament epistles became inadequate as guides for Christian** communities as they began to evolve into **more complicated and integrated** organizational structures throughout the Mediterranean world. Herein lies the problem. **Integration and infiltration of paganism and the world structure brought discontent with the Word of God, and changes were sought to appease the culture**. Additionally, there was **censorship** of the **Bible** both by **restricting Bibles** from those "lacking instruction" and by **censoring translations** thought to "encourage deviations" from official Catholic doctrines. (142)

By the fourth century (during the time of Constantine), **bishops** had established themselves as administrators of local churches. They also recognized their role in governing the affairs of nearby churches **in councils** as well as their responsibility to confront questions that touched upon the interests of the **universal Church**.

A *bishop* is an overseer; a spiritual superintendent, ruler, or director. This role was applied to Christ as an example. Titus 1:7-8 describes the office of bishop, "For a **bishop** must be **blameless**, as the steward of God; not self-willed, not soon angry, not given to wine, no striker, **not given to filthy lucre**; But a lover of hospitality, a lover of good men, sober, just, holy, temperate."

The Catholic bishops developed their own guiding canons. The word *canon* at that time meant "rule." It did not mean "law." Christian churches began to produce canons that were publicly circulated. These rules were **recognized as authoritative** by all the "Christian" Catholic communities.

Constantine went so far as to elevate the authority of bishops in Christian communities. He issued a law that bishops could hear legal cases **between Christians**. Constantine also used the church council to deal with **doctrinal** and **disciplinary** problems **within the church**.

In 314 AD, the first significant council issued 25 canons that dealt with a **variety of problems** in the church. These canons dealt with the discipline of the clergy, the alienation of ecclesiastical property, chastity, sex with animals, adultery, murder, and magic. [118] **These were the problems of the early Catholic church!**

Eventually Constantine's **Council of Nicaea** established 325 canons as a structure for the church that paralleled the secular organization of the Roman Empire. Religion became even more mired into the **political arena**. It wasn't long until bishops began to write letters to the "Pope" for clarification of the canon laws. The oldest letter for clarification was from Constantine's time. It asked for clarification to problems of ecclesiastical doctrine, discipline, and governance. [118] Roman Catholic canon law became and is today a fully developed **legal system.** [22]

Today there are **two sets** of recognized Canon Law, one from **1917** and a revision in **1983**. The latter supersedes the former. The 1917 code contains 2,414 canons with 26,000 citations. The 1983 code contains 1,752 canons organized into seven books. [24, 31, 130]

The word *pope* is from the Greek ('páppas'), meaning 'father.' In the early centuries of Christianity, this title was applied to **all bishops**. [116] There is no record of bishops being **appointed as popes** until the sixth century. [115] The most powerful office in the Roman priesthood was that of **pontifex maximus**. Constantine held this title. The *pontifex maximus* was the chief high priest of the **College of Pontiffs**. The *College of Pontiffs* was one of the four major priestly colleges.

During the Kingdom of Roman history, the pontiffs were primarily **advisers of the kings**. Originally their responsibility was limited to supervising both **public** and **private sacrifices**, but after the expulsion of the last Roman king in 510 BC, the College of Pontiffs became religious advisers to the **Roman Senate.** Their duties involved advising the Senate on **issues pertaining to the gods,** the supervision of the **calendar**, and thus the supervision of **ceremonies** with their **specific rituals**, and the **appeasement of the gods** upon the appearance of **omens** (foretelling the future).

These advisers determined the **days** on which **religious** and political meetings could be held, when **sacrifices** could be offered, **votes** cast, and **senatorial decisions** brought forth. **They came to <u>replace the religious authority</u> that was once held by the king**. When "Christianity" became the official religion of the Roman Empire, they began using the title *pontifex maximus* to emphasize **the <u>authority of the pope</u>**.

The term *chief priests* in the New Testament in Mark 15:1 is translated as **Pontifices** in the Latin Vulgate and *high priest* as **Pontifex** in Hebrews 2:17. [117]

"But the **<u>chief priests</u>** moved the people, that he should rather release **Barabbas** unto them" (Mark 15:1).

"Then the band and the captain and officers of the Jews **took Jesus**, and bound him, And **led him away to Annas first**; for he was father in law to Caiaphas, **which was the <u>high priest</u>** that same year" (John 18:12-13).

This reference is to the Jews who held the high priestly office and had **power in the Senate.** They had much affluence in <u>public affairs</u>. Emperor Gratian in 376 AD refused the title of Pontifex Maximus, and from then on it was bestowed upon the **bishop of Rome. From this point forward,** the bishop of Rome was the **Supreme Priest** <u>to the **pagans**</u> and the **head of the Christian Catholic church.** **Paganism and Christianity flowed together** under the leadership of the Pontifex Maximus, ultimately to be called **the Pope.** [138]

"Wherefore in all things it behoved him [**JESUS**] to be made like unto his brethren, that he [Jesus] might be a merciful and **faithful <u>high priest</u>** in things pertaining to God, to make reconciliation for the sins of the people" (Hebrews 2:17).

This reference is to Christ because **He offered Himself** as a **sacrifice** to God and has entered into the heavenly sanctuary where He continually intercedes on our behalf. He has power in the heavens and affluence before God almighty. **JESUS IS THE HIGH PRIEST! HE HAS ALL AUTHORITY!**

"And Jesus came and spake unto them, saying, **<u>All power is given unto me in heaven and in earth</u>**" (Matthew 28:18).

The title, *pontifex maximus*, **suggests the pope is equal** to not only the status of the Jewish high priest **but <u>also the status of Jesus Christ!</u>**

The Catholic church recognizes Apostle Peter as the first Bishop (Pope) of Rome appointed by Christ. Bible believing Christians do not believe that Peter or Jesus would approve of such an appointment. This nomination came **after his death of martyrdom,** in Rome of course. **Rome <u>martyrs</u> the apostles, then <u>promotes</u> them to <u>sainthood,</u> then charges a <u>fee</u> to visit their <u>memorial</u> and to see the "Holy Relics."**

An example of a canon in Book Two, *The People of God,* under the Roman Pontiff, Cannon 331 reads, "The bishop of the Roman Church, in whom continues the office given by the Lord uniquely to Peter, the first of the Apostles, and **to be transmitted to his successors, is the head of the college of bishops, the <u>Vicar of Christ</u>, and the pastor of the universal Church on earth.** By virtue of his office he possesses supreme, full, immediate, and universal ordinary power in the Church, which he is always able to exercise freely." [131] Often the pope was called "**our Lord God**" and <u>**believed he had the power to change the authoritative Word of God and nullify what Jesus did.**</u>

As we stated earlier, **Peter or Jesus Christ has nothing to do with this doctrine.** A *vicar* is a representative, deputy, or substitute; anyone acting "in the person of" or agent for a superior. **We do not need a representative to access the throne of God.** Remember, antichrist means "**instead of**" Christ. We access the throne **directly through Jesus Christ**, who is *THE WAY, THE TRUTH, THE LIFE.*

Jesus said to him, **"I am the way, the truth, and the life. No one comes to the Father except through Me"** (John 14:6).

Adding laws to the Bible comes with a curse. John warns in Revelation 22:18-19, "For I testify unto every man that heareth the words of the prophecy of this book, **If any man shall add unto these things, God shall add unto him the plagues** that are written in this book: And **if any man shall take away from the words of the book of this prophecy, God shall take away his part out of the book of life, and out of the holy city,** and from the things which are written in this book."

There are seven sacraments or ceremonies necessary for salvation in the Catholic Church. They are: Baptism, Confirmation, Eucharist (Communion), Penance (Reconciliation, Confession), Matrimony (Marriage), Holy Orders (ordination to the diaconate, priesthood, or episcopate) and Anointing of the Sick. [127]

These sacraments are orally taught and are called **catechism.** *Catechism* is a summary or exposition of doctrine and serves as a learning introduction to the Sacraments in the teaching of children and adult converts. The format is often in the form of **questions** followed by **answers** to be memorized. [128]

Catholics must follow not only the Bible, but the *Apocrypha*, biblical text not part of the Bible, but is considered canon law. Catholics must also follow church tradition, and they are under the pope's authority. Followers believe the church determines what is true and what is not. **This makes the church a higher authority than Scripture.** Christians believe the Bible, the inspired Word of God, is **the ultimate test of all truth** and the **Holy Spirit is the teacher**. Jesus said in John 14:26, "But the Comforter, which is the Holy Ghost, whom the Father will send in my name, **he shall teach you all things**, and bring all things to your remembrance, whatsoever I have said unto you."

Today, the roots of the Catholic church **are at the center** of Western civilization values, ideas, science, laws, and the institution of the Protestant churches. **Denominations** and **non-denominations** are the **descendants of spiritual Babylon**. The first universities in Europe were established by the **Catholic church**. Some older cathedral schools became universities. Many **masonic temples** are housed in former **universities** and **schools**.

Remembering that the word *Catholic* means "universal," and the Catholic church is "ecumenical," it is no surprise that the church strives to join all religions as one. Specifically, the backers of the Abrahamic religions' agenda is **politically driven to bring all religions together under one god, the antichrist.**

A long-running argument exists over whether Christians and Muslims worship the same God. [135] Catholic Catechism Paragraph 841, written in 1964, refers to the Catholic church's relationship with the Muslims. It says, "The plan of salvation also includes those **who acknowledge the Creator**, in the first place <u>amongst whom are the Muslims</u>; these profess to **hold the faith of Abraham, and <u>together with us</u> they adore the one, merciful God**, mankind's judge on the last day." [136] Muslims worship **Allah**, but Catholics say they worship the **God of Abraham**. **Be not deceived.** More will be written on the Muslim faith in the next chapter.

In 2022, the pope addressed a delegation of the *World Jewish Congress*, saying the shared religious heritage of **Jews** and **Christians** should be an incentive to act together **for fraternity** and **peace** in a broken world. The Jews, as we have already explored, do not believe that Jesus Christ is a divine being. **Jesus is the prince of peace**! Therefore, it would be impossible to say that the belief system of Judaism and Christianity can unite. Amos 3:3 says, "Can two walk together, unless they are agreed?"

Often Christians believe that two religions can come together for social, human needs, or community benefit; however, true Christians must follow the Word. The list of irreconcilable differences between **what the Bible says** and what the Roman Catholic Church says make a joint mission between the two impossible. Colossians 3:17 says, "And whatsoever ye do in word or deed, **do all in the name of the Lord Jesus**, giving thanks to God and the Father by him." Paul said, "Above all, Christians must promote Jesus Christ. For I determined **not to know any thing among you, save Jesus Christ, and him crucified**" (1 Corinthians 2:2).

We are called to bring to the world the **salvation message** of the gospel **in all our deeds**. Sharing the death and resurrection of Christ brings glory to God and **should influence our interaction with the world**. This is not the purpose when differing groups come together for a social or humanistic cause.

Catholicism makes salvation a long, complicated process with no assurance of eternal life and forgiveness of sin. Baptism, mass, confession, prayers to Mary and the saints, good works, and purgatory are all **added** to faith in Christ. By contrast, the Bible teaches salvation by faith is in Jesus Christ **alone**.

Reformation

In the sixteenth century, Martin Luther led an uprising called the Reformation. He was a professor of moral theology at the University of Wittenberg, Germany. He wrote a thesis with ninety-five points against the Catholic religion. [139] One predominantly well-known Catholic method of exploitation in the Middle Ages was the practice of selling indulgences, **a monetary payment of penalty to absolve one of past sins** or to **release one from purgatory after death**. It was the **marketing of indulgences** that led Luther to publish his famous *Ninety-Five Point Theses*. [166]

Examples of points from Luther's thesis include:

2. Only God can give salvation, not a priest.

48. The pope should have more desire for devout prayer than for ready money.

79. He who says that the cross with the pope's arms solemnly set on high, has as much power as the cross of Christ, blasphemes God.

86. Again, why does not the pope build St. Peter's with his own money, since his riches are not more ample than those of Crassus, rather than with money of poor Christians?

Luther's theses were considered to have been the **launching pad** of the **Protestant Reformation**. [139] Luther claimed <u>repentance was required by Christ in order for sins to be forgiven</u> and that <u>salvation was a free gift.</u> Other leaders, such as **Charles Spurgeon** and **John Wycliffe**, joined Luther's efforts. Wycliffe advocated the **translation of the Bible** into the **common language** so that **all could read it** without having to go through the pope. [140] Additionally, he had come to regard the scriptures as the **only reliable guide** to the truth about God. He maintained that all **Christians should rely on the Bible** rather than the unreliable and frequently self-serving teachings of popes and clerics. **The reformers wrote that the pope was the Antichrist.**

Later, **William Tyndale** was the first person to produce an English translation of the Bible directly from the Hebrew and Greek texts.

Foxe's Book of Martyrs says, Tyndale said, "I defy the pope, and all his laws." [101] In August 1536, he was condemned. **He was strangled and his body burned at the stake.** His last prayer was

"Lord, open the King of England's eyes." The prayer was partially answered in 1539 when King Henry VIII required every parish church in England to make a copy of the English Bible available to its parishioners. [274]

Protestant was the name given to those who protested the Roman church. The basis of their **protests** was that the church could not dispense salvation. [139]

Rome was desperate to counter the reformation. (See the section, Christian Zionism.) **They could no longer control the printing press** as more **Bibles were produced** and the true Word of God was reaching many. The Protestant movement was gaining ground, and many Catholics were converted.

Counter-Reformation

The word *infidel* is one known to those of the Catholic faith. The term applies to all who are unaware of the true God; **those who have not pledged their fidelity**; those who are betrothed to various kinds of pagans; and, those, such as the Jews and Muslims, who do not recognize Jesus as the Messiah or Christ. [159]

In the past, the Catholic church has sought to wipe out the infidels. The Crusades were a series of military campaigns first inaugurated and sanctioned by the papacy that were undertaken between the eleventh and thirteenth centuries. Originally, the Crusades were Christian holy wars to recapture Jerusalem and the Holy Land from the Muslims, but many other targets were sought at this time as well.

For example, the riotous mobs accompanying the first three Crusades attacked the Jewish "infidels" who were in Germany, France, and England. Many were put to death. This resulted in strong feelings of ill will on both sides for centuries. One example of terroristic acts was when the crusaders stormed Jerusalem on July 15, 1099. They drove the Jews into one of the synagogues and there burned them alive.

Killing Muslims, Jews, or heretics was **regarded as an act of merit**, rewarded by paradise, and during this time, **forced conversion** was prevalent. Many chose death rather than to renunciate their faith. [158]

The idea of a counter reformation began with the Roman Catholic *Council of Trent* in 1545. The Council issued denunciations of what they believed to be heresies committed by **supporters of Protestantism**. They also issued key statements and explanations of the church's doctrine and teachings. These included: scripture, the biblical canon, traditions, original sin, justification, salvation, the sacraments, the mass, and the worship of saints. [147]

During the Council of Trent, the following was declared:

- Tradition is of equal authority with the Bible.
- Denial of Reformation doctrine, particularly such as "salvation by grace through faith alone."
- Proclamation of eternal damnation upon anyone not believing in the Catholic doctrine.

Examples include:

- If anyone shall deny that the body and blood together with the soul and divinity of our Lord Jesus Christ, and therefore entire Christ, are truly, really, and substantially contained in the sacrament of the most holy Eucharist; and shall say that He is only in it as a sign, or in a figure, or virtually – **let him be accursed**. (Canon 1)
- If anyone calls the bread and wine transubstantiation, **let him be accursed**. (Canon 2)
- If anyone believes the ungodly is justified by faith, **let him be accursed**. (Canon 9)
- **Scriptures are for the priesthood only** (prohibited to anyone in the laity without written permission from one's superior) – to violate this was [and still is in most "Catholic countries" today] considered a mortal sin). [148]

The *Society of Jesus*, also known as the **Jesuits**, was founded just before the Council of Trent in 1540 by Ignatius of Loyola and six companions, with the approval of Pope Paul III. Ignatius was a wounded Spanish knight who had a religious conversion. He transferred his **military background** and experience into a religious venture where he would accept orders from the Catholic headship as **"the Secret Service of the Vatican."** [154]

Many believe the Jesuits were raised up in the name of Christ to **attack the true Christians**. The Counter-Reformation was viewed as a plot to **counter the reformation** with the formation of a **wicked society** called the **Society of Jesus**. It is also believed the **Jesuits** birthed the official organization of **Freemasonry**. [144] However, in many references, the **Jews claim ownership** as well as a goal to **rebuild the third temple** in **Jerusalem**. Here are a few references to Jewish ownership of Freemasonry, although evidence shows they are intertwined with both groups.

- The *Jewish Tribune*, New York, 10/28/27, Cheshvan 2, 5688, Vol. 91, No. 18: **"Masonry is based on Judaism**. Eliminate the teachings of Judaism from the Masonic ritual and what is left?"
- *The Jewish Guardian*, 4/12/22, **"Freemasonry is born out of Israel."** [435]
- *La Verite Israelite*, Jewish paper 1861, IV, page 74, **"The spirit of Freemasonry is the spirit of Judaism** in its most fundamental beliefs; it is its ideas, its language, it is mostly organization, the hopes which enlighten and support Israel. Its crowning will be that **wonderful prayer house of which Jerusalem will be the triumphal center and symbol."**
- *An Encyclopedia of Freemasonry*, Philadelphia, 1906: "Each Lodge is and must be a symbol of **the Jewish temple**; each Master in the Chari, a representative of the Jewish King; and **every Mason a personification of the Jewish workman**."

Both orders, Freemasonry and the Jesuits, are listed as two of the world's most dangerous secret societies. [154] From the age of seven, Adam Weishaupt was raised attending a Jesuit school. He later became a Jesuit Catholic priest and the founder of the Illuminati. The Illuminati was founded May 1, 1776, with a secret plan to merge all occult systems into one powerful global organization. The primary union was the <u>Illuminati with Freemasonry</u>. [275]

The Jesuits' order was formed in 1540, one year after the first Bible was printed in England. The specific purpose was to overthrow the Reformation. [139] The *Great Bible of 1539* was the first authorized edition of the Bible in English, authorized by King Henry VIII of England to be read aloud in the church services of the Church of England. [144]

The Society of Jesus' symbol is IHS, which is a Christogram meaning Jesus Christ in Greek. It is a deceiving symbol with a credible name but a malicious agenda. The symbol is displayed on many buildings throughout Rome still today. (*See Photo*).

But evil men and seducers shall wax worse and worse, deceiving, and being deceived (2 Timothy 3:13).

IHS members are expected to accept orders to go anywhere in the world, where they might be required to live in extreme conditions. Ignatius, the leading founder of IHS, was a nobleman who had a military background. The opening lines of the founding deceptive document declared that "the society was founded for whoever desires to serve as a soldier of God, to strive especially for the defense and propagation of the faith, and for the progress of souls in Christian life and doctrine." Jesuits are thus sometimes referred to as God's soldiers or God's marines. This sounds good until we dig deeper. Members of the society participated in the Counter-Reformation. In addition to deception, this organization is charged with being dedicated to magic. [155]

The society has a way to resist and lure the population back to Catholicism. Enticement comes through education, social programs, and infiltration, to advance the cause of the Catholic church. [139]

The following is the text of the *Jesuit Extreme Oath of Induction* as recorded in the *Journals of the 62nd Congress* in 1913.

Many references to the Jesuit Oath can be found in research. A portion of the ceremony when a Jesuit of the minor rank is to be elevated to command is below.

Jesuit Ceremony

The following is an excerpt from the Jesuit Ceremony.

"The subject is conducted into the Chapel of the Convent of the Order, where there are only three others present, the principal or Superior standing in front of the altar. On either side stands a monk, one of whom holds a **banner of yellow and white, which are the Papal colours**, and the other a **black banner with a dagger and red cross** above a **skull and crossbones**, with the word **INRI**, [which in English translates to **Jesus the Nazarene, King of the Judeans**]. [146, 407] and below them the words **USTUM NECAR REGES IMPIUS**. The meaning of which is: It is just to **exterminate or annihilate impious or heretical Kings, Governments, or Rulers**. [145]

Upon the floor is a **red cross** at which the postulant or candidate kneels. The Superior hands him a **small black crucifix**, which he takes in his left hand and presses to his heart, and the Superior at the same time presents to him a **dagger**, which **he grasps by the blade and holds the point against his heart**, the Superior still holding it by the hilt, and thus addresses the postulant:"

<u>Jesuit Oath</u>

The oath taken by Jesuit members is very controversial and menacing. It has many characteristics of the oaths for Freemasonry. The following is an excerpt.

(The Superior speaks:)

"My son, heretofore you have been taught to act the **dissembler**: among Roman Catholics to be a Roman Catholic, and **to be a spy even among your own brethren; to believe no man, to trust no man. Among the Reformers, to be a <u>Reformer</u>;** among the Huguenots, to be a Huguenot; **among the Calvinists, to be a Calvinist; among other Protestants, generally to be a Protestant; and obtaining their confidence, to seek even to preach from their pulpits, and to denounce with all the vehemence in your nature our holy religion and the pope; and even to descend so low as to**

become a Jew among Jews, that you might be enabled to gather together all information for the benefit of your Order as a faithful soldier of the pope.

<u>You have been taught to plant insidiously the seeds of jealousy and hatred between communities, provinces, states that were at peace, and to incite them to deeds of blood, involving them in war with each other, and to create revolutions and civil wars in countries</u> that were independent and prosperous, cultivating the arts and the sciences and enjoying the blessings of peace; to take sides with the combatants and **to act secretly with your brother Jesuit, who might be engaged on the other side, but openly opposed to that with which you might be connected, only that the Church might be the gainer in the end,** in the conditions fixed in the treaties for peace and that the end justifies the means.

You have been taught your **duty as a spy**, to gather all statistics, facts and information in your power **from every source;** to **ingratiate yourself into the confidence of the family circle of Protestants** and heretics **of every class** and character, **as well as that of the merchant, the banker, the lawyer, among the schools and universities, in parliaments and legislatures, and the judiciaries and councils of state, and to be all things to all men, for the Pope's sake**, <u>whose servants we are unto death</u>. You have received all your instructions heretofore as a novice, a neophyte, and have served as co-adjurer, confessor and priest, but you have not yet been invested with all that is necessary to command in the **Army of Loyola** in the service of the pope.

You must serve the proper time as the instrument and executioner as directed by your superiors; for none can command here who has not consecrated his labours with the blood of the heretic; **<u>for without the shedding of blood no man can be saved.</u>** Therefore, to fit yourself for your work and make your own salvation sure, you will, in addition to your former oath of obedience to your order and allegiance to the pope, repeat after me." [145]

"We are warned in the Word, "And that because of **false brethren unawares brought in, who came in privily <u>to spy out</u>**

our liberty which we have in Christ Jesus, **that they might bring us into bondage**" (Galatians 12:4).

The significance of the order recently resurfaced due to the fact that on March 13, 2013, (3/13/13) Pope Francis began his papacy. **He is the first Jesuit pope, thus being a member of the Jesuit organization, IHS.** He joined the Jesuits in 1960 and became a priest in 1969. This was a significant appointment. There is a history of tense relations between IHS and the Holy See. [143] The IHS organization was suppressed for a period of time from 1759 to 1814 due to political and economic impacts relating to issues such as trade disputes. [164]

In 2018, Archbishop Carlo Maria Viganò, former apostolic nuncio to the United States (2011-2016), accused Pope Francis as being guilty of covering up decades of **homosexual predation** and abuse of high-ranking bishops. [150, 152]

Vigano commented in 2019 in an interview with *Inside the Vatican* that there has been a **60-year-old Jesuit plan of insurrection** and he stated that it has **come to fruition under Pope Francis.** The referenced plan involves a connection with Marxism, which is cause for concern. [165]

He stated, "What we are now seeing is the **triumph of a 60-year-old plan**, the successful execution of a well-thought out plan to bring a new sort of thinking into the heart of the Church, a thinking rooted in elements of Liberation Theology containing strands of Marxism, little interested in traditional Catholic liturgy or morality or theology, but rather focused on 'praxis' in the field of **social justice**. And now this plan has achieved one of its supreme goals, **with a Jesuit on the See of Peter . . .**" [21, 149]

Evidence indicates that Pope Francis is furthering the cause by **infiltrating the homosexual agenda into church doctrine and is said to be promoting Jesuits** on a regular basis. For example, he installed the Venezuelan Marxist and communist Fr. Arturo Sosa as the head of the Jesuit order. Also, in the headlines is the Jesuit pro-LGBT propagandist Fr. James Martin, who Pope Francis turned into a "consultor" to the Vatican's Secretariat for Communications. He has published a book deliberately challenging the Church's teaching on homosexual behavior. [151, 152, 156]

Pope Francis has proclaimed his delight in bringing disorder in the dioceses. Rush Limbaugh recognized this as Marxism and Michael Savage called him "Lenin's pope." Francis responded by saying, "I have met many Marxists in my life who are good people." [32, 153]

In an interview with Jesuit editors, Francis stated, "I was never a right-winger." He stated that the church was **"obsessed"** with **abortion** and **gay marriage**, yet it has been stated that the Jesuit order is one of the **most pro homosexual** orders of any Catholic institution or assembly. [156]

Once one has received Jesuit training, it transfers into the way in which they serve the church. [155]

Brannon Howse, producer and writer for "Worldview Report" recently did a report entitled, *"Evidence Joe Biden Is a Jesuit Ally of Jesuit Pope Frances to Bring Down America."* In it he discusses the plan to divide the world into ten regions. He associates this with Revelation 17:3, "I saw a woman sit upon a scarlet coloured beast, full of names of blasphemy, having seven heads and **ten horns**" (Revelation 17:3).

He states that Joe Biden is a disciple of many Jesuits. He says the term *social justice* was coined by a Catholic priest. He emphasizes Archbishop Vigano's warning about the infiltration of the Freemasons and Jesuits into the Catholic church. Many Catholic leaders are joining the warning. [156] There are some who say this is the agenda of Kamala Harris with having a father who has a reputation as being a Marxist. Marxism is intertwined with social justice. [449]

For many decades, Malachi Martin, former Catholic and Jesuit priest, has spoken out about these issues. Martin consistently warned that Freemasons and Communists were infiltrating the Catholic Church, **working together to destroy Christianity**. He also warned long before Pope Frances that the Catholic Church would end up with a **Communist pope**. Martin wrote many books about the infiltration of the **Freemasons**, the **Jesuits**, and the **false global church**. Martin was so troubled he requested a release from his Catholic and Jesuit vows. His request was granted in 1965. He died a suspicious death in 1999 from "a fall" in his Manhattan apartment. The documentary, *Hostage to the Devil*, claims that Martin was pushed from a stool by a demonic force. [157]

Howse supports the notion that there is a hidden plan. He cites the 1819-1820 Grand Masters of the Lodges document, *Permanent Instruction*. It refers to the establishment of the republic of brotherhood and **world peace**, the total annihilation of **Catholicism** and even **Christianity**. The plan was to **"wait for a pope suitable for our purposes, because with such a pope, we could effectively crush the Rock on which God built his Church."**

Jesus told Peter in Matthew 16:18, "And I say also unto thee, That thou art Peter, and **upon this rock I will build my church; and the gates of hell shall not prevail against it.**"

The goal was to make the younger secular clergy and "religious" receptive to the hidden doctrine, then have these representatives occupy "responsible positions." This group would then elect the future pope. Pope Francis seems to fit this description. The document goes on to state that the dream of **secret societies is to have a pope as their ally**.

In 2010, eighty-five-year-old Reverend Amorth, chief exorcist in the Vatican for the last twenty-five years, confessed, "The devil resides in the Vatican." He said the consequences of the devil's work are evident as there **are cardinals who don't believe in Jesus and bishops who are linked with the devil**. He pointed to the **pedophilia** and **murder** within the church. [160]

As early 1972 Pope Paul VI talked about the "smoke of Satan" that hovered in the Vatican. The pedophilia scandal in the church is an example of the **spirit of antichrist** of which he speaks.

The word *Vatican* means "**Divining Serpent**," and is derived from the word *Vatis*, which means, Diviner, and the word, *Can*, which means **serpent**. Vatican City and St. Peter's Basilica were built on the ancient pagan site called the "mountain of prophecy."

The word *Basilica* is derived from the word *basilisk*, which means a **mythological snake**. Basilik is known as the **king of the serpents** because its Greek name *basiliscus* means "little king." [161] Why would anyone name a church after a serpent?

In the Harry Potter stories, Basilisk was a giant serpent. The Basilisk origins proved that the **reptilian creature** is one of the most dangerous creatures in the wizard world. [162]

Basilicas are Catholic church buildings that have a designation conferring special privileges given by the Pope. This chapter has presented several monumental Christian basilicas that were constructed during the latter reign of Constantine the Great. As shown, a basilica is typically built as a **shrine over the tomb of a Christian martyr**.

From the early 4th century, Christian basilicas, along with their associated catacombs, were used for burial of the dead. The name was later applied to Christian churches that adopted the same basic plan. [385]

The *Hall of the Pontifical Audiences* or the *Paul VI Audience Hall* is where the pope addresses the general audiences. Interestingly, **it is a church in the shape of a snake head**. When looking at the outside of the building, one can see the narrow rounded front with nostrils, the eyes in the middle, the wide back, and the curve at the top. There are two windows on each side of the building that resemble the **eyes of a viper**. There is also a slit in the center of the eye-shaped windows that resembles a reptile eye. A simple Google search will display the demonic shape and interior design of this "church."

Inside the Hall are **two pillars** at the front of the stage which represent **fangs**. The lights above appear as snake scales. In between the two fangs is the *La Resurrezione Statue*. It is proclaimed to be a statue of Christ rising from a ghoulish atomic apocalypse. The side view of the statute **evolves into a reptile snake**. The combination of all these elements: shapes, eyes, fangs, scales, and statues, is too much of a coincidence to ignore. [163] The **pope speaks from between the "fangs" of the serpent figure.**

There are three types of popes: the **white** pope, representing the head of the **Catholic church**; the **black** pope, representing the head of the **Jesuits**; and the **gray** pope, representing the head of the bloodline families of the **Illuminati**. It is said the black and gray popes are two of the most powerful figures in the world. [388]

Information in this chapter only scratches the surface of Catholicism and the contrast to the doctrine of Christ. However, in summary there are **two basic false teachings** of Catholicism that clearly classify it as a false doctrine rather than the true church of Jesus Christ. These **two identifiers alone** are enough to discern the direction of this false religion. The Word of God is the plumbline for discernment. These two basic errors are:

Although Roman Catholicism teaches the Bible is the Word of God, the apocryphal books are added to the Scriptures. Church tradition and the words of man, that is, **the word of popes and councils, are elevated to a greater level of authority than the Word of God.** This places Roman Catholicism under God's curse of adding to the Word (Deuteronomy 4:2; Revelation 22:18-19). [138]

Roman Catholicism teaches faith in Jesus Christ is necessary for salvation; however, **it denies the truth of the gospel by adding** sacraments, good works, and purgatory as **additional requirements for forgiveness of sin and for eternal life.** This is a false gospel, which places the Roman Catholic Church under another curse from God. (Galatians 1:6-10) [138]

Catholicism is not a religion of Abraham. One is deceived if they believe Catholicism teaches the way of Christ. There are true Christians who are bound to the Catholic way of life, many who are seeking truth and a way out. The devil in the details is being revealed. Truth cannot be suppressed forever. **"For there is nothing covered, that shall not be revealed; neither hid, that shall not be known"** (Luke 12:2).

Diana Ketterman

Islam versus Christianity

The soft-spoken, bright-eyed Palestinian, Samir, stood before my desk as he introduced his sister, Amani. She shyly smiled and clasped her hand in mine. Our eyes met and I knew I would enjoy having these two siblings as my high school students.

The Muslim students were conscientious, polite, and excelled with detail in all their work. Samir was going to be a doctor. Amani was still trying to decide. Their work propelled them to the top of the class and soon we were off traveling to national competitions for business and industry.

I grew close to them as people and appreciated their tenacity to grow and learn. I admired them as they gained national recognition for their efforts.

Unexpectedly, Samir contacted me with horrible news. A genetic defect had been found with Amani's heart. She was in intensive care in a prestigious hospital in Washington, DC. She might not survive. Amani had requested that I come see her.

It was with a heavy heart that I drove the couple of hours to the city. Amani lay in the hospital bed with tubes and wires from head to toe. Her face was covered with a clear mask. I touched her seventeen-year-old olive-skinned hand and then wrapped my fingers into hers, praying under my breath.

Slowly her brown eyes opened and found their way to mine. Just as when we first met, we locked eyes. She whispered, "Miss Ketterman, you came!"

"Of course, I came," I stammered, holding back the tears.

She whispered, "Don't cry. What will be will be." No fear of death!

I said, "May I pray for you?"

"Yes," she whispered.

I do not remember the prayer, but somehow it gave me peace and honor to have this opportunity.

A few days later I was making my way down the school hallway where I met the tall principal of the school who was walking toward me. He had a serious look on his face. His eyes met mine as he stopped and paused. I waited for him to speak. He said softly, "Amani is gone."

No! I thought. *It's not fair*. My face became distorted as I fought back the tears. She was such a kind, good, hard-working student.

He said, "The family has requested that you attend the funeral. It will be a Muslim funeral in the city. You will probably be the only non-Muslim there. You must go tomorrow as they will bury her within 24 hours after passing." I choked back the lump in my throat as I hung my head and whispered, "Thank you for allowing me to go."

I arrived at the Islamic Mosque, and the information the principal had given me was accurate. I was the only non-Muslim attending. When I entered the room, the family came quickly to greet me. The lifeless body was wrapped in white linen from head to toe and lying on the floor on a rug-like blanket. She was surrounded with family and friends, who were crying and talking.

The family motioned for me to join them around her body. I obliged, grabbing the hands of her siblings. I couldn't understand the language they were speaking, but I melded with their broken hearts.

Suddenly they grew quiet. All eyes were on me. Samir said, "My family would like for you to speak."

I wasn't prepared to speak, but I seized the moment, honored to give a good report of Amani's humble and kind spirit and the privilege I had to have known her and her kind family. It was an experience I will never forget. I think of her often and believe God was preparing me to have a heart for the Muslims to come to know Him.

The Religion of Islam

Islam is the name of the religion that Muslims follow. The word *Islam* means "submission" [to **Allah**]. Allah is the Arabic word for God. Muslims are monotheistic and believe in **Allah as the sole deity**, however, Allah has **99 names** and research shows the name Allah refers to the **moon god, Hubal**. [195] Remember, Abraham's father was a moon god worshipper.

The religion of Islam states that **Judaism and Christianity** are earlier versions of **Islam**. The Islamic tradition recognizes many of the Jewish and Christian prophets, including **Abraham**, **Moses**, and **Jesus**. Islam **does not teach** that **Jesus is the Son of God**, nor do they believe in **salvation**. Their basic beliefs include remembrance of God, repentance, fear of God, and hope in God's mercy. [170] Imam is the name given to religious leaders of Islam.

Muhammad

Muhammad (570-632), an Arab, is **believed** by Muslims to be a descendant from **Abraham's son Ishmael**. Muhammad claimed to be a prophet and messenger of Allah. He founded Islam in 610 AD. [185]

Muhammad was **orphaned** around the age of six and raised by his grandfather. [196] When he was forty years old, he reported being visited by the angel Gabriel while in a cave. It was then that he said he received his **first revelation from God**. In 613 AD, he started public evangelization proclaiming that God is One, and that complete **submission to Allah** was **the way**. [185]

Muhammad taught that Muslims are accountable **to Allah** on Judgment Day. At this time, Allah will either punish or forgive his followers.

Muslims see Islam as the final, complete, and correct revelation in the monotheistic tradition of the three "Abrahamic" faiths.

Ninety-three percent **(93%) of Arabs are Muslim**, but **not** all **Muslims are Arabs.** Arabs are not a race. Rather, the word *Arab* refers to those who speak Arabic as their primary language. Remember also, *Semite* refers to those who **speak the Semitic language**.

Arabs are united by culture and by history. [186] **Ishmaelites** and **Palestinians** are **Arabian** groups. Ninety-**eight percent of all Palestinians are Muslim.** [187] Jewish **tradition** equates the descendants of Ishmael, the Ishmaelites, with Arabia. However, the **Muslim faith is not from Ishmael but rather Muhammad.**

Today, there are over a **hundred million people** in the world who call themselves **Arabs.** [182, 183] Not all Arabs are Ishmaelites. Arabs can be Moabites, **Israelites**, Amorites, Ishmaelites, Edomites, or Midianites. These groups of people are **mixed in ethnicity** and **in country**.

Who Are the Palestinians?

Who are the Palestinians? Who are the Ishmaelites? The term *Palestine* is referenced in the Bible, and is associated with the area called Philistia within the land of Canaan. [188]

Palestine today includes the West Bank of modern Israel, East Jerusalem, and the Gaza Strip as its territory. Today Palestinian Arabs occupy these territories in Israel. The entirety of the Gaza Strip has been under **Israeli occupation** since the **1967** Six-Day War. [188] The war was fought between Israel and a combination of Arab states, mainly Egypt, Syria, and Jordan, on June 5-10, 1967. [189] For the first time in **almost two millennia,** the ancient Jewish holy places in Jerusalem were under the control of modern Jews. [193, 7)

The **Oslo Accords** was signed in Washington, DC under President Bill Clinton by Yitzhak Rabin and Yasser Arafat at the White House in 1993. [190]

As a result of the Oslo Accords of 1993–1995, in 1993, the West Bank was divided into 165 Palestinian regions and put under **limited** Palestinian Authority control. Two hundred remaining Israeli settlements are under **full modern Israeli control.** The Gaza Strip, a territory that borders Egypt, has been ruled by the militant Islamic group **Hamas** since 2007. [190] Several sources state that Hamas has been **funded by Israel to weaken the Palestinian Authority.** [377] Together, the **Gaza Strip** and the **West Bank,** a landlocked territory that borders Jordan and the Dead Sea, make up the **State of Palestine.** [191]

Let's go back to the beginning. The story of Ismael is in Genesis 16 and reads as follows:

"Now Sarah Abram's wife bare him no children: and she had an handmaid, an Egyptian, whose name was **Hagar.** And Sarai said unto Abram, Behold now, the LORD hath restrained me from bearing: I pray thee, **go in unto my maid**; it may be **that I may obtain children** by her. And Abram hearkened to the voice of Sarai. And Sarai Abram's wife took Hagar her maid the Egyptian, after Abram had dwelt ten years in the land of Canaan, and gave her to her husband Abram to be his wife. And he went in unto Hagar, and she conceived: and when she saw that she had conceived, **her mistress was despised in her eyes.** And Sarai said unto Abram, **My wrong be upon thee**: I have given my maid into thy bosom; and when she saw that she had conceived, **I was despised in her eyes: the LORD judge between me and thee. But Abram said unto Sarai, Behold, thy maid is in thy hand; do to her as it pleaseth thee. And when Sarah dealt hardly with her, she fled from her face"** (Genesis 16:1-6).

Ishmael was Sarah's **"good idea,"** but it produced a product of the flesh. Ishmael **looked like Abraham**, but he had **an Egyptian heart** like his mother, **Hagar,** who was an **Egyptian** handmaiden.

When a child is born, its ethnicity is of the **mother** (Hosea 5:7). Therefore, Ishmael was considered Egyptian.

Shepherds are an abomination to Egyptians. This brought spiritual conflict to the Israelites. Yet, the Egyptian ethnicity must be considered. Remember Joseph's two children, Ephraim and Manasses had an Egyptian mother; **yet they became Israelite tribes**.

The **Angel of the Lord** met Hagar in the desert. The Angel told Hagar she would bear a son and call his name Ishamel. The Angel of the Lord was Jesus! (Genesis 6:13; John 6:46).

Hagar was then instructed **to return** and **submit to Sarai**. The angel gave information about Ishmael in verses ten and twelve. He said, "I will multiply thy seed exceedingly, that it shall not be numbered for multitude." Then he said, "And he [Ishmael] will be a **wild man; his hand will be against every man**, and **every man's hand against him**; and he shall dwell in the presence of all his brethren" (Genesis 16:12).

So, Hagar returned to Abram and Sarai and had a son. Interestingly, the name, **Ishmael**, means **"God will hear."** Ishmael was brought up under the **godly teaching of Abraham until he was around the age of fourteen to sixteen.**

Ishmael was **Abraham's first child**. He was conceived out of the will of God. When Ishmael was **thirteen** years old, he was **circumcised at the same time** as all other males in Abraham's household. Abraham was 86 years old when Ishamel was born (Genesis 16:16). There is no record in scripture where God spoke to Abraham from the age of 86 to age 100, for thirteen years. **Thirteen is the number of rebellion.**

God promised Ishmael he would beget **twelve princes** and **a great nation** (Genesis 17:20-27). We contrast this with Jacob out of whom came the **twelve tribes** of Israel and the promise that God would make him (Israel) **a great nation. Both had a <u>promise</u> but one had a <u>covenant</u>.**

"And God said unto Abraham, Let it not be grievous in thy sight because of the lad, and because of thy bondwoman; in all that Sarah hath said unto thee, hearken unto her voice; **for in Isaac shall thy seed be called. And also of the son of the bondwoman will I make a nation, <u>because he is thy seed</u>**" (Genesis 21:12-13).

Things did not work out so well between Sarai (later named Sarah) and Hagar. One day Sarah saw Ishmael mocking her and her son, Isaac (Genesis 21:9), so she demanded that Abraham send the mother and boy packing.

This was very difficult for Abraham. Genesis 21:11 says, "And the thing was **very grievous in Abraham's sight because of his son**." But the Lord commanded him to do as Sarah asked.

"And Abraham rose up early in the morning, and took bread, and a bottle of water, and gave it unto Hagar, putting it on her shoulder, and the child, and **sent her away**: and she departed, and **wandered in the wilderness** of Beersheba" (Genesis 21:14).

Ishmael grew up and became a skillful **archer**, and he settled in the wilderness of Paran. **Paran** is Mecca in **Saudia Arabia**.

Ishmael's mother, Hagar, arranged for Ishmael to marry a woman from the land of **Egypt, her country** (Genesis 21:20-21). Spiritually, Egypt represents "**the world**."

As prophesied, Ishamel produced a nation. Ishmael fathered twelve sons as promised in Genesis 17 and 25.

"And **these are the names of the sons of Ishmael**, by their names, according to their generations: the firstborn of Ishmael, Nebajoth; and Kedar, and Adbeel, and Mibsam, And Mishma, and Dumah, and Massa, Hadar, and Tema, Jetur, Naphish, and Kedemah" (Genesis 25:13).

The Descendants of Ishmael

Ishmael's numerous descendants settled near the eastern border of **Egypt** in the Wilderness of Shur in **Saudi Arabia** [301] and lived in **hostility toward all of their relatives** (Genesis 25:18). [167] Many of the Ishmaelites became **Bedouins** or desert dwellers. I have had the opportunity to visit with several Bedouins as well as stay overnight accommodations in a tent in the Jordanian desert. (*See Photo*). The Bedouins are wonderful hosts; however, they have an edge of sharpness when communicating, especially if the Bible is mentioned.

Ishmael's first son was Nebayot. The tribe of Nebayot (Nabajoth) were renowned for **sheep raising** (Isaiah 60:7). Nabajoth is specifically mentioned by the Jewish historian **Josephus**, who identified the **Nabataeans** of his time with Ishmael's eldest son. Today when traveling through Jordan, one can see the occasional shepherd in the fields with their flocks. (*See Photo*). One must wonder if the **trait came from Abraham, since shepherding is not an Egyptian line of work.**

Ishmael's daughter married **Esau**. Esau was **Ishmael's half-brother**. Esau, who sold his birthright and blessing, to his younger brother, Jacob, was an **Edomite**. This brought a mix into the family.

God gave the **land of Petra** or Mont Seir to **Esau's family**, the Edomites. Edom means "**red**." When Esau was born, he was ruddy or red. Today the red mountains in Jordan can be seen from the town of Eilat, Israel. (*See Photo*).

"I have given **Mount Seir** to Esau as a possession" (Deuteronomy 2:5).

"So Esau dwelt in **Mount Seir. Esau is Edom"** (Deuteronomy 36:8).

Petra was the capital city of **Edom**, built by the **Edomites**. [378] The magnificent ruins at Petra attest to **the greatness which Edom once knew, much like Rome.** When the **Israelites** came from **Egypt during the Exodus,** about 1445 BC, the Edomites still occupied this region. [301] (*See Photo*).

Some of the **Edomites** emigrated to **Judea**, where Jesus taught. They became known as "Idumaeans." They **opposed the Jews** during the rebuilding of the second temple at Jerusalem under Ezra, and later, the rebuilding of the city walls of **Jerusalem** under Nehemiah.

King Herod, also known as Herod the Great, the ruler of the Roman province of Judea during the time of Jesus, was **an Edomite**; therefore, **Edom** became associated with **Rome**. [168]

Before emerging as a powerful kingdom, the **Nabataeans**, the descendants of Ishmael's oldest son, Nabutoli, of Petra, Jordan [232] were **Bedouin nomads** who used their knowledge of desert water sources to become successful **traders**. [192] The Nabateans' spice trade specialized in **frankincense**, and the route ran through **Petra**, where the cisterns were guarded as they maintained control of the trade. Petra became the capital of Rome. [187] Today spices are still a hot commodity in Petra. (*See Photo*).

Ishmael's second son was **Kedar**. The Kedarites were the main **military power** of the sons of Ishmael (Isaiah 21:16-17) and were in constant conflict with the Assyrians. Kedar had settled in the land of **Paran**, where Ishmael and his mother had lived. (Genesis 21:21) Paran is modern day **Mecca** in **Saudia Arabia**. [379]

Prior to Muhammad, the Ishmaelites as a group worshipped **pagan idols,** mainly of stone. [187] The chief deity of the Kedarites was Atarsamain, or the **morning star** of heaven, the counterpart of the Mesopotamian god, **Ishtar, the god of Easter**. Later their worship also included a fertility god called **Orotalt** and a sky goddess known as **Allat**. Later, **Allat** would be referred to in the masculine form as **Allah**. [380]

As prophesied in Genesis 16, **the spirit of the Edomites** and **Ishmaelites** have cried out for centuries for **complete destruction** of **the Israelites** as an attempt to remove **the painful memory** associated with the **rejection** from the those who had the promise from God, the Israelites.

Muslims worship in a mosque. The **Kaaba** is the first most holy place for Muslims. Kaaba means "**cube**." (See the Baroque Architecture section.) The Kabba is a stone building at the center of Islam's most important mosque and holiest site. No one knows the origin date for the building of the Kabba. It was a polytheist (many gods) sanctuary before Islam. Prior to Islam, the Kaaba was a holy site for the various Bedouin tribes. Once every lunar year, Bedouin people would make a **pilgrimage to Mecca.** [381]

There is a **black rock** in the eastern corner of the **Kaaba.** According to Muslim **tradition**, the **black stone** dates back to the time of **Adam and Eve**. [382] Historically, a **black stone** is a symbol of darkness, calamity, dishonor, and condemnation. [407]

A statue of the **moon god, Hubal**, the **principal idol of Mecca**, and statues of other pagan deities are placed in or around the Kaaba. [381]

The Hubal statue was a human figure believed to control acts of **divination**, which was performed by tossing arrows before the statue. The direction in which the arrows pointed answered questions asked of the idol. I cringe as I am reminded of the **Magic 8 Ball** I had as a child. We would ask the ball a question, shake it, and the ball would display an answer on the bottom when turned over. **Was it a ball for Baal**?

The syllable, "**bal**" of HuBAL is thought to refer to the Moabite **god, Baal**. There are claims that worship of Allah evolved from the worship of Hubal, thus **making Allah a "moon god"** too. [383]

According to Islam, the Kaaba was rebuilt several times throughout history. They believe it was rebuilt by Abraham and Ishmael, after returning to the valley of Mecca. Tradition says Abraham was commanded by Allah to leave his wife Hagar and Ishmael in Mecca. **However, these teaching are not biblical.**

The **second most holy place** for Muslims is **in Israel** on the **Temple Mount**. It is the **Dome of the Rock** and the Al-Aqsa Mosque. The Dome of the Rock is a shrine where the deity Allah is worshiped. (*See Photo*).

The Dome of the Rock was built in 516 BC to **replace Solomon's temple** and the **second temple by Herod** the Great, which was destroyed by the Romans in 70 AD. The Dome of the

Rock is built on Mount Moriah. Mount Moriah has historical and religious significance to Christians, Jews, and Muslims.

King David bought the site as a threshing floor, known as Mount Moriah, as outlined in 2 Corinthians 3:1.

Significance of Dome of the Rock

While the building the Dome of the Rock is prominent to Muslims, this holy site is relevant to many faiths.

Jews recognize the Dome of the Rock for the following reasons: God commanded **Abraham to sacrifice** Isaac on this spot, known as Mount Moriah, in Genesis 22. It is where Solomon built the first temple; It is where Nehemiah and Zerubbabel built the second temple; and it is where Herod the Great restored the second Temple.

Christians recognize the Dome of the Rock for the following reasons: The site is where Abraham brought Isaac for the sacrifice and where **God brought the ram in Isaac's place**. Jesus was dedicated to the Lord at the temple which stood here. The temple is where Jesus taught, and where He overturned the money tables. Jesus prophesied against the physical temple at this spot, and he later **replaced the physical temple with Himself, the New Covenant.**

Muslims recognize the Dome of the Rock for the following reasons: The site is the third most holy site in Islam. It is believed that Muhammad ascended to Allah from the Temple Mount. The Dome of the Rock is a **Muslim shrine** that marks the location from where the Muslims believe Muhammad ascended. [173]

After the Roman Catholic Crusaders captured Jerusalem in 1099, the Dome of the Rock was then **turned into a church** by a **Catholic** sect. The nearby **Al-Aqsa prayer hall** became a royal palace for a while, and then for much of the 12th century it was the headquarters of the **Knights Templars**, who are associated with the **Catholics** and **Freemasonry**. [172]

Ramadan is the ninth month of the Muslim calendar. It is a time of fasting for Muslims. The period begins and ends with a **crescent**

moon. [169] The Dome of the Rock is holds significant importance for Muslims during this Islamic holy month.

The **crescent moon** is a widespread motif in Islamic symbolism; however, **it is not Islamic** in origin nor exclusive to the religion. **The source of the crescent moon goes back to the Moon god**, which is the god of Sin from **Land of Ur** where **Abraham was from**. [178]

Ishtar, the fertility goddess (relating to eggs), was the daughter of the **god of Sin**. [179] Connected with the moon is Sin's role as the god of oracles. The meaning of Oracle is a person through whom a deity is believed to speak. [176] Remember Oracle is synonymous with the word Vatican!

The **five-pointed star** and **crescent** finial on top of many mosques represent the Creator and the five pillars of Islam. [175] The five required pillars of Islam are:

1) Testament that there is one God and Muhammad is his messenger
2) Prayer five times daily
3) Fast during Ramadan
4) Charity to the poor
5) Pilgrimage once in their lifetime to Mecca, Saudi Arabia, to the Kaaba

Minarets can be seen at the entrance of many cities. They serve as landmarks and symbols of Islam's presence. [174] These **tall towers** are generally used to project the Muslim call to prayer.

It is common for **Arabs** and **Jews** to refer to each other as "cousins." [183] One of the most stirring stories in the Bible is when half-brothers **Isaac** and **Ishmael** came together to bury their father.

We are told in Genesis 25:8-9, "Then Abraham gave up the ghost, and died in a good old age, an old man, and full of years; and was gathered to his people. **And his sons Isaac and Ishmael buried him in the cave of Machpelah,** in the field of Ephron the son of Zohar the Hittite, which is before Mamre." (*See Photo*).

Abraham's burial site is the last fully surviving structure built by King Herod. Herod built it between 31 and 4 BC.

Over the centuries the wounded heart of rejection, of not being "the chosen," the favored or receiving the firstborn blessings, has continued in the hearts of the Ishmaelites. This has led to hatred, bitterness, anger, and jealousy.

In Psalm 83, the **spirits of Edomites** and the **Ishmaelites** cry out for complete destruction of Israel so that the memory of Israel (the pain) will be removed. Many associate this with the modern day Israel; however, this is **the antichrist spirit** crying out against **the Israel of God**.

Destruction is a distraction. Destruction does not heal pain. Out of **rejection** and **bitterness** another religion, another **"way"** was born. However, it is not "the way." It is not God's way. The Quran was written as guidance **against God's law. The only answer is forgiveness**.

God made a way! Jesus is the Way! Redemption for the Arabian people is promised:

"Cretes and **Arabians, we do hear them speak in our tongues the wonderful works of God.**"

"In that day shall **there be an altar to the Lord in the midst of the land of <u>Egypt</u>,** and a pillar at the border thereof to the Lord. And it shall be for a sign and for a witness unto the Lord of hosts **in the land of <u>Egypt</u>: for they shall cry unto the Lord because of the oppressors, and he shall send them a saviour,** and a great one, and **he shall deliver them.** And **the Lord shall be known to <u>Egypt</u>,** and the <u>**Egyptians shall know the Lord in that day,**</u> and shall do sacrifice and oblation; yea, they shall vow a vow unto the Lord, and perform it. And the Lord shall smite Egypt: he shall smite and **heal it: and they shall return even to the Lord,** and he shall be intreated of them, and **shall heal them**" (Acts 2:11; 19:19-22).

And it shall come to pass <u>**in that day, that the Lord shall set his hand again the second time to recover the remnant of his people**</u>, which shall be left, from Assyria, and **from Egypt,** and from

Pathros, and from Cush, and from Elam, and from Shinar, and from Hamath, and from the islands of the sea (Isaiah 11:11).

This prophecy is coming true. According to *Joel News*, **almost 25 percent of Muslims who come to Jesus encounter Him through dreams and visions.**

These supernatural occurrences are taking place all around the Islamic world as God is bringing healing to the Ishmaelites. Many are coming to Christ in this unique way. This phenomenon is well-documented in the Muslim world. Men and women, **without knowledge of the gospel** or contact among Christians in their community, **have experienced visions of Jesus Christ** and they are coming to know Him. Hallelujah! [184]

The **Quran** is the book composed of sacred writings accepted by Muslims as revelations made to Muhammad by Allah through the angel Gabriel. It is believed that Muhammad **did not write the Quran**, as some say **he did not know how to write**. It was written in 661 AD. It compiles **oral** and **written** traditions believed to be a description of the words and actions of Muhammad. It is the basis for **Islamic law**. [30]

In Islam, the word *infidel* refers to all non-Muslims. It is a derogatory term used to describe an unbeliever, non-Muslims, a Muslim of a differing sect, or an apostate from Islam. [181] It refers to "people not of the book."

The Qur'an is very unrelenting to "infidels." It teaches the following relating to those who are in this category:

- The unbelievers are your sworn enemies. (Sura 8:58)
- Seek out your enemies relentlessly. (Sura 2:216)
- You shall not plead for traitors. (Sura 8:58)
- Allah does not love the treacherous or the sinful. (Sura 4:107)
- Kill the pagans wherever you may find them. (Sura 8:58)

Sharia Law

Sharia Law is derived from the Quran. Sharia governs prayers, business transactions, and individual rights, as well as criminal and governmental laws. **It is enforced by the government**. [171] Examples from the Quran include the following [413, 414]:

- Sura 3:28 - "Muslims must not take the infidels as friends."
- Sura 3:85 - "Any religion other than Islam is not acceptable."
- Sura 5:33 - "Maim and crucify the infidels if they criticize Islam."
- Sura 8:12 - "Terrorize and behead those who believe in Scriptures other than the Koran."
- Sura 8:60 - Muslims must muster all weapons to terrorize the infidels.
- Sura 8:65 - The unbelievers are stupid; urge the Muslims to fight them.

Often the term *Jihad* is associated to Sharia. In classical Islamic law (Sharia), Jihad refers to an **armed struggle** against **unbelievers**, in other words, a **Holy War**. [180] These wars are viewed by others as **terrorism**. Most Christians believe these attacks have nothing to do with war or religious revolution. The victims are usually **innocent Christians** who were specifically targeted and abused solely **because of their faith in Jesus Christ.**

Freemasonry is connected to **Allah** through the Shriners. In order to be a *Shriner*, one must be a third-degree master Freemason. The Shriners wear a red hat with a black tassel called a **"Fez."** This refers to Fez, Morocco, where there have been numerous verified massacres of **both Jews and Christians** by many Muslim conquerors. The Fez is a distinctly **Muslim symbol** and is a **badge of honor**, commemorating the Muslim conquest of the area. The Shriner hat has the Arabic pagan god symbols of the **Crescent Moon and Star**, now the symbol of Islam. Many say the red hats represent the Muslim murderers who dipped their caps in the blood of the victims as a testimony to Allah. [416, 417, 418]

The **Shriners' oath** is sworn on the Bible and **the Koran**, in the name of Mohammed, and invoke Masonry's horrific consequences upon themselves. [415] The oath states:

"I do hereby, upon this Bible, **and on the mysterious legend of the Koran**, and its dedication to the **Mohammedan faith**, promise and swear and vow . . . that I will never reveal any secret part or portion whatsoever of the ceremonies . . . and now upon this sacred book, by the sincerity of a **Moslem's oath** I here register this irrevocable vow . . . in willful violation whereof **may I incur the fearful penalty of having my eyeballs pierced to the center with a three-edged blade, my feet flayed and I be forced to walk the hot sands upon the sterile shores of the Red Sea until the flaming sun shall strike me with livid plague, and may <u>Allah, the god of Arab, Moslem, and Mohammedan</u>, the god of our fathers, support me to the entire fulfillment of the same. Amen. Amen. Amen."

From September 11, 2001, to September 23, 2023, there have been more than 44,001 deadly Islamic terror attacks. In the last thirty days at the time of this writing, there have been 55 Islamic attacks in 20 countries, in which 330 people were killed and 331 injured. [180] Not all Muslims participate in these extremist types of attacks, just as not all Christians participate in what the Bible teaches.

The Fields Are White to Harvest

The **Quran** teaches Jesus did not die on the cross, but rather it was Judas or Simon the Cyrene, the man who carried Jesus' cross, who was crucified in Jesus' place. Therefore, if Jesus did not die for our sins on the cross, He did not resurrect from the dead. **Jesus' death, burial, and resurrection is the cornerstone of the Christian faith.** <u>Without it there is no Christianity</u>. It is the Christian message. [194]

The Bible has many prophetic references relating to the Arabians and the **remnant** he will bring **out of Egypt**. Remember **Hagar** was an **Egyptian,** and **Ishmael** had an **Egyptian** heart.

In that day shall five cities **in the land of Egypt** speak the language of Canaan, and swear to the LORD of hosts; one shall be called, **the city of destruction**.

In that day **shall there be an altar to the LORD in the midst of the land of Egypt,** and a pillar at the border thereof to the LORD.

And it shall be for a sign and for a witness unto the LORD of hosts in the land of Egypt: **for they shall cry unto the LORD because of the oppressor**s, and he shall send them a saviour, and a great one, and **he shall deliver them**.

And the LORD shall be known to Egypt, and the Egyptians shall know the LORD in that day, and shall do sacrifice and oblation; yea, **they shall vow a vow unto the LORD, and perform it**.

And the LORD shall smite Egypt: he **shall smite and heal it**: and **they shall return even to the LORD**, and he shall be intreated of them, and **shall heal them**.

Whom the LORD of hosts shall bless, saying, **blessed be Egypt my people**, and Assyria the work of my hands, and Israel mine inheritance (Isaiah 19:19-25).

The Abrahamic covenant incorporates the WHOLE EARTH. It is a blessing and a promise to ALL NATIONS of THE WORLD (Romans 4:13).

Behold, I say unto you, Lift up your eyes, and **look on the fields; for they are white already to harvest** (John 4:35).

The angel of the Lord found Hagar (Genesis 16:7) **where God finds us all**: by the fountain of water, representing the Word of God, **in the wilderness.** He instructed Hagar to *return, submit, and obtain* the promise. [384]

<u>The promise and the opportunity to be a part of the Israel of God is also for the descendants of Ishmael</u>, as **God is no respecter of persons** (Acts 10:34).

Religion Definitions

There has been a twisting of the definitions of the "Abrahamic religions." Society has strayed from the Word of God and thus perception has changed over the years **from truth to lies**, from light to darkness, from good to evil, from life to death. Due to these changes, **the definition of words**, theologies, education, etc., have changed. We know that **Jesus Christ, our Savior, is the same yesterday, today, and forever** (Hebrews 13:8). Neither He nor His Word change (Malachi 3:6).

Below is a table showing the difference in the definition changes of the "Abrahamic" religions over a period of 200 years.

Judaism –Definition	
1828 Dictionary	The religious doctrines and rites of the Jews, as enjoined in the laws of Moses. <u>Judaism was a temporary dispensation</u>.
2023 MW Dictionary	A religion developed among the ancient Hebrews and characterized by belief in one transcendent God who has revealed himself to Abraham, Moses, and the Hebrew prophets and by a religious life in accordance with Scriptures and <u>rabbinic</u> traditions.

Islam –Definition	
1828 Dictionary	The true faith according to the Mohammedans (followers of Mohammed).
2023 MW Dictionary	The religious faith of Muslims including belief in <u>Allah as the sole deity</u> and in Muhammad as his prophet.

Catholicism –Definition	
1828 Dictionary	Universal or general; as the Catholic church. Originally this epithet was given to the Christian church in general, but is now appropriated to the <u>Romanish church</u>, and in strictness there is no Catholic church, or universal Christian communion. Liberal, not narrow minded. A papist.
2023 MW Dictionary	<u>Roman Catholic</u>; of, relating to, or forming the church universal.

Christianity – Definition	
1828 Dictionary	The religion of Christians; or the system of doctrines and precepts <u>taught by Christ</u> and recorded by the evangelists and apostles.
2023 MW Dictionary	The religion derived from Jesus Christ, based on the Bible as sacred scripture, and professed by Eastern, <u>Roman Catholic</u>, and Protestant bodies.

Third Blood Moon Warning

Do Not Be Distracted

The third warning the Lord gave me for the church as a result of my blood moon experience was, "**Do not be distracted**."

"And this I speak for your own profit; not that I may cast a snare upon you, but for that which is comely, and that **ye may attend upon the Lord <u>without distraction</u>**" (1 Corinthians 7:35).

Distraction, in the 1828 Webster Dictionary, means, "**separation; confusion from a multiplicity of objects <u>crowding on the mind</u>** and calling the attention different ways; **perturbation of mind**; perplexity; **confusion** of affairs; tumult; disorder; as **political distractions**; madness; a state of **disordered** reason; **folly** in the extreme or amounting to **insanity**."

It is interesting that **distraction** is synonymous with "**confusion**." **Remember**, Babylon means **confusion**, mixing and mingling.

Webster states, "On the supposition of the truth of the birth, death, and resurrection of Jesus Christ, <u>**irreligion** or **indifference**</u> is **nothing better than distraction**." [(395)]

Distraction puts one in spiritual danger of idolatry. What are you focused on? Today's society is being conditioned to distraction. Most are having trouble staying focused. Research shows that a human's attention span is eight seconds. This is less than a goldfish whose attentiveness is nine seconds. [454]

Today there are many things in the world that grab our attention and cause panic and confusion, such as: wars, rumors of wars, pestilence, false teachings, earthquakes, famines, eschatology, jobs, education, family, country, on and on and on. **We must learn to recognize the distractions and separate <u>from</u> the world <u>to</u> Christ.**

There are two women in the Bible, the bride of Christ and the harlot. We must come out of Babylon, the harlot. Babylon is a spirit. It is a spirit of **confusion** because of **mixing** and **mingling** with the **world**. When we open the **"gate of the gods"** and let in the world, we come into a state of **bondage**.

Our **bodies** are the **temple** of the Holy Spirit, and the Lord wants to **tabernacle among us**. He cannot do that if we are distracted. Distraction leads **<u>to our own confused way</u>, producing temples of antichrist,** "instead of Christ."

"I saw a woman sit upon a scarlet coloured beast, full of names of **blasphemy**, having seven heads and ten horns. And the woman was arrayed in purple and scarlet colour, and decked with gold and precious stones and pearls, having a golden cup in her hand full of **abominations** and **filthiness** of her **fornication**: And upon her forehead was a name written, *Mystery,* ***Babylon the great, the mother of harlots and abominations of the earth.* And** I saw the woman **drunken with the blood of the saints**, and with the blood of the martyrs of Jesus: and when I saw her, I wondered with great admiration" (Revelation 17:3).

"Go to, let us build us a city and **a tower** [*twist, magnify, pyramid*], whose top may reach unto heaven; and **let us make us a name**" (Genesis 11:1 ,4).

Sudden destruction is coming to **the harlot church**. Paul speaks of this in 1 Thessalonians 5:3, "For when they shall say, Peace and safety; then sudden destruction cometh upon them, as travail upon a woman with child; and **they shall not escape.**"

Magnifying anything other than the Lord Jesus will lead us astray. We must submit our will to His will. Our will <u>must become</u> His will. Our mind <u>must become</u> His mind. We must take our thoughts captive (2 Corinthians 10:5). To help us understand how Christ can be formed in us (Galatians 6:16) let's distinguish between the tabernacle, the temple, and the church.

Tabernacle means *"habitation."* It is the temple sanctuary and includes all representations of the **heavenly**. He inhabits the praises of His people (Psalm 22:3). Are you spending time with Him? If not, how can He reside within you?

"And I saw no temple therein: **for the Lord God Almighty and the Lamb are the temple of it**" (Revelation 21:22).

Temple means "to *dwell*." Where and on what is our heart and mind dwelling? What are we thinking about? Where do we go and what do we do in our daily lives? **Where do we dwell?**

"Know ye not that **ye are the temple of God**, and that **the Spirit of God dwelleth in you**?" (1 Corinthians 3:6).

Temple also represents a palace. There are two characteristics of a temple. There are **priests** in the temple, and it is a **holy place**.

"And when the builders laid the foundation of the temple of the Lord, they **set the priests** in their apparel with trumpets, and the Levites the sons of Asaph with cymbals, to praise the Lord" (Ezra 3:10).

"O God, the heathen are come into thine inheritance; **thy holy temple** have they defiled" (Psalm 79:1).

Church means "of or belonging to the Lord" [ISBE] or "an assembly of believers". [PCE] The church is universal. It is not a physical building. It is the whole body of Christian believers. Jesus is the *Rock* upon which the church must be built. Christians are those who believe Jesus Christ is God.

"And I say also unto thee, That thou art Peter, and upon this rock [Jesus] I will build my church; **and the gates of hell shall not prevail against it**" (Matthew 16:18).

The Kingdom Is within You

The church is a universal body of believers with individual temples where the kingdom of God dwells or tabernacles. **It is the habitation of Christ.** It is the **light**, the **Holy City** set on a hill.

Jesus said to the Pharisees, "The kingdom of God does not come with observation; nor will they say, 'See here!' or 'See there!' For indeed, **the kingdom of God is within you**" (Luke 17:20-21).

Moses was given the pattern for the tabernacle in the wilderness. **Both temples**, built by **Solomon** and **Herod**, were defiled and destroyed. **Jesus changed the priesthood with the New Covenant.** He became the tabernacle! **The tabernacle is Jesus**. The tabernacle **built by Moses was given to us as an earthly pattern** for the **spiritual tabernacle.**

"According to all that I shew thee, **after the pattern of the tabernacle**, and the pattern of all the instruments thereof, even so shall ye make it" (Exodus 25:9).

There was a **physical tabernacle** here on earth. It has been replaced by the **spiritual tabernacle** in heaven. There the Song of Moses and the Song of the Lamb will be sung. Those who are overcomers will sing these songs!

"And I saw as it were a sea of glass mingled with fire: and **them that had gotten the victory over the beast**, and over his image, and over his mark, and over the number of his name, stand on the sea of glass, having the harps of God.

And they sing the **song of Moses** the servant of God, and the **song of the Lamb**, saying, Great and marvellous are thy works, Lord God Almighty; just and true are thy ways, thou King of saints.

Who shall not fear thee, O Lord, and glorify thy name? for thou only art holy: for all nations shall come and worship before thee; for thy judgments are made manifest.

And after that I **looked, and, behold, the temple of the tabernacle of the testimony in heaven was opened**" (Revelation 15:2-5).

The **church** is a **temple tabernacled In and through** *JESUS*, after the pattern given to Moses. Our bodies are individual temples. Together, we are a corporate spiritual temple, the city of God, the New Jerusalem, His bride.

"Now therefore ye are no more strangers and foreigners, but fellow citizens with the saints, and of the household of God; And are built upon the foundation of the apostles and prophets, **Jesus Christ himself being the chief corner stone**; In whom all the **building fitly framed together groweth unto an holy temple in the Lord: In whom ye also are builded together for an habitation of God through the Spirit**" (Ephesians 2:20).

Do you have abominations in your temple? Ezekiel was given a vision and the Lord showed him the *SECRETS* of the temple. They involved idols and the worship of the **Sun god** instead of **the SON OF GOD**.

"And he brought me to the door of the court; and when I looked, behold a hole in the wall. Then said he unto me, Son of man, dig now in the wall: and when I had digged in the wall, behold a door. [*SECRETS!*] And he said unto me, Go in, and behold the **wicked abominations** that they do here. So I went in and saw; and behold every form of creeping things, and abominable beasts, and **all the idols of the house of Israel**, portrayed upon the wall round about. And there stood before them seventy men [Sanhedrin] of the ancients of the house of Israel, and in the midst of them stood Jaazaniah the son of Shaphan, with every man his censer in his hand; and a thick cloud of incense went up. Then he brought me to the door of the gate of the Lord's house which was toward the north; and, behold, there sat women weeping for **Tammuz** [worship of the Babylonian **sun god**; festivals; orgies]" [PCBE] (Ezekiel 8:7-12).

Tammuz is still celebrated in both the **Catholic** and **Protestant** churches. Therefore, we can summarize if **Catholicism** is the harlot, the **Protestant** churches are the descendants of the harlot.

In a world filled with **lies**, we waiver from the **truth**. What do you believe? How do you form your opinions? Do you know, that you know, that you know? How do you know what you know? Can you give an answer for what you believe and why?

An *opinion* is the judgment which the **mind** forms. A *belief* is a persuasion of the **truth**, on the ground of **evidence**, distinct from personal knowledge. A belief can be held regardless of knowledge and science, it comes from the heart. **At some point, God will deal with the kingdom of our hearts.**

Faith is the belief where the assent of the **mind** or understanding of the **truth is what God has revealed**, founded on the **testimony** of the sacred writers, the **Word of God.**

Is what you believe **opinion, persuasion, or faith**? [28]

"I know whom I have believed, and **am persuaded** that he is able to keep that which I have committed unto him against that day" (2 Timothy 1:12).

To *know* means knowledge is obtained, not by mere intellectual activity **but by operation of the Holy Spirit** consequent upon **acceptance of Christ.**

To *know* is the **connection** or **union** as between man and woman. To *know* is by **observation** and **experience**. The Greek refers to the inception of knowledge and the progress in knowledge. We must have a constant and **progressive** experience of **knowing Him** (Matthew 4:13).

The word *knew* in Matthew 7:23, "I never **knew** you" means "I have never been in approving connection with you." We must *study to show ourselves approved* (2 Timothy 2:15).

The word *know* in Matthew 25:12, "I **know** you not" means "You stand in no relation to me."

The scariest words ever are found in Matthew 7:23.

"Not every one that saith unto me, Lord, Lord, shall enter into the kingdom of heaven; **but he that doeth the will of my Father** which is in heaven. Many will say to me in that day, **Lord, Lord**, have we not prophesied in thy name? and in thy name have cast out devils? and in thy name done many wonderful works? And then will I profess unto them, <u>**I never knew you**</u>**: depart from me, ye that work iniquity.**"

I may not like **His will**, but **His will** is "**The Way.**" Do you think Jesus wanted to die on the cross? Not at all, but like Jesus, **we must submit our will to the Father's will**. Jesus said in John 5:30, "I seek not mine own will, **but the will of the Father**."

There are many rewards for **submitting our will to His will**.

"He therefore that **ministereth to you** the Spirit, and **worketh miracles** among you" (Galatians 3:5).

"For it is God which worketh in you both to will and **to do of his good pleasure**" (Philippians 2:13).

"But the manifestation of the Spirit is given to every man **to profit** withal" (1 Corinthians 12:7).

We must ask ourselves: **Did I do it *MY WAY*?** Do I trust God's way even though I don't understand it? Do I turn to Him in *EVERY SITUATION*? Doing it **His way** keeps us under the umbrella of His **protection**.

"**If ye abide in me, and my words abide in you**, ye shall ask what ye will, and it shall be done unto you. **Herein is my Father glorified, that ye bear much fruit**" (John 15:7-8).

Faith is of the **mind** and **heart**, our **thoughts** and **emotions. We must change our mindset to please God and do it <u>His way</u>.**

"**Without faith** it is impossible to please God" (Hebrews 11:1).

"For we walk **by faith** and **not by sight**" (2 Corinthians 5:7).

"With the **heart** man believeth **to righteousness**" (Romans 10:6).

The **faith of the gospel** is that **emotion** of the **mind**, which is called **trust** or **confidence**, exercised towards the moral **character** of God, and particularly of the **Savior**.

FAITH is an affectionate practical confidence **in the testimony of God**. **FAITH** is a firm, cordial belief **in the truth of God**, in all the **declarations of His Word**.

Hebrews 11 lists the *Faith Wall of Fame*. Many names are on the list, including: Abel, Enoch, Noah, Abraham, Sara, Issac, Jacob, Joseph, Moses, Joshua, Rahab, Samson, David, Samuel, and many others.

"These all died in faith, **not having received the promises, but having seen them afar off, and were persuaded of them**, and embraced them, and confessed that they were strangers and pilgrims on the earth" (Hebrews 11:13).

[Moses] "Choosing **rather to suffer affliction with the people of God, than to enjoy the pleasures of sin for a season**; Esteeming the reproach of Christ greater riches than the treasures in Egypt: **for he had respect unto the recompence of the reward**" (Hebrews 11:25-26).

Gateways to the **mind** can lead to the **heart**. <u>**The eyes and the ears are gateways.**</u>

"So then **faith** cometh by **hearing**, and **hearing by the word of God**" (Romans 10:17).

"While we **look** not at the things which are **seen**, but at the things which are not seen: for the things which are **seen** are **temporal**; but the things which **are not seen** are **eternal**" (2 Corinthians 4:18).

The **EYE** and **EAR** gates, often through **movies** and **music**, change our **mindsets**. Media brings **knowledge**, whether it be false or true, to our knowledge, to **KNOW**. Listening and looking *forms a knowing*. It produces *thoughts*.

These **gateways** are often opened with the use of **technology**. Our *beliefs* are formed, and our **faith** can become good or bad, depending the content coming through the **gateways** of the **eyes** and **ears** to our **hearts** and **minds**.

<u>We must give the costliest parts of ourselves to Christ</u>. Our **time, talent**, and **treasure** must be His. Refer back to the seven separations of Abraham and **examine what you need to separate from**.

We must be *faithful* to have *faith*. We must be faithful to sit at His feet; faithful to spend alone time in the secret place; faithful to read His Word every day; faithful to be quiet in His presence; faithful to thank him; faithful to praise Him; faithful to repent, faithful to ask for sanctification and cleansing; faithful to grow in wisdom and knowledge; faithful to commune with him in time and communion; faithful to proclaim His Word to others; and faithful to trust Him.

It's not about going to church; growing up in a Christian family; reading a devotional; listening to a teacher; volunteering; being a good person; teaching Sunday school; going on a mission trip, or anything else, "I did . . .." It's about *knowing Christ* **so that He can** *dwell in you*.

Unbelief is the greatest enemy of *knowing* Christ. Remember the Exodus. The Israelites were murmuring, complaining, and forgetting what God did. They had a spirit of unbelief. Therefore, **none of the original Israelites ever saw the Promised Land.** Only Joshua and Caleb and the young descendants of the murmurers went in.

"Take heed, brethren, lest there be in any of you an **evil heart of unbelief**, in departing from the living God" (Hebrews 3:12).

"They could not enter in **because of unbelief**" (Hebrews 3:19).

"For he that is entered into his rest, he also hath ceased from his own works, as God did from his. Let us labour therefore to enter into that rest, **lest any man fall after the same example of unbelief**" (Hebrews 4:10-11).

"**Because of unbelief they were broken off,** and thou standest by faith. Be not highminded, but fear: For if God spared not the natural branches, take heed lest he also spare not thee" (Romans 11:20-21).

Having faith like Abraham means being faithful to come to the altar, humbling ourselves before God. It is hard to bend our knees in prayer when we have unbelief or lose our faith. However, the spirit of Life in Christ will draw us back to Him when we repent and bring a sacrifice of gratitude. A daily prayer might go like this:

Thank You, Father, for being my Father. Thank You for: sending Your only begotten Son to save me; the sacrifice of Jesus; the blood of Jesus that covers me, adopting me into Your family; making me a joint-heir to Your kingdom; sending Your Holy Spirit to give me power over all power of the enemy; guiding me in all truth and teaching me; for the prayers and intercession of Jesus for me; for living in me; eternal life, Your Word; angels that surround me who minister to me and protect me. I ask that Your Holy Spirit guide me to plant and water the seeds of Your Word in the world around me. Help me to bear fruit for those around me. Shine through me as a light in a dark world. Make me salt to remove corruption. Deliver me from evil and thank You for perfecting that which concerns me.

Making the Word of God of No Effect

I was a favorite in the prestigious organization to say the benediction at gatherings and sometimes large events. I spent time with the Lord before the preparation of each prayer, knowing the Holy Spirit would be speaking through me to many people from many walks of faith. I believe those in attendance were receptive to the prayers I prepared because they could feel the passion of the Holy Spirit speaking through me.

I was asked to give the blessing over a large event where about 500 people were in attendance. There were community leaders, politicians, and business associates. With passion I delivered the prayer, being lead by the Holy Spirit.

The next day, a phone call came from the local Rabbi. He said, "You do a great job at saying the prayers, but you are not following the rules of the club."

I said, "What rule am I breaking?"

He said, "**You cannot end your prayers with 'in Jesus' name'.** The oaths of the association do not allow it."

I was shocked! What kind of oath did I take? I knew I would have to resign. I could not be a part of anything, no matter how much I liked the association or the people or the work performed. I must not allow anything, or anyone take the place of my being able to stand for Jesus Christ.

As my research grew, I realized that many in the group were Freemasons. Many seemingly "good" common organizations with "good" people have freemasonry characteristics. For example, **all faiths have to be held as equal in notable groups** such as Rotary International, Boy and Girl Scouts, Lions Club, etc. One cannot stand for Jesus Christ if someone else is there who is against Christ taking precedence. Be very careful of the oaths you take and with whom you form a spiritual agreement.

Paul says in Galatians 4:16, "Am I therefore become your enemy, because I tell you the truth?"

Everything boils down to **"Who or what do you worship?"** Who is the God of **Judaism, Islam,** and **Catholicism**? <u>Jesus Christ is the God of those who are the seed of Abraham.</u>

The "Christian" churches and our families have been infiltrated and mingled with traces of many other religions.

We must heed Ezekiel's warning regarding the danger of being taken captive due to <u>rebellion against truth</u>, **"Son of man, you dwell in the midst of a rebellious house, which has eyes to see but does not see, and ears to hear but does not hear; for they are a rebellious house. <u>Therefore, son of man, prepare your belongings for captivity</u>"** (Ezekiel 12:2-3).

But **they refused to hearken**, and **pulled away the shoulder, and stopped their ears**, that **they should not hear**. Yea, **they made their hearts as an adamant stone**, lest they should hear the law, and the words which the LORD of hosts hath sent in his spirit by the former prophets: **therefore came a great wrath from the LORD of hosts** (Zechariah 7:11-12).

Because Jesus is **the Way, the Truth, and the Life**, <u>every other path is antichrist</u> (John 14:6). The Bible is clear that we all must go through Jesus.

Often, we make the Word of God of no effect due to the traditions of man (Mark 7:13). The traditions handed down from our parents, the traditions we start in our families, and the things we do because we want to fit in or like how it makes us feel often supersede the Word of God. We must separate from those things which are not Biblical. **One of the most widespread traditions is Freemasonry** as it's characteristics are embedded in MANY organizations.

Christians and Freemasonry

Freemasonry is one example of occult infiltration in the church, society, business, courts, education, and family that is common across the board. Freemasons believe in **universalism**; all paths will get one to the grand lodge in the sky.

Most churches are run by Freemasons behind the scenes. Freemasons control by using money, power, and influence. Targets are drawn in through the lure of helping with business, brotherhood, influence, and prestige.

The **first degree** of Freemasonry is the **Entered Apprentice**. This is where the oaths begin. The "brother" is blindfolded.

"Whose minds the god of this world [age] has blinded, who do not believe, lest the light of the glorious gospel of Christ, who is the image of God, should shine on them" (2 Corinthians 4:4).

This ritual is where we get the term, *hoodwinked*. A steward leads the blind man into the "Holy Place" with three raps on the door. A voice from inside: "Who comes here?"

The steward replies: "A **poor *blind* candidate** who desires to be brought into *LIGHT*. . .." <u>Isn't a Christian already in the light</u>? The prearranged "right" answers are coordinated with pre-arranged questions. The candidate is told how to reply.

Jesus said to the church, "Behold, **I stand at the door, and knock**: if any man hear my voice, and open the door, I will come in to him, and will sup with him, and he with me" (Revelation 3:20).

The candidate is **led by a cable tow to the light**.

Jesus said, "If any man serve Me, **let him follow Me**" (John 12:26).

The candidate takes his shirt off and **bows before an altar**, before the **Worshipful Master**.

<u>**Jesus is the only one to whom we bow**</u>.

A sharp instrument is pointed at the candidate's chest and the candidate vows to **never reveal the secrets**. The **first-degree oath** taken is as follows:

"Binding myself under no less a penalty than that of **having my throat cut across, my tongue torn out by its roots,** and buried in the rough sands of the sea at low-water mark, where the tide ebbs and flows twice in twenty-four hours, **should I ever knowingly or willingly violate this my solemn oath and obligation as an Entered Apprentice Mason. So help me God,** and keep me steadfast in the due performance of the same."

The candidate is led around the room and asked more questions. Then he must **kiss an open Bible**, representing kissing Jesus goodbye at the **altar of Baal.**

"But Jesus said unto him, **Judas, betrayest thou the Son of man with a kiss**?" (Luke 22:48).

The **second-degree oath** of the **Fellow Craft** reads,

"Binding myself under no less a penalty than that of **having my left breast torn open, my heart plucked out, and given as a prey to the wild beasts of the field and the fowls of the air as a prey**."

The **third-degree oath** of the **Master Mason** reads,

"Binding myself under no less a penalty than that of ha**ving my body severed in two, my bowels taken from thence and burned to ashes**, the ashes scattered to the four winds of heaven, **so that no more trace or remembrance may be had of so vile and perjured a wretch as I, should I ever knowingly or willingly violate this my solemn obligation as a Master Mason**. So help me God, and keep me steadfast in the due performance of the same." [419, 432, 434]

There are "**Christians**" taking these vows. In the **seventh degree,** the ritual is essentially **Hindu** where one learns they worship a god called **Jabulon,** which is worship of the **Babylonian god Baal** and the **Egyptian god Osiris.** [418]

When at the seventh degree, the candidate **swears to keep all the secrets** of a companion of his degree, **murder and treason not excluded.** [437]

At the **seventeenth degree,** the secret password is given **to get one into eternity.** The password is **Abaddon.** Abaddon is the name of the **destroyer** that came **out of the pit of hell** in the tribulation. [418]

"And they had a king over them, **which is the angel of the bottomless pit, whose name in the Hebrew tongue is Abaddon [the minister of death, a destroying angel],** but in the Greek tongue hath his name Apollyon" (Revelation 9:11).

Abaddon is the name they believe will get them into **the grand lodge in the sky when they die.** When in actuality, the password, Abaddon, **will summon** the **destroyer** of the **bottomless pit.**

We expect these things from the world, but **these are the oaths of many "Christians" in the church.** Freemasons are allowed to do rituals in churches, particularly when holding **funerals**. The message of Salvation, a call to accept Jesus Christ is **not given** at a Masonic funeral.

Many church boards and pastors are Freemasons. **This is just the surface of what goes on in this secret society**. These people need to be **fired from our church boards** if they refuse to **renounce** this occult and **repent** and **turn to Jesus Christ as the true light**.

Be ye not unequally yoked together with unbelievers: for what fellowship hath **righteousness with unrighteousness**? and what communion hath **light with darkness**? (2 Corinthians 6:14).

David and Donna Carrico state in their book, *The Egyptian, Masonic, Satanic Connection*, that Freemasonry is an organization that **deceives good men**. They state, "**Not all masons are bad people**." However, Freemasons are **responsible** "for the **actions** and **doctrines** that the **masonic lodge perpetrates**" and if involved, "**Your hands are not clean**." [436]

"Wherefore **come out from among them**, and **be ye separate, saith the Lord**, and **touch not the unclean thing**; and I will receive you" (2 Corinthians 6:17).

Thank God for forgiveness and DELIVERANCE! Those who have come out of Freemasonry and repented have exposed what goes on behind closed doors. Actual footage of these rituals has been recorded for authenticating the reports. [418]

"Fear them not therefore: **for there is nothing covered, that shall not be revealed; and hid, that shall not be known. What I tell you in darkness, that speak ye in light: and what ye hear in the ear, that preach ye upon the housetops. And fear not them which kill the body, but are not able to kill the soul**: but rather fear him which is able to destroy both soul and body in hell" (Matthew 10:26-28).

Hollywood and the **music industry** are big influences on Christians. **Freemasonry** is profound throughout **Hollywood**. The movie, *The National Treasure,* has been used as a promotional and recruiting tool. The music industry is involved with **symbolism**

promotion, hand signs, stances, etc. Freemasonry runs the **political system**, the Supreme Court, judges, court systems, shipping, and the global world.

Allegiance is first solely to protecting the brotherhood. Freemasonry **supersedes the Constitution, the Bill of Rights, and the law of the land**. For example, masonic judges overseeing a Freemason involved in a court case, when the hand signal is given, the judge is **bound** by the bloody oaths of Freemasonry **to rule in favor** of the Freemason on trial. **He must release the brother. The Freemason agenda is not God's agenda.**

This book is to get the truth out about **many different ways Satan deceives. How can Christians know unless they are told?** Once one knows, they are responsible for standing for truth.

Each individual Christian must do their duty to dispel darkness by teaching the truth, the light of Christ. **When we turn on the light, the darkness must flee.** We must be the **salt** and the **light** of the world. (Matthew 5:13-14).

"And **have no fellowship with the unfruitful works of darkness**, but **rather reprove them**" (Ephesians 5:11).

"Therefore **to him that knoweth to do good, and doeth it not, to him it is sin**" (James 4:17).

"How beautiful upon the mountains are the feet of him that **bringeth good tidings**, that publisheth peace; that bringeth good tidings of good, that **publisheth salvation**; that saith unto Zion, Thy God reigneth!" (Isaiah 52:7).

It's time to wake up and seek truth! The spiritual state of the church is dire. Most are in a state of **confusion** and **deception** and do not know Truth. Matthew 15:9 says, **"In vain they do worship me,** teaching for **doctrines the commandments of men."**

Doctrinally and **politically**, the apostate church has become **contaminated** by religious tradition.

We must **repent and turn** so we can be **overcomers**, the people of Zion. On Mount Zion, the holy place, there is change and transformation. Zion is for those who are pressing toward the high calling of Christ Jesus (Philippians 3:14). Matthew 21:44 says, "**And whosoever shall fall on this stone shall be broken.**" We must be **broken and mourn** for the state in which we become.

If you have taken the Freemasonry oath, married someone who has, or had parents who took it; **you must seek deliverance**. God is able to release you from the curses associated with the oaths.

If you are a part of any organization where you have taken an oath, please examine the oath, and ask the Holy Spirit to show you truth.

David and Donna Carrico have ministered to many for years to help those be set free from Freemasonry and other soul ties. They give four prayers one can say personally to be set free [455] I encourage you to look up and read the scriptures given and in your own words repent, renounce, ask for cleansing from iniquity, and break the curse. For additional information, you can review the reference noted.

1) Prayer of **Repentance** (Acts 2:38, 3:19, Luke 13:3, 2 Corinthians 6:2).
2) Prayer of **Renunciation** (Romans 12:2, 2 Corinthians 4:2, Luke 14:33).
3) Prayer of **Cleansing from Iniquity** (Psalm 51:2, Ezekiel 36:25, Isaiah 1:18)
4) Prayer to **Break the Curse** (Exodus 20:5, Ephesians 4:27, Galatians 3:13, Isaiah 54:17, Romans 8:2)

But above all things, **my brethren, swear not, neither by heaven, neither by the earth, neither by any other oath**: but let your yea be yea; and your nay, nay; lest ye fall into condemnation (James 5:12).

The Chosen Remnant

The primary verse the Lord gave me the night I saw the unscheduled crescent moon over the Sea of Galilee was Joel 2:31-32.

"The sun shall be turned into darkness, and **the moon into blood, before the great and the terrible day of the Lord come.** And it shall come to pass, **that whosoever shall call on the name of the Lord shall be delivered: for in mount Zion and in Jerusalem shall be deliverance, as the Lord hath said, and in the remnant whom the Lord shall call**" (Joel 2:31-32).

The three warnings are as follows:

Warning	Scripture
Do not be DECEIVED	*"Take heed that no man deceive you."* Matthew 24:4
The Lord IS ONE LORD	*"Hear, O Israel, the Lord our God is one Lord"*. Deuteronomy 6:4 and Mark 12:29
Do not be DISTRACTED	*"that ye may attend upon the Lord without distraction."* 1 Corinthians 7:23

Deception and discrepancy abound, but we must stand up and proclaim JESUS CHRIST is the Lord, our God, the *ONE LORD*.

Jesus said, "I am the way, the truth, and the life: <u>no man cometh unto the Father, but by me</u>" (John 14:6).

The "One Lord" verse is given in both the Old Testament (Deuteronomy 6:4) and reiterated by Jesus in the New Testament. This verse is **the Law of Christ**. Jesus addressed it to one of the scribes in Mark 12:29, saying, "The **first of all the commandments** is: '**Hear, O Israel, the Lord our God, the Lord is one**. And thou shalt love the Lord thy God <u>with all thy heart</u> [*desires, affections*], and with <u>all thy soul</u> [*will, emotions*], and with <u>all thy mind</u> [*understanding, thoughts*], and with all thy strength [*ability, might*]: this is the first commandment."

God was addressing His people in this verse. He is calling His people to *know* the one true God and to *love* Him with everything within our **being**.

There is one true God (Yahweh, Jehovah). He is Jesus Christ (Yeshua), born in Bethlehem of **Judaea** (Matthew 2:10), called out of Egypt (Hosea 11:1), grew up in **Nazareth**, of **Galilee** (Matthew 2:23), suffered many things in **Jerusalem** (Matthew 16:21), was transfigured on **Mt. Hermon** (Matthew 17:2), died on **Golgotha** (Luke 23:33), rose from the grave and was first seen in **Emmaus** (Luke 24:28), ascended to heaven on the **Mount of Olives** (Matthew 28:16-20), is seated at the right hand of God the Father in **Heaven** (Colossians 3:1), interceding for His children (Romans 8:34), is coming back to the **Mount of Olives** (Zechariah 14:4), where He will reign as King of Kings in the **Holy city, the *NEW* Jerusalem** (Revelation 21:2) and those who are faithful will have eternal life with Christ in **the world to come** (Mark 10:30).

Many are distracted and need deliverance to come to Christ. The Lord is calling His remnant! **It will be a terrible day for those who are deceived and do not recognize who the one Lord is. It will be a great day for those who know the Lord, our God, Yahweh, Jehovah, JESUS CHRIST.**

Jesus was here first, and He will be here last. Hebrews 12:2 says, "Looking unto Jesus the **author and finisher of our faith**; who for the joy that was set before him endured the cross, despising the shame, and is set down at the right hand of the throne of God."

Many are distracted by end time events, but **the End is Jesus**. "**I am** the Alpha and the Omega, the Beginning and **the End**," says the Lord, "who is and who was and who is to come, the Almighty" (Revelation 1:8).

Old Jerusalem is the **physical Jerusalem**, the city of **bondage**. **New Jerusalem** is the **heavenly Jerusalem**, the city of **freedom**. Which one do you have your eyes fixed on?

"But he who was of the **bondwoman** was born according to the **flesh**, and he of the **freewoman** through **promise**, which things are symbolic. For these are the two covenants: the one from Mount Sinai which gives **birth to bondage**, which is Hagar— for this Hagar is Mount Sinai in Arabia, and **corresponds to Jerusalem which now is**, and is in **bondage** with her Children but the **Jerusalem above is free, which is the mother of us all**" (Galatians 4:22-26).

The Hebrews (Israelites) and Arabs were physical descendants of Abraham, but **EVERYONE** can share in the blessings of Abraham by putting their faith in Jesus Christ for salvation. The plan of God, as His promise to Abraham proclaims, was for ***"ALL FAMILIES OF THE EARTH BE BLESSED"*** (Genesis 12:3); not an **ethnicity** or **race**, but to those who are faithful (Hebrews 11).

The Biblical connection of Abraham to **Judaism** changed when the priesthood changed with the New Covenant (Hebrews 7:12). Jesus fulfilled the law, and the old order was no longer valid after His resurrection (Hebrews 8:13). The true church has always been the **Israel of God** and still is (Galatians 6:16).

"Jesus fulfills every preparatory and anticipatory aspect of the history of redemption in the Old Testament in general—and in the history of Israel in particular—because **He is the true Israel of God**. He recapitulates—summarizes and repeats—Israel's history in His own experience and work in order to secure for His people the blessings promised to Abraham'" (2 Corinthians 1:20). [38]

There is no direct biblical connection of Abraham to **Islamic religion**; but rather to the Arab **people**, through Ishmael.

Abraham did not father the "**Abrahamic religions**." These three religions are built on **idolatry** and **traditions of men**. We know that the **traditions** of man make the **Word of God of no effect** (Mark 7:13). The Bible explicitly warns us. Colossians 2:8 says, "Beware lest any man spoil you through philosophy and **vain deceit, after the tradition of men**, after the rudiments of the world, and not after Christ."

Many worship the "process," rather than sitting at the feet of Christ. Paul says in Romans 1:21-22, "Professing themselves to be wise, they became fools, and **changed the glory of the uncorruptible God into an image** made like to corruptible man."

There is agreement that Abraham was the first human being to have **one God**. The "Abrahamic religions" share teachings from the Torah, the first five books of the Bible written by Moses, but none of them solely worship Jesus Christ as God. Therefore, the "one true God" is not the same as the "one god" of these three religions.

The Bible is very clear that just because one was a physical descendant from Abraham does not mean one is of the **spiritual seed** of Abraham.

Jesus says, "**If ye were Abraham's children, ye would do the works of Abraham**. But now ye seek to kill me, a man that hath told you the truth, which I have heard of God: this did not Abraham" (John 8:39-40).

JESUS IS THE SEED of ABRAHAM. JESUS INHERITS ALL THE BLESSINGS OF ALL THE COVENANTS. JESUS IS THE HEIR TO THE LAND. JESUS IS THE HEIR TO THE THRONE TO RULE THE LAND. He must be recognized and worshiped as King of Kings if we are to share in the inheritance with Him.

Most versions of the Bibles after the King James version replaced the word, *seed*, with the word, *descendants*. **This switching of the reference to Christ as *the seed* to a physical people has brought mass confusion.**

All of Abraham's descendants can share in the blessings of Abraham by putting their faith in Jesus Christ, THE SEED, for salvation. When one accepts Jesus Christ as their Savior, they are grafted into the root and thus anyone, no matter their physical descent, can become a spiritual Jew (Romans 11:17). Jesus is the root.

Christianity is the only religion that believes Jesus Christ is God, and the individual has ultimate authority to access the throne of God. Christianity is the only religion where their God died for them to give them eternal life. Christianity believes that the Holy Spirit can give revelation of truth and interpretation of scripture **to individuals** (John 16:13).

Abraham "looked for a city which hath foundations, whose builder and maker is God" (Hebrews 11:10).

Stay focused on Jesus! Keep your eyes on spiritual Jerusalem. We must be covered in the blood of the lamb, proclaim a testimony, and not love our lives unto death (Revelation 12:11). **We must be prepared for the great and terrible day of the Lord.**

"Jesus answered and said unto them, Destroy this temple, and in **three days** I will raise it up. But he spake of the **temple of his body**" (John 2:19, 21).

The third day is here. The **Jews** and **Zionists** are trying to raise up their physical temple **on the third day**. But remember, JESUS, the **true temple, arose on the third day!**

"Arise, shine; for thy light is come, and the glory of the Lord is risen upon thee. For, behold, the darkness **shall cover the earth**, and **gross darkness the people**: but the Lord shall arise upon thee, and his glory shall be seen upon thee. And the Gentiles shall come to thy light, and kings to the brightness of thy rising" (Isaiah 60:1-3).

We have a ministry to tell **the TRUTH!** Those who do not believe cannot **KNOW the TRUTH**. Their minds **are blinded** and they walk in darkness. **The TRUTH** is within those who belong to Christ Jesus. **The TRUTH** is a light that shines in the darkness.

"Therefore, since **we have this ministry**, as we have received mercy, we do not lose heart. But we have renounced the hidden things of shame, **not walking in craftiness** nor handling the word of God **deceitfully**, but by manifestation of the truth commending ourselves to every man's conscience in the sight of God. But even if our gospel is veiled, it is veiled to those who are perishing, whose minds **the god of this age has blinded, who do not believe**, lest the light of the gospel of the glory of Christ, who is the image of God, should shine on them. For **we do not preach ourselves, but Christ Jesus the Lord**, and ourselves your bondservants for Jesus' sake. For it is the God who commanded **light to shine out of darkness**, who has shone in our hearts to give the light of the knowledge of the glory of God in the face of Jesus Christ" (1 Corinthians 4:1-6).

My personal belief, based upon prayer, revelation, and research, is that **America's birth was mixed with good and evil**. The **pilgrims** brought the **doctrine of Christ** and presented their dreams for America through the *Mayflower Compact*. It was **superseded** by the *Declaration of Independence*, which is a very **powerful document**. However, many of the **founding fathers** were **Freemasons** and the system was infiltrated by the **Jesuits**, and the spirit of antichrist.

Even the monetary system in America has been deceiving with the, *"In God We Trust"* slogan. Which God? Whose God? How many gods?

Can you imagine the upheaval if it said, "In Jesus Christ we trust?" That would be promoting of *truth*, because *Jesus* is the only way. **He is the Truth!** So if America is under "God" and not "Jesus Christ," is it truly or was it ever under Jehovah God? Which "god" have we been under? All "other gods" are "of this world" and have infiltrated our country, schools, media, churches, government, homes, and personal lives.

One may observe a partial overview of the impact of the infiltration and the downfall of America in the chart below. "And that because of **false brethren unawares brought in**, who came **in**

privily to spy out our liberty which we have in Christ Jesus, that they might bring us into bondage" (Galatians 12:4).

Look closely at what has infiltrated the United States since we have been blessing the physical nation of Israel instead of Jesus, the seed of Abraham.

Year	Event
1620	Mayflower Compact
1717	Modern Freemasonry
May 1, 1776	Illuminati (Jesuits)
July 4, 1776	Declaration of Independence
1777	Illuminati merged with Freemasonry
1906-1915	Azusa Street Revival
1909	Scofield Bible First Version
6/28/1914	World War I
1916	First Jewish Justice appointed to US Supreme Court
4/2/1917	President Wilson declared War on Germany
1917	Scofield Bible Second Version
1917	First Catholic Canon Law
11/2/1917	Balfour Declaration
1924	Dallas Theological Seminary promoted Dispensationalism
1929	The Vatican became a Country
1935	Billy Graham promoted Scofield Bible and

	"Sinner's Prayer"
1945	United Nations
1947	Dead Sea Scrolls found
1947	Separation of Church & State
1948	Television in Homes
1948	National Israel
1948	First International Mental Health Conference
1948	World Health Organization
1948	First Computer Program Written
1962	No Prayer in School
1963	John F Kennedy Assassination
1967	Term, "Conspiracy Theory" Coined
1969	Woodstock
1969	Gay Rights Movement
1970	Hal Lindsay's Late Great Planet Earth
1971	The First Women's Liberation March
1971	World Economic Forum
1973	Roe v. Wade
1973	Watergate Hearings
1975	Microsoft
1975	John Hagee's Christians United for Israel
1976	New Age Movement
1977	Sex, Drugs, Rock and Roll
1978	Jimmy Carter Recognized Noahide Laws

1982	Ronald Reagan Signed Noahide Laws
1983	Second Catholic Cannon Law
1986	Burning Man Festival
1990	The World Wide Web
1991	George H Bush signed Noahide Laws
1993	Homosexuals in Military
1993	Terrorist Bombing NYC
1995	Tim LaHaye Left Behind Series
2000	RU-486 Abortion Pill
2000	Emergent Church Movement
2001	9/11
2002	George W. Bush Roadmap for World Peace
2007	George W. Bush proclaims, 'Education and Sharing Day, USA' (Noahide)
2010	Transgender Movement
2013	First Jesuit Pope
2016	Antisemitism Defined
2016	Barack Obama Declares 'Education and Sharing Day, USA' (Noahide)
2016	Barack Obama signed 21st Century Cures Act
2018	Donald Trump moves US Embassy to Jerusalem
2019	Donald Trump Champion of Noahide Laws
2019	Mormon *The Chosen* TV Series
2020	Donald Trump Abram Accords

2022	Biden proclaims, 'Education and Sharing Day, USA' (Noahide)
2024	Antisemitism Law
2024	Netanyahu addresses Congress

The Lord is calling a remanent. Will you be a part? We must continually go back to the Scriptures as our only source for **Truth**. His Word is **Truth**. His Word is above His Name (John 17:17; Psalm 138:2).

We must:

- get on our knees in the secret place and ask the Holy Spirit to teach us **ALL TRUTH**.
- **not believe** based upon admiration, respect, influence, money, and status.
- always remember to be Bereans, checking the conclusions and reasoning of others against the **plumb line of God's Word.**

"They [Bereans] received the word with all readiness of mind, and **searched the scriptures daily, whether those things were so**" (Acts 17:11).

Truth died and was buried. **Truth** arose and ascended. **Truth** now reigns from heaven. [311] **Truth** is a person. **Do you know Truth**?

"The sun shall be turned into darkness, and the moon into blood, before the great and the terrible day of the Lord come. And it shall come to pass, that **whosoever shall call on the name of the Lord shall be delivered**: for in mount Zion and in Jerusalem shall be deliverance, as the Lord hath said, **and in the remnant whom the Lord shall call**" (Joel 2:31-32).

The great and terrible day of the Lord is coming. Call on the name of the Lord for deliverance today. The Lord, **who is Truth**, is calling you to be **His remnant which will be delivered.**

The power of darkness will be defeated, and the remnant will soon be delivered. **Are you ready for the great and terrible day of the Lord? <u>Only those who know Truth will be.</u>**

Appendix

Song of Moses, Old Testament (Exodus 15)

Then sang Moses and the children of Israel this song unto the Lord, and spake, saying, I will sing unto the Lord, for he hath triumphed gloriously: the horse and his rider hath he thrown into the sea.

The Lord is my strength and song, and he is become my salvation: he is my God, and I will prepare him an habitation; my father's God, and I will exalt him.

The Lord is a man of war: the Lord is his name.

Pharaoh's chariots and his host hath he cast into the sea: his chosen captains also are drowned in the Red sea.

The depths have covered them: they sank into the bottom as a stone.

Thy right hand, O Lord, is become glorious in power: thy right hand, O Lord, hath dashed in pieces the enemy.

And in the greatness of thine excellency thou hast overthrown them that rose up against thee: thou sentest forth thy wrath, which consumed them as stubble.

And with the blast of thy nostrils the waters were gathered together, the floods stood upright as an heap, and the depths were congealed in the heart of the sea.

The enemy said, I will pursue, I will overtake, I will divide the spoil; my lust shall be satisfied upon them; I will draw my sword, my hand shall destroy them.

Thou didst blow with thy wind, the sea covered them: they sank as lead in the mighty waters.

Who is like unto thee, O Lord, among the gods? Who is like thee, glorious in holiness, fearful in praises, doing wonders?

Thou stretchedst out thy right hand, the earth swallowed them.

Thou in thy mercy hast led forth the people which thou hast redeemed: thou hast guided them in thy strength unto thy holy habitation.

The people shall hear, and be afraid: sorrow shall take hold on the inhabitants of Palestina. (This is the land in modern Israel today).

Then the dukes of Edom shall be amazed; the mighty men of Moab, trembling shall take hold upon them; all the inhabitants of Canaan shall melt away.

Fear and dread shall fall upon them; by the greatness of thine arm they shall be as still as a stone; till thy people pass over, O Lord, till the people pass over, which thou hast purchased.

Thou shalt bring them in, and plant them in the mountain of thine inheritance, in the place, O Lord, which thou hast made for thee to dwell in, in the Sanctuary, O Lord, which thy hands have established.

The Lord shall reign for ever and ever.

For the horse of Pharaoh went in with his chariots and with his horsemen into the sea, and the Lord brought again the waters of the sea upon them; but the children of Israel went on dry land in the midst of the sea. (Exodus 15:1-19)

Song of Miriam (Exodus 15)

And Miriam the prophetess, the sister of Aaron, took a timbrel in her hand; and all the women went out after her with timbrels and with dances.

And Miriam answered them, Sing ye to the Lord, for he hath triumphed gloriously; the horse and his rider hath he thrown into the sea. (Exodus 15:20-21)

My Refuge and My Fortress (Psalm 91)

He that dwelleth in the secret place of the most High shall abide under the shadow of the Almighty.

I will say of the Lord, He is my refuge and my fortress: my God; in him will I trust.

Surely he shall deliver thee from the snare of the fowler, and from the noisome pestilence.

He shall cover thee with his feathers, and under his wings shalt thou trust: his truth shall be thy shield and buckler.

Thou shalt not be afraid for the terror by night; nor for the arrow that flieth by day;

Nor for the pestilence that walketh in darkness; nor for the destruction that wasteth at noonday.

A thousand shall fall at thy side, and ten thousand at thy right hand; but it shall not come nigh thee.

Only with thine eyes shalt thou behold and see the reward of the wicked.

Because thou hast made the Lord, which is my refuge, even the most High, thy habitation;

There shall no evil befall thee, neither shall any plague come nigh thy dwelling.

For he shall give his angels charge over thee, to keep thee in all thy ways.

They shall bear thee up in their hands, lest thou dash thy foot against a stone.

Thou shalt tread upon the lion and adder: the young lion and the dragon shalt thou trample under feet.

Because he hath set his love upon me, therefore will I deliver him: I will set him on high, because he hath known my name.

He shall call upon me, and I will answer him: I will be with him in trouble.

I will deliver him, and honour him.

With long life will I satisfy him, and shew him my salvation.

Song of Moses, New Testament (Revelation 15)

And they sing the song of Moses the servant of God, and the song of the Lamb, saying, Great and marvellous are thy works, Lord God Almighty; just and true are thy ways, thou King of saints.

Who shall not fear thee, O Lord, and glorify thy name? for thou only art holy: for all nations shall come and worship before thee; for thy judgments are made manifest. (Revelation 15:1-4)

Photos by the Author

Protests in Israel, February 13, 2023

Blood Moon
Sea of Galilee

February 14, 2023

Border Fence,
2017

Signs of Coming
Messiah
2023

Click to add title

Buildings by
King Herod

**Cave of the Patriar
Abraham's Grave
2023**

Masada, 2017

Church of the Holy Sepulcher

Wailing Wall

Solar Fields

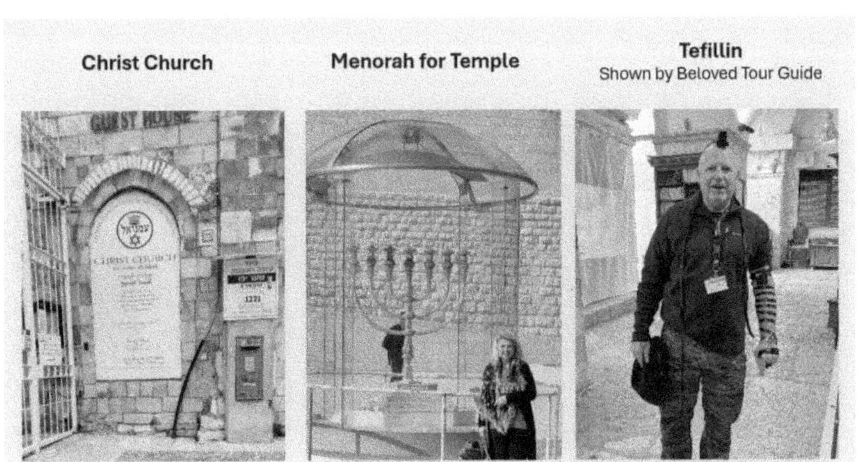

Christ Church

Menorah for Temple

Tefillin
Shown by Beloved Tour Guide

Dome of the Rock

Caesarea Maritime

Underground Tunnel

Sanhedrin Synagogue

Circle of Freemasonry
Eilat, Israel

Eilat, Israel
Red Mountains
of Jordan in background

Akeldama Field

Emmaus

Spices Trade Route, Petra

Shepherds in Field, Jordan

Ancient City of Petra

Vatican Square, Rome

St. Peter's Square with Egyptian Obelisk

St. Peter's Basilica

St. Peter's Square from top of Basilica

Stories in the Ceiling

Wall around Vatican City

Baroque Architecture with Masonic Floors

Jesuit Logo

Statutes of gods

Circus Animals

Palatine Hill

Appian Way

Arch of Titus

Arch of Constantine

Diana Ketterman

Roman Coliseum

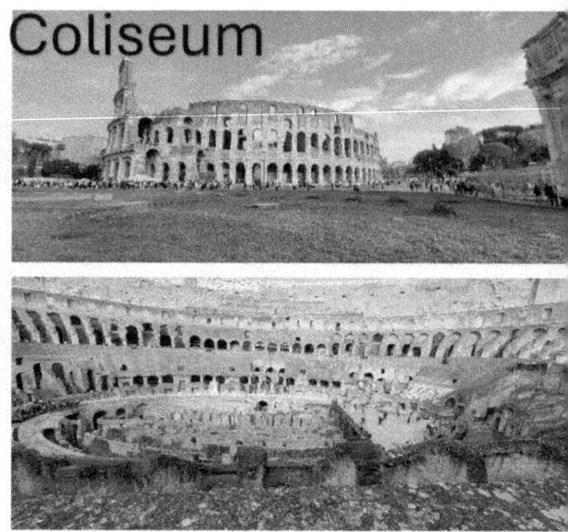

St. Paul's Church

gods over the City

Faces of Popes on Ceiling

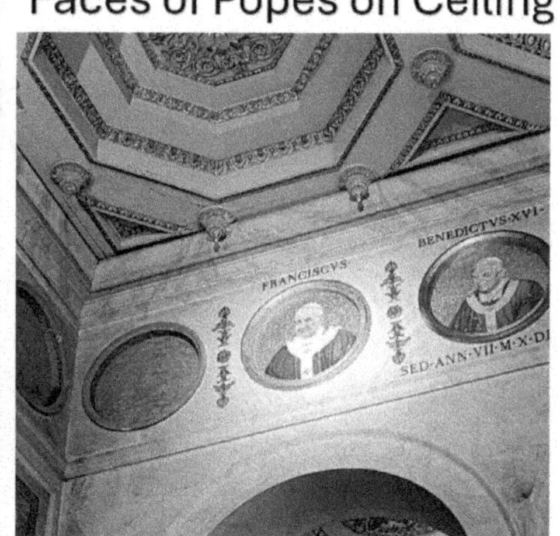

About the Author

Diana Ketterman is a minister, researcher, educator, pastoral counselor, and grief recovery specialist. Her desire is to see others grow in the wisdom and revelation in the knowledge of Jesus Christ. She accepted Christ and was baptized at the age of seven. By the age of twelve, she was enrolled in Bible correspondence courses.

Diana has twenty-three years in education and fifteen years working for the federal government.

Additional books by Diana Ketterman available on Amazon are:

End Notes

1) Religion, Three Religions, One God, https://www.pbs.org/wgbh/globalconnections/mideast/themes/religion/index.html, Accessed 5/26/23

2) Cave of the Patriarchs, http://www.israelandyou.com/cave_of_the_patriarchs/, Accessed 6/1/23

3) A microcosm of Palestinian struggle: One family's life in Hebron, https://www.aljazeera.com/features/2022/4/26/microcosm-palestinian-struggle-one-familys-life-hebron, Accessed 6/1/23

4) Roman Catholicism, https://www.britannica.com/topic/Roman-Catholicism/The-emergence-of-Roman-Catholicism, Accessed 6/3/23

5) WEF "Great Reset" King Charles Boasts He Is Direct Descendant of Muhammad, https://thepeoplesvoice.tv/wef-great-reset-king-charles-boasts-he-is-direct-descendant-of-muhammad/, Accessed 6/3/23

6) The Apocalypse of Abraham, Together with the Testament of Abraham, Trans. By G.H. Box and Dr. Moses Gaster, Lost Antiquities Books, Chicago, IL, 2011, p. 53

7) Abdullah II of Jordan, https://en.wikipedia.org/wiki/Abdullah_II_of_Jordan, Accessed 6/3/23

8) Ur of the Chaldeans, The Old Testament and Archaeology, https://www.christianstudylibrary.org/article/ur-chaldeans, Accessed 6/4/23.

9) Strongs Concordance [H3068] Y'hovah p. 109

10) Catholicism and Natural Moral Law, https://www.dummies.com/article/body-mind-spirit/religion-spirituality/christianity/catholicism/catholicism-and-natural-moral-law-192631/, Accessed 6/4/23

11) What Are Tefillin?, https://www.chabad.org/library/article_cdo/aid/1918251/jewish/What-Are-Tefillin.htm, Accessed 6/4/23

12) Society of Jesus, S—ciety of Jesus - New World Encyclopedia, Accessed 6/4/23

13) Are there any limitations on the Power of the Pope? https://canonlawmadeeasy.com/2008/02/08/are-there-any-limitations-on-the-power-of-the-pope/, Accessed 6/4/23

14) Who was Herod the Great?, https://www.gotquestions.org/Herod-the-Great.html, Accessed 6/5/23

15) Was Esau's Descendants in Rome?, https://12tribehistory.com/was-esaus-descendants-in-rome/, Accessed 6/5/23

16) Whore of Babylon, https://en.wikipedia.org/wiki/Whore_of_Babylon , Accessed 6/5/23

17) Catholic Church, https://en.wikipedia.org/wiki/Catholic_Church#cite_note-26, Accessed 6/5/23

18) Oracle, https://www.merriam-webster.com/dictionary/oracle , Accessed 6/5/23

19) Oracle, https://en.wikipedia.org/wiki/Oracle , Accessed 6/5/23

20) The History of the Roman Catholic Church and the Holy See, https://www.superprof.com/blog/vatican-city-history/, Accessed 6/5/23

21) What does the term "holy see" mean?, https://catholicstraightanswers.com/what-does-the-term-holy-see-mean/ , Accessed 6/5/23

22) Who Is The Whore Of Babylon? (And Why Does It Matter?), https://ca.thegospelcoalition.org/columns/ad-fontes/who-is-the-whore-of-babylon-and-why-does-it-matter/, Accessed 6/5/23

23) Babylon, https://en.wikipedia.org/wiki/Babylon, Accessed 6/5/23

24) Canon Law, https://en.wikipedia.org/wiki/Canon_law, Accessed 6/5/23

25) Military of ancient Rome, https://en.wikipedia.org/wiki/Military_of_ancient_Rome, Accessed 6/5/23

26) Augustus, https://en.wikipedia.org/wiki/Augustus , Accessed 6/5/23

27) Strongs, Israel, [H3478; G2474], p. 124.

28) Webster's American 1828 Dictionary of the English Language, Walking Lion Press, West Valley City, UT, 2010

29) The Abraham Accords, https://www.standwithus.com/theabrahamaccords, Accessed 6/6/23

30) Quran, https://en.wikipedia.org/wiki/Quran, Accessed 6/10/23

31) Catholic Bible, https://en.wikipedia.org/wiki/Catholic_Bible Accessed 6/10/23

32) 5 lessons from Pope Francis' commitment to Muslim-Catholic dialogue, https://www.americamagazine.org/faith/2023/03/03/pope-francis-muslim-christian-dialogue-244833 , Accessed 6/10/23

33) What is the difference between Christianity and Judaism? https://www.gotquestions.org/difference-Christianity-Judaism.html , Accessed 6/10/23

34) SHOCKING TRUTHS ABOUT SHARING THE GOSPEL IN ISRAEL, https://www.oneforisrael.org/israel/shocking-truths-about-sharing-the-gospel-in-israel/ , Accessed 6/10/23

35) History of Judaism, https://www.coursehero.com/study-guides/atd-fscj-worldreligions/history-2/ , Accessed 6/10/23

36) Kabbalah, https://en.wikipedia.org/wiki/Kabbalah, Accessed 6/10/23

37) Zohar, https://en.wikipedia.org/wiki/Zohar, Accessed 6/10/23

38) Who Is the True Israel of God? https://tabletalkmagazine.com/posts/who-is-the-true-israel-of-god/ , Accessed 6/10/23

39) Abraham Accords, https://en.wikipedia.org/wiki/Abraham_Accords#cite_note-:0-6 Accessed 7/2/23

40) Abraham Accords special envoy bill passes US House, https://ejpress.org/abraham-accords-special-envoy-bill-passes-us-house/ Accessed 7/2/23

41) Father Abraham, https://www.ifcj.org/learn/holy-land-moments/daily-devotionals/father-abraham Accessed 7/2/23

42) Moses, G., The Apocalypse of Abraham, *Together with the Testament of Abraham*, Lost Antiquities Books, London Society of Biblical Archaeology, 1886, p. 55

43) The Rabbis' Dilemma: A Look at Isaiah 53, https://jewsforjesus.org/learn/the-rabbis-dilemma-a-look-at-isaiah-53 Accessed 7/2/23

44) The Forbidden Chapter: Isaiah 53 in the Hebrew Bible, https://www.youtube.com/watch?v=cGz9BVJ_k6s Accessed 7/2/23

45) Christianity vs. Judaism, https://www.diffen.com/difference/Christianity_vs_Judaism Accessed 7/2/23

46) Hexagram, https://en.wikipedia.org/wiki/Hexagram Accessed 7/2/23

47) Hebrew Bible, https://en.wikipedia.org/wiki/Hebrew_Bible Accessed 7/2/23

48) Halacha, https://www.merriam-webster.com/dictionary/halakha Accessed 7/2/23

49) THE SATANIC VERSES OF THE JEWISH TALMUD AND ZIONISM, https://hshidayat.wordpress.com/2014/01/07/the-satanic-verses-of-the-jewish-talmud-and-zionism/ Accessed'7/2/23

50) The Talmud is Judaism's Holiest Book Important READ, https://www.indybay.org/newsitems/2002/08/13/1406441.php Accessed 7/2/23

51) What is the definition of the term Gnostic?, https://www.gotquestions.org/gnostic-definition.html Accessed 7/2/23

52) The History of the Talmud, https://www.simpletoremember.com/articles/a/talmud-history/ Accessed 7/2/23

53) What is the Zohar?, https://www.gotquestions.org/Zohar.html Accessed 7/2/23

54) 1666 — REDEMPTION THROUGH SIN: SABBATEAN TIES TO ROTHSCHILDS, THE ILLUMINATI AND NEW WORLD ORDER, https://truthcomestolight.com/1666-redemption-through-sin-sabbatean-ties-to-rothschilds-the-illuminati-and-new-world-order/, Accessed 7/2/23

55) The Satanic Cult That Rules the World, The Satanic Cult That Rules the World | Astute News, Accessed 7/2/23

56) America's Theological Social Contract: The Mayflower Compact, https://religiousfreedominstitute.org/eric-patterson-amp-rebecca-blessing-americas-theological-social-contract-the-mayflower-compact/, Accessed 7/2/23

57) Adam Weishaupt, https://en.wikipedia.org/wiki/Adam_Weishaupt, Accessed 7/2/23

58) FAMOUS MASONS, https://mdmasons.org/about-md-masons/famous-masons/ Accessed 7/2/23

59) Prophetic Anticipation Builds: Unblemished Red Heifers for Temple Ceremony Soon Come of Age, https://www2.cbn.com/news/israel/prophetic-anticipation-builds-unblemished-red-heifers-temple-ceremony-soon-come-age Accessed 7/2/23

60) From Texas to Israel: Red heifers needed for Temple arrive, https://www.jpost.com/judaism/article-717650 Accessed 7/2/23

61) Jewish Prayers: The Shema, https://www.jewishvirtuallibrary.org/the-shema, Accessed 7/15/23

62) What Is Idolatry?, https://www.myjewishlearning.com/article/idolatry-the-ultimate-betrayal-of-god/, Accessed 7/15/23

63) Seven Laws of Noah, https://en.wikipedia.org/wiki/Seven_Laws_of_Noah, Accessed 7/15/23

64) The New Sanhedrin, https://israelmyglory.org/article/the-new-sanhedrin/, Accessed 7/15/23

65) Maimonides, https://en.wikipedia.org/wiki/Maimonides#Works, Accessed 7/15/23

66) The Noahide Laws, https://www.myjewishlearning.com/article/the-noahide-laws/, Accessed 7/15/23

67) What's the real purpose behind "The Underground Sanhedrin Synagogue" in Jerusalem, https://stateofthenation.co/?p=52415 Accessed 7/15/23

68) Rabbi Yosef M'zrachi: 6'Bi'lion People Don't Deserve To Live, https://rumble.com/v1twv6q-rabbi-yosef-mizrachi-6llion-people-dont-deserve-to-live.html, Accessed 7/15/23

69) Ronald Reagan proclaims Jewish Noahide Law is the morality of America and all faiths, https://stopnoahidelaw.blogspot.com/2019/03/ronald-reagan-proclaims-jewish-noahide.html, Accessed 7/15/23

70) Menachem Mendel Schneerson, https://en.wikipedia.org/wiki/Menachem_Mendel_Schneerson, Accessed 7/15/23

71) NOAHIDE LAWS PASSED BY CONGRESS-1991, https://seemytruth.wordpress.com/2010/04/14/noahide-laws-passed-by-congress-1991-death-by-guillotine/, Accessed 7/15/23

72) DONALD J. TRUMP: CHAMPION OF NOAHIDE LAW, https://www.jewishlifeleague.org/pro-life-blog/donald-j-trump-champion-of-noahide-law, Accessed 7/15/23

73) Pompey, https://en.wikipedia.org/wiki/Pompey, Accessed 7/15/23

74) Institute of Noahide Code INC in UN and DC events 2018, https://noahide.org/institute-of-noahide-code-inc-in-un-and-dc-events-2018/, Accessed 7/15/23

75) The Threat of Newly Formed Right- Wing Israeli Government – A Warning to Christians, https://israelinewslive.org/the-threat-of-newly-formed-right-wing-israeli-government-a-warning-to-christians/, Accessed 7/15/23

76) Public Law 102-14, H.J. Res 104, https://noahide.org/public-law-102-14-h-j-res-104/, Accessed 7/15/23

77) Why Many Jewish People Think Christianity Is Antisemitic, https://jewsforjesus.org/learn/why-many-jewish-people-think-christianity-is-antisemitic, Accessed 7/16/23

78) Talking About Ritual Magick, https://fraterbarrabbas.blogspot.com/search/label/Zohar, Accessed 7/16/23

79) What is Kabbalah?, https://reformjudaism.org/beliefs-practices/spirituality/what-kabbalah, Accessed 7/16/23

80) Spiritual Contract, https://www.preparingyou.com/wiki/Spiritual_Contract, Accessed 7/16/23

81) Samaria, https://en.wikipedia.org/wiki/Samaria, Accessed 7/22/63

82) Haller, John, Behold He Comes, Last Days Bible Conference, Alberta, Canada, May 5, 2003

83) Pool of Siloam to Open in Jerusalem After 2,000 Years, https://greekreporter.com/2023/01/03/pool-siloam-open-jerusalem-after-2000-years/, Accessed 7/22/23

84) Hershberg, Rabbi Greg, Beth Yeshua International

85) Adam Weishaupt, a human devil, https://www.amazon.com/Weishaupt-human-devil-Gerald-Winrod/dp/B0006C00FM, Accessed 7/24/23

86) In Israel, a Civil War Is No Longer Unthinkable, https://www.haaretz.com/opinion/2023-02-09/ty-article-opinion/.premium/in-israel-a-civil-war-is-no-longer-unthinkable/00000186-36b0-dd98-a1b6-7fbeba490000, Accessed 7/24/23

87) Christianity and paganism, https://en.wikipedia.org/wiki/Christianity_and_paganism, Accessed 7/29/23

88) Constantine the Great, https://en.wikipedia.org/wiki/Constantine_the_Great, Accessed 7/29/23

89) Donation of Constantine, https://en.wikipedia.org/wiki/Donation_of_Constantine, Accessed 7/29/23

90) Nero, https://en.wikipedia.org/wiki/Nero, Accessed, 7/29/23

91) Nero Persecutes The Christians, 64 A.D., http://www.eyewitnesstohistory.com/christians.htm, Accessed 7/29/23

92) Origins of Christmas, https://www.allaboutjesuschrist.org/origin-of-christmas.htm, Accessed 7/31/23

93) Easter, https://www.worldhistory.org/Easter/, Accessed 7/31/23

94) Sol (Roman Mythology), https://en.wikipedia.org/wiki/Sol_(Roman_mythology), Accessed 7/31/23

95) MARCH 7, 321 AD – CONSTANTINE'S SUNDAY LAW, https://sabbathsentinel.org/2016/10/13/constantine-march-321-ad/, Accessed 7/31/23

96) What is Mardi Gras? History, Meaning and Origin of the Holiday, https://www.newsweek.com/what-mardi-gras-history-meaning-origin-holiday-1488897, Accessed 7/31/23

97) Moriel Ministries, https://www.moriel.org/

98) Constantine I, https://www.yahfatheroflights.com/constantine-l-and-hillel-ll.html, Accessed 7/31/23

99) What is the origin of the Roman Catholic Church?, https://www.gotquestions.org/origin-Catholic-church.html, Accessed 7/31/23

100)   Persecution of Christians in the Roman Empire, Persecution of Ch–istians i— the Roman Empire - Wikipedia, Accessed 7/31/23

101)   Foxe, John, Foxe's Book of Martyrs, pg. 3-5, Chapter XII

102) Winrod, Gerald, Martin Luther and the Reformation, Defender Publishers, Wichita, KS, pg. 19

103) Sol Invictus, https://en.wikipedia.org/wiki/Sol_Invictus, Accessed 8/1/23

104) First Council of Constantinople, https://www.britannica.com/topic/Nicene-Creed, Accessed –/3/23

105) 3: The Perfect Number - Trinity Symbolism in World Religious Traditions, https://www.ancient-origins.net/human-origins-religions/3-perfect-number-trinity-symbolism-world-religious-traditions-005411, Accessed, 8/3/23

106) Ecumenism, https://en.wikipedia.org//wiki/Ecumenism, Accessed 8/3/23

107) 501(c)3 Organizations, https://en.wikipedia.org/wiki/501(c)(3)_organization, Accessed 8/3/23

108) Sol Invictus and Christmas, https://penelope.uchicago.edu/~grout/encyclopaedia_romana/calendar/invictus.html, Accessed 8/4/23

109) Week, https://en.wikipedia.org/wiki/Week, Accessed 8/4/23

110) 14 Facts About Esau Everyone Should Know, https://www.chabad.org/library/article_cdo/aid/4937157/jewish/14-Facts-About-Esau-Everyone-Should-Know.htm, Accessed 8/5/23

111) How Esau Became Rome, https://www.mayimachronim.com/how-esau-became-rome/, Accessed 8/5/23

112) Second Temple, https://en.wikipedia'org/wiki/S"cond_Temple#Herod's_Temple, Accessed 8/5/23.

113) Christian martyrs in the Colosseum, https://mariamilani.com/ancient_rome/rome_gladiator_christians.htm, Accessed 8/5/23.

114) Ignatius of Antioch, https://en.wikipedia.org/wiki/Ignatius_of_Antioch, Accessed 8/5/23

115) Papal Appointment, https://en.wikipedia.org/wiki/Papal_appointment, Accessed 8/5/23

116) Pope, https://en.wikipedia.org/wiki/Pope, Accessed 8/5/23

117) College of Pontiffs, https://en.wikipedia.org/wiki/College_of_Pontiffs, Accessed 8/5/23

118) A Short History of Canon Law from Apostolic Times to 1917, legalhistorysources.com/Canon

Law/ShortHistoryCanonLaw.htm?fbclid=IwAR2JEaq2bLWNgpwgSUO1X-8neYSoYK2Hhaygh0ruGu73cNn_Q7aDzHbwL0A#The Apostolic and Conciliar Age, Accessed 8/25/23

119) Theodosius I, https://en.wikipedia.org/wiki/Theodosius_I, Accessed 8/7/23

120) Disputation of Paris, https://en.wikipedia.org/wiki/Disputation_of_Paris, Accessed 8/7/23

121) Talmud, https://en.wikipedia.org/wiki/Talmud, Accessed 8/7/23

122) 8 Reasons Why Rome Fell, 8 Reasons Why Rome Fell | HISTORY, Accessed 8/7/23

123) Proven Truth: How Paganism and Idolatry Started in the Church, Proven Truth: How Paganism and Idolatry Started in the Church (seekthegospeltruth.com), Accessed 8/7/23

124) Diocletianic Persecution, Diocle—ianic Persecution - Wikipedia, Accessed 8/7/23.

125) The "Nimrod" Tree – "NIMROD" – The LORD of Christmas, https://christmaspagandeception.wordpress.com/2013/07/02/the-nimrod-tree-nimrod-the-lord-of-christmas/, Accessed 8/13/23

126) Frazer, Sir James, George, The Golden Bough, Kindle, Accessed 8/13/23

127) Sacrament, https://en.wikipedia.org/wiki/Sacrament, Accessed 8/13/23

128) Catechism, https://en.wikipedia.org/wiki/Catechism, Accessed 8/13/23

129) Augustus, https://en.wikipedia.org/wiki/Augustus, Accessed 8/13/23

130) Code of Canon Law, https://www.britannica.com/topic/Code-of-Canon-Law, Accessed 8/13/23

131) CODE OF CANON LAW, https://www.vatican.va/archive/cod-iuris-canonici/cic_index_en.html, Accessed 8/13/23

132) The Rosary, https://letgodbetrue.com/bible-topics/index/heresies/the-rosary/, Accessed 8/14/23

133) What is transubstantiation?, https://www.gotquestions.org/transubstantiation.html, Accessed 8/14/23

134) Vatican City, https://en.wikipedia.org/wiki/Vatican_City, Accesssed 8/14"23

135) Pope Frances in M"rocco: "L""t us build bridges" between Christianity and Islam, https://www.americamagazine.org/faith/2019/03/30/pope-francis-morocco-let-us-build-bridges-between-christianity-and-islam, Accessed 8/14/23

136) Catholic Catechism Paragraph 841, https://www.zionhebraiccongregation.com/blog/841, Accessed 8/14/23

137) Torrell, John S., Christian Dynamic Course I, European-American Evangelist Crusades, Sheridan, CA. p 273.

138) Roman Catholicism, Cult of Roman Catholicism (eaec.org), Accessed 8/20/23

139) A Lamp in the Dark: The Untold History of the Bible Documentary, Christian Pinto & Adullam Films, https://youtu.be/UlEaYhLXSNQ, Accessed 8/20/23

140) Radiate Crown, https://en.wikipedia.org/wiki/Radiate_crown, Accessed 8/21/23

141) On Mithraism and Freemasonry, https://www.mithraeum.eu/liber/on-mithraism-and-freemasonry_1996, Accessed 8/21/23

142) Censorship of the Bible, https://en.wikipedia.org/wiki/Censorship_of_the_Bible, Accessed 8/21/23

143) Pope Francis, https://en.wikipedia.org/wiki/Pope_Francis, Accessed 8/26/23

144) Great Bible, https://en.wikipedia.org/wiki/Great_Bible, Accessed 8/26/23

145) The Jesuit Oath, https://www.alamoministries.com/content/english/Antichrist/jesuitoath.html, Accessed 8/26/23

146) Jesus, King of the Jews, https://en.wikipedia.org/wiki/Jesus,_King_of_the_Jews, Accessed 8/26/23

147) Council of Trent, Council of Trent - Wikipedia, Accessed 8/28/23

148) Timeline of Roman Catholicism, Timeline of Roman Catholicism (eaec.org), Accessed 8/28/23

149) The Jesuits and the Long Plan, https://insidethevatican.com/news/letter-44-2019-jonah/, Accessed 8/28/23

150) The Papacy in Jesuitical Captivity: Archbishop Viganò and the "60-Year-Old Plan", https://catholicfamilynews.com/blog/2019/08/25/the-papacy-in-jesuitical-captivity-archbishop-vigano-and-the-60-year-old-plan/, Accessed 8/28/23

151) Arturo Sosa, https://en.wikipedia.org/wiki/Arturo_Sosa, Accessed 8/28/23

152) The Papacy in Jesuitical Captivity: Archbishop Viganò and the "60-Year-Old Plan",

https://catholicfamilynews.com/blog/2019/08/25/the-papacy-in-jesuitical-captivity-archbishop-vigano-and-the-60-year-old-plan/, Accessed 8/28/23

153) Neumayr, George, The Political Pope: How Pope Francis Is Delighting the Liberal Left and Abandoning Conservatives, Center Street, NY, 2017, p. 8, Kindle, Accessed 8/28/23

154) Jackson, James, The World's Most Dangerous Secret Societies, Make Profits Easy, LLC, 2015, p. 175, Kindle, Accessed 8/28/23

155) Zagami, Leo, Pope Francis: The Last Pope? Money, Masons, and Occultism in the Decline of the Catholic Church, Consortium of Collective Consciousness Publishing, p. 63, Kindle, Accessed 8/28/23

156) Evidence Joe Biden Is a Jesuit Ally of Jesuit Pope Frances to Bring Down America, https://www.worldviewweekend.com/tv/video/evidence-joe-biden-jesuit-ally-jesuit-pope-frances-bring-down-america, Accessed 9/1/23

157) Malachi Martin, https://en.wikipedia.org//wiki/Malachi_Martin, Accessed 9/1/23

158) The Crusades, https://www.newworldencyclopedia.org/entry/The_Crusades, Accessed 9/1/23

159) Infidel, https://www.newworldencyclopedia.org/entry/I'fidel, A''cessed 9/1/23

160) Pope's Exorcist Says the Devil Is In the Vatican, https://abcnews.go.com/Travel/chief-exorcist-rev-gabriele-amorth-devil-vatican/story?id=10073040, Accessed 9/1/23

161) The Vatican, The Cult of Cybele, and the King of Serpents on the Hill of Prophecy, https://thepathtolife.home.blog/2019/08/09/the-vatican-the-cult-of-cybele-and-the-king-of-serpents-on-the-hill-of-prophecy/, Accessed 9/1/23

162) Harry Potter: The Basilisk Origin Explained, https://screenrant.com/harry-potter-the-basilisk-origin-explained/, Accessed 9/1/23

163) The Pope's Audience Hall Of Dark Secrets, https://malonepost.com/posts/the-popes-audience-hall-of-dark-secrets, Accessed 9/1/23

164) Suppression of the Society of Jesus, https://en.wikipedia.org/wiki/Suppression_of_the_Society_of_Jesus, Accessed 9/14/23

165) New Marxist phase of the Jesuits, https://www.traditioninaction.org/RevolutionPhotos/A701-Sosa.htm, Accessed 9/14/23

166) Reformation, https://www.pbs.org/faithandreason/theogloss/refor-body.html, Accessed 9/14/23

167) Edomites Descendants of Esau, https://amazingbibletimeline.com/blog/edomites-descendants-of-esau/, Accessed 9/23/23

168) King Herod the Great: King of Judea, https://historycooperative.org/king-herod-of-judea/, Accessed 9/23/23

169) Ramadan, https://www.britannica.com/topic/Ramadan, Accessed 9/23/23

170) Who Wrote the Quran and When?, https://www.learnreligions.com/compilation-of-the-quran-2004545, Accessed 9/23/23

171) Christianity vs. Islam, https://www.diffen.com/difference/Christianity_vs_Islam, Accessed 9/23/23

172) Dome of the Rock, https://en.wikipedia.org/wiki/Dome_of_the_Rock, Accessed 9/25/23

173) Temple Mount, https://en.wikipedia.org/wiki/Temple_Mount, Accessed 9/25/23

174) Minaret, https://en.wikipedia.org/wiki/Minaret, Accessed 9/25/23

175) Design and symbolism of the mosque, https://www.bbc.co.uk/bitesize/guides/zvm96v4/revision/7, Accessed 9/25/23

176) Oracle, https://www.merriam-webster.com/dictionary/oracle, Accessed 9/25/23

177) The History of the Roman Catholic Church and the Holy See, https://www.superprof.com/blog/vatican-city-history/, Accessed 9/25/23

178) Chaldean Religion, https://www.globalsecurity.org/military/world/iraq/history-chaldean-religion.htm, Accessed 9/25/23

179) Ishtar, http://www.mythencyclopedia.com/Ho-Iv/Ishtar.html, Accessed 9/25/23

180) Islamic Terror on Christians, https://www.thereligionofpeace.com/attacks/christian-attacks.aspx, Accessed 9/25/23

181) Infidel, https://www.newworldencyclopedia.org/entry/Infidel, Accessed 9/25/23

182) Who is an Arab? https://www.africa.upenn.edu/K-12/Who_16629.html, Accessed 9/25/23

183) Arabs, https://en.wikipedia.org/wiki/Arabs, Accessed 9/26/23

184) How Muslims meet Jesus in dreams and visions, https://jesus.net/how-muslims-meet-jesus-in-dreams-and-visions/, Accessed 9/27/23

185) Muhammad, https://en.wikipedia.org/wiki/Muhammad, Accessed 9/29/23

186) Facts about Arabs and the Arab World, https://adc.org/facts-about-arabs-and-the-arab-world/, Accessed 9/29/23

187) The International Standard Bible Encyclopedia, Volume I, Hendrickson Publishers, Peabody, MA, p. 218

188) State of Palestine, https://en.wikipedia.org/wiki/State_of_Palestine, Accessed 9/29/23

189) Six Day War, https://en.wikipedia.org/wiki/Six-Day_War, Accessed 9/29/23

190) Oslo Accords, https://en.wikipedia.org/wiki/Oslo_Accords, Accessed 9/29/23

191) West Bank, https://en.wikipedia.org/wiki/West_Bank, Accessed 9/29/23

192) Who were the Nabataean?, https://arabiannightsrum.com/about-wadi-rum/learn/nabataean/, Accessed 10/1/23

193) 1967 war: Six days that changed the Middle East, https://www.bbc.com/news/world-middle-east-39960461, Accessed 10/7/23

194) HOW DOES ISLAM UNDERSTAND THE DEATH AND RESURRECTION OF JESUS? https://www.blueletterbible.org/Comm/stewart_don/faq/islam/12-how-does-islam-understand-the-death-and-resurrection-of-jesus.cfm, Accessed 10/10/23

195) Islam: Truth or Myth?, https://www.bible.ca/islam/islam-moon-god-hubal.htm, Accessed 10/10/23

196) The Life of Muhammad, https://www.pbs.org/muhammad/timeline_html.shtml, Accessed 10/10/23

197) The Complete Apocrypha, 2018 Edition With Enoch, Jasher, & Jubliees, Covenant Press, p. 306

198) The International Standard Bible Encyclopaedia, Hendrickson Publishers, Peabody, MA. 1939, p. 163

199) The Popular and Critical Bible Encyclopaedia and Scriptural Dictionary Fully Defining and Explaining all Religious Term Including Biographical, Geographical, Historical Archaeological and Doctrinal Themes, Chicago, The Howard-Servance Company, 1904

200) Sin (Mythology), https://en.wikipedia.org/wiki/Sin_(mythology), Accessed 12/27/23

201) The Legacy of Noah's Sons, https://www.learnreligions.com/sons-of-noah-701191, Accessed 12/27/23

202) Autumnal Equinox, https://www.britannica.com/science/autumnal-equinox, Accessed 12/27/23

203) Joseph (Genesis), https://en.wikipedia.org/wiki/Joseph_(Genesis), Accessed 1/7/24

204) Egyptian Obelisk, https://www.worldhistory.org/Egyptian_Obelisk/, Accessed 1/10/24

205) Humbaba, https://en.wikipedia.org/wiki/Humbaba, Accessed 1/20/24

206) City of Biblical Abraham Brimmed With Trade and Treasure, https://web.archive.org/web/20160312174803/http://news.nationalgeographic.com/2016/03/160311-ur-iraq-trade-royal-cemetery-woolley-archaeology/, Accessed 1/20/24

207) Abraham or Abram, https://amazingbibletimeline.com/blog/abraham-or-abram/, Accessed 1/20/24

208) Daniel, https://en.wikipedia.org/wiki/Daniel_(biblical_figure), Accessed 1/20/24

209) Chronology: Abraham to the Exodus, https://bibletopicexpo.wordpress.com/2017/01/30/chronology-abraham-to-the-exodus/, Accessed 1/28/24

210) A Worldly Faith, https://www.moodymedia.org/sermons/strength-journey/worldly-faith/, Accessed, 2/5/24

211) Statue of Molech, Pagan Deity of Child Sacrifice, Displayed at Colosseum, https://www2.cbn.com/news/news/statue-molech-pagan-deity-child-sacrifice-displayed-colosseum, Accessed 2/11/24.

212) Grand Lodge of the State of Israel, https://freemasonry.org.il/en/mwgm-message/, Accessed 3/16/24

213) Tabernacling with God, Psalm 91 - Living Under the Shadow of His Wings (oneforisrael.org), Accessed 3/16/24

214) Sanhedrin, https://en.wikipedia.org/wiki/Sanhedrin, Accessed 3/17/24

215) The New Sanhedrin, https://israelmyglory.org/article/the-new-sanhedrin/, Accessed 3/17/24

216) Pharisees Today? https://hebrewnations.com/articles/quora/judaism/pharisees.html, Accessed 3/17/24

217) The Influence of the Orthodox Jews in the Community, https://www.kibin.com/essay-examples/the-influence-of-the-orthodox-jews-in-the-community-z2XWP850, Accessed 3/17/24

218) Rhythmic Chanting and Mystical States across Traditions, https://www.ncbi.nlm.nih.gov/pmc/articles/PMC7828722/, Accessed 3/17/24

219) The Book of Jasher, https://sacred-texts.com/chr/apo/jasher/9.htm, Accessed 3/17/24

220) Temple Institute, https://en.wikipedia.org/wiki/Temple_Institute, Accessed 3/17/24

221) Freemasons, the Third Temple, and the Antichrist, https://christianobserver.net/freemasons-the-third-temple-and-the-antichrist/, Accessed 3/17/24

222) Want world peace? 'Build 3rd Temple', https://www.timesofisrael.com/want-mideast-peace-build-the-3rd-temple/, Accessed 3/17/24

223) Interfaith Dialogue, https://en.wikipedia.org/wiki/Interfaith_dialogue, Accessed 3/17/24

224) Why can't religions coexist peacefully?, https://www.gotquestions.org/religions-coexist.html, Accessed 3/24/24

225) Tolerance, https://www.merriam-webster.com/dictionary/tolerance, Accessed 3/24/24

226) Diversity, equity, and inclusion, https://en.wikipedia.org/wiki/Diversity,_equity,_and_inclusion, Accessed 3/24/24

227) The Gift Tax Made Simple, https://turbotax.intuit.com/tax-tips/estates/the-gift-tax-made-simple/L5tGWVC8N#GoTo-What-is-the-gift-tax-, Accessed 3/24/24

228) Orwell Today https://www.orwelltoday.com/stagedevents.shtml, Accessed 3/24/24

229) Masonic Motto: Ordo Ab Chao, https://www.universalfreemasonry.org/en/article/ordo-ab-chao, Accessed 3/24/24

230) Ur, https://en.wikipedia.org/wiki/Ur, Accessed 3/24/24

231) The Chosen Series, 10 Critical Concerns, A Lighthouse Trails Publication, Roseburg, OR, p. 7.

232) A Giant Statue Of Molech Has Been Put Up Right At The Entrance To The Colosseum In Rome – End Of The American Dream, A Giant Statue Of Molech Has Been Put Up Right At The Entrance To The Colosseum In Rome – End Of The American Dream - The Book Of Revelation, Accessed 3/30/34

233) Visit Akeldama (The fields of Blood) in Jerusalem, https://slavaguide.com/sites/visit-akeldama-the-fields-of-blood-in-jerusalem, Accessed 3/30/24

234) When it Comes to Education, the Federal Government is in Charge of ... Um, What?, https://www.gse.harvard.edu/ideas/ed-magazine/17/08/when-it-comes-education-federal-government-charge-um-what, Accessed 4/1/24

235) SOCIAL JUSTICE AND THE COMMUNIST INDOCTRINATION OF AMERICA'S JUDICIAL SYSTEM, https://www.movieguide.org/news-articles/social-justice-and-the-communist-indoctrination-of-americas-judicial-system.html, Accessed 4/1/24

236) Emergent Church, https://bereanresearch.org/emergent-church/, Accessed 4/1/24

237) What is the emerging / emergent church movement?, https://www.gotquestions.org/emerging-church-emergent.html, Accessed 4/1/24

238) The Relationship Between Ecumenism and Freemasonry, https://www.jeremiahproject.com/deceptions/relationship-ecumenism-freemasonry/, Accessed 4/5/24

239) Promise Keepers and Ecumenism, https://www.jeremiahproject.com/culture-war/promise-keepers-and-ecumenism/, Accessed 4/5/24

240) (ECT) Evangelicals and Catholics Together, https://www.jeremiahproject.com/deceptions/ect-evangelicals-catholics-together/, Accessed 4/5/24

241) Reaffirmation of Support for the LGBTQ+ Community, https://ncchurches.org/2019/06/reaffirmation-of-support-for-the-lgbtq-community/, Accessed 4/5/24

242) Inanna, https://en.wikipedia.org/wiki/Inanna, Accessed 4/5/24

243) Tribe of Dan, https://en.wikipedia.org/wiki/Tribe_of_Dan, Accessed 4/6/24

244) Where are the Ten Lost Tribes, https://www.pbs.org/wgbh/nova/israel/losttribes.html, Accessed 4/8/24

245) Matthew Henry :: Commentary on Ezekiel 47, https://www.blueletterbible.org/Comm/mhc/Eze/Eze_047.cfm, Accessed 4/8/24

246) KV00-V13b Kelley Varner "The Seven Separations Of Abraham", KV00-V13b Kelley Varner "The Seven Separations Of Abraham" (youtube.com), Accessed 4/13/24

247) Pope Francis ranked among this year's 50 most prominent Jews, https://www.lastampa.it/vatican-insider/en/2013/11/14/news/pope-francis-ranked-among-this-year-s-50-most-prominent-jews-1.35955863/, Accessed 4/13/24

248) Hitler's Grandfather Was A Jew, https://trove.nla.gov.au/newspaper/article/98241616, Accessed 4/13/24

249) The Y Chromosome Pool of Jews as Part of the Genetic Landscape of the Middle East, https://www.ncbi.nlm.nih.gov/pmc/articles/PMC1274378/, Accessed 4/14/2

250) Virtually all "Jews" are not the Seed of Abraham, https://www.city-data.com/forum/history/1823838-virtually-all-jews-not-seed-abraham.html#ixzz5NtU7lrul, Accessed 4/14/24

251) Hebrew School of Virginia, https://www.facebook.com/RuachReformationAssemblies/posts/1508680662570146/, Accessed 4/14/24

252) Josephus, F., The Antiquities of the Jews, Kartindo Publishing House, p. 3-26.

253) Bernstein, J., In Racist Marxist Israel: The Life of an American Jew, 1984, First Noontide Press, Costa Mesa, CA.

254) Schurer, E., A History of the Jewish People in the time of Jesus Christ, First Division, Volume II, 1890, p. 269

255) Tammuz, https://www.newworldencyclopedia.org/entry/Tammuz, Accessed 4/14/24

256) History of Palestine, https://en.wikipedia.org/wiki/History_of_Palestine, Accessed 4/15/24

257) Ottoman Empire, https://en.wikipedia.org/wiki/Ottoman_Empire, Accessed 4/15/24

258) Al-Aqsa Mosque, https://en.wikipedia.org/wiki/Al-Aqsa_Mosque, Accessed 4/15/24

259) Dome of the Rock, https://en.wikipedia.org/wiki/Dome_of_the_Rock, Accessed 4/15/24

260) Kingdom of Jerusalem, https://en.wikipedia.org/wiki/Kingdom_of_Jerusalem, Accessed 4/15/24

261) First Crusade, https://en.wikipedia.org/wiki/First_Crusade, Accessed 4/15/24

262) King of Jerusalem, https://en.wikipedia.org/wiki/King_of_Jerusalem, Accessed 4/15/24

263) Church of the Holy Sepulchre, https://en.wikipedia.org/wiki/Church_of_the_Holy_Sepulchre, Accessed 4/15/24

264) Syriac Orthodox Church, https://en.wikipedia.org/wiki/Syriac_Orthodox_Church, Accessed 4/15/24

265) Regardie, Israel. The Complete Goldendawn, ISBN 978-0875426631, p. 299

266) The History and Practice of Magic (Secaucus, NJ: University Books, published by arrangement with Lyle Stewart, 1979), Vol. II, p. 304.

267) Hebrew Bible, https://en.wikipedia.org/wiki/Hebrew_Bible#cite_note-Tov_2014-3, Accessed 4/19/24

268) Hexagram, https://en.wikipedia.org/wiki/Hexagram#cite_note-8, Accessed 4/19/24

269) Modern attempts to revive the Sanhedrin, https://en.wikipedia.org/wiki/Modern_attempts_to_revive_the_Sanhedrin, Accessed 4/20/24

270) Hang Onto Your Seats! Sanhedrin Wants To Replace United Nations, https://beastwatchnews.com/sanhedrin-wants-to-replace-united-nations/, Accessed 4/20/24

271) HERE WE GO!! ONE WORLD RELIGION, | The Abraham Accords Summit | The New Religion | Chrislam, 12/17/22, https://ugetube.com/watch/here-we-go-one-world-religion-the-abraham-accords-summit-the-new-religion-chrislam_QnBeA7SRmiHtDVQ.html, Accessed 4/23/24

272) Ancient Mesopotamian Transgender and Non-Binary Identities, https://www.academuseducation.co.uk/post/ancient-mesopotamian-transgender-and-non-binary-identities, Accessed 4/23/24

273) Exploring Aelia Capitolina, Hadrian's Jerusalem, https://followinghadrian.com/2014/11/05/exploring-aelia-capitolina-hadrians-jerusalem/, Accessed 4/23/24

274) William Tyndale: Life and Death of the Father of the English Bible, https://www.biblestudytools.com/bible-study/topical-studies/translator-william-tyndale-strangled-and-burned-11629961.html, Accessed 4/23/24

275) The history of the Illuminati, https://www.heritagedaily.com/2021/11/the-history-of-the-illuminati/142001, Accessed 4/23/24

276) Repeal The Jewish Noahide Laws In The USA, https://stopnoahidelaw.blogspot.com/2020/09/repeals-jewish-noahide-laws-in-usa.html, Accessed 4/23/24

277) WASHINGTON DC – THE CITY ON SEVEN HILLS, https://www.gnosticwarrior.com/washinton-dc-is-this-the-city-of-seven-hills-that-will-be-destroyed.html, Accessed 4/25/24

278) The Circus Maximus in Rome, https://www.biblestudy.org/biblepic/circus-maximus-in-rome.htmlm Accessed 4/25/24

279) Semitic, https://en.wikipedia.org/wiki/Semitic, Accessed 5/4/24

280) Predictions and Claims for the Second Coming, https://en.wikipedia.org/wiki/Predictions_and_claims_for_the_Second_Coming, Accessed 5/17/24

281) Christology, https://www.merriam-webster.com/dictionary/Christology, Accessed 5/17/24

282) Eschatology, https://www.merriam-webster.com/dictionary/eschatology, Accessed 5/17/24

283) A DISPENSATIONALIST CALCULATION ERROR, https://www.ministrymagazine.org/archive/2002/08/a-dispensationalist-calculation-error.html, Accessed 5/19/24

284) Covenant Theology, https://www.gotquestions.org/covenant-theology.html, Accessed 5/17/24

285) Christian Zionism, https://en.wikipedia.org/wiki/Christian_Zionism, Accessed 5/17/24

286) Christian Zionism, https://en.wikipedia.org/wiki/Christian_Zionism#cite_note-43, Accessed 5/19/24

287) https://web.archive.org/web/20190616205126/https://www.palestine-studies.org/sites/default/files/jq-articles/Pages%20from%20JQ%2076%20-%20Kuttab.pdf

288) Kuttab, J. Palestinian Evangelicals and Christian Zionism, https://web.archive.org/web/20190616205126/https://www.palestine-

studies.org/sites/default/files/jq-articles/Pages%20from%20JQ%2076%20-%20Kuttab.pdf, Accessed 5/19/24

289) Plymouth Brethren, *https://en.wikipedia.org/wiki/Plymouth_Brethren, Accessed 5/17/24

290) 1972 Encyclopedia Judaica Jerusalem, pg. 1154, 1034-1039

291) Martin Luther, https://en.wikipedia.org/wiki/Martin_Luther, Accessed 5/17/24

292) The History of the Counter Reformation in a Nutshell, https://deeptruths.com/wp/the-history-of-the-counter-reformation-in-a-nutshell/, Accessed 5/17/24

293) Ribera, https://en.wikipedia.org/wiki/Francisco_Ribera, Accessed 5/17/24

294) Willie_Martin_Studies, https://israelect.com/reference/WillieMartin/Ignatius_Loyola.htm, Accessed 5/19/24

295) The Jesuit Connection to the Assassination of Abraham Lincoln, https://www.truthontheweb.org/abe.htm, Accessed 5/19/24

296) Did The Jesuits Assassinate Lincoln?, https://www.patheos.com/blogs/mcnamarasblog/2013/02/did-the-jesuits-assassinate-lincoln-3.html, Accessed 5/19/24

297) The Apostles' Creed: Its History and Origins, https://www.logos.com/grow/the-apostles-creed-its-history-and-origins/, Accessed 5/19/24

298) Rober Bellarmine, https://en.wikipedia.org/wiki/Robert_Bellarmine, Accessed 5/17/24

299) King James I Biography, https://www.jesus-is-lord.com/kingbio.htm, Accessed 5/19/24

300) Mayflower Compact, https://en.wikipedia.org/wiki/Mayflower_Compact, Accessed 5/20/24

301) The Exodus Route: Wilderness of Shur, https://bible.ca/archeology/bible-archeology-exodus-route-wilderness-of-shur-ishmaelites-midianites-amalekites.htm, Accessed 6/2/24

302) The little known fascination Newton had with the Jewish Temple, https://www.jpost.com/israel-news/newtons-temple-596350, Accessed 5/20/24

303) Newton Manuscripts, https://www.nli.org.il/en/discover/humanities/newton-manuscripts, Accessed 5/20/24

304) Isaac Newton, https://en.wikipedia.org/wiki/Isaac_Newton, Accessed 5/20/24

305) The first Christian Zionist?, https://www.ynetnews.com/articles/0,7340,L-3416287,00.html, Accessed 5/20/24

306) George Washington Masonic National Memorial, https://en.wikipedia.org/wiki/George_Washington_Masonic_National_Memorial, Accessed 5/20/24

307) Manuel Lacunza, https://en.wikipedia.org/wiki/Manuel_Lacunza, Accessed 5/17/24

308) Edward Irving, https://en.wikipedia.org/wiki/Edward_Irving, Accessed 5/17/24.

309) Catholic Apostolic Church, https://encyclopedia2.thefreedictionary.com/Irvingites, Accessed 5/17/24

310) Samuel Maitland, https://en.wikipedia.org/wiki/Samuel_Roffey_Maitland, Accessed 5/17/24

311) Varner, Kelley, *Whose Right It Is*, Destiny Image Publishers, Shippensburg, PA, 1995, Chapter six.

312) John Nelson Darby, https://en.wikipedia.org/wiki/John_Nelson_Darbym Accessed 5/17/24

313) Orson Hyde, https://en.wikipedia.org/wiki/Orson_Hyde, Accessed 5/17/24

314) BYU Jerusalem Center, https://en.wikipedia.org/wiki/BYU_Jerusalem_Center, Accessed 5/17/24

315) The Restored Church of Jesus Christ and the Holy Land, https://byustudies.byu.edu/article/the-restored-church-of-jesus-christ-and-the-holy-land-beginnings/, Accessed 5/21/24

316) William Blackstone, https://en.wikipedia.org/wiki/William_E._Blackstone, Accessed 5/17/24

317) The Prophetic Faith of Our Fathers, vol. 3, https://m.egwwritings.org/en/book/1582.3752#3771, Accessed 5/21/24

318) The History Of Dispensationalism, https://christianobserver.net/the-history-of-dispensationalism/, Accessed 5/21/24

319) C. I. Scofield, https://en.wikipedia.org/wiki/C._I._Scofield, Accessed 5/17/24

320) Clarence Larkin, https://en.wikipedia.org/wiki/Clarence_Larkin, Accessed 5/17/24

321) Kolbe Report 11/25/23, https://kolbecenter.org/kolbe-report-11-25-23/, Accessed 5/21/24

322) George Dealey, https://en.wikipedia.org/wiki/George_Dealey, Accessed 5/21/24

323) Bloodlines of the Illuminati, Fritz Springmeier

324) Edmond James de Rothschild, https://en.wikipedia.org/wiki/Edmond_James_de_Rothschild, Accessed 5/17/24

325) Rothschild Dynasty, The Balfour Declaration and War in Syria, https://whtt.org/rothschild-dynasty-balfour-agreement-creation-israel/, Accessed 5/21/24

326) Revelation and the Rothschild connection, https://proliberty.com/observer/20090404.htm, Accessed 5/21/24

327) The Rothschilds: Controlling the World's Money Supply for More Than Two Centuries, https://www.donaldwatkins.com/post/the-rothschilds-controlling-the-world-s-money-supply-for-more-than-two-centuries, Accessed 5/21/24

328) The ultimate proof of partnership, https://www.jpost.com/opinion/the-ultimate-proof-of-partnership-589815, Accessed 5/21/24

329) Larkin, Clarence, *Dispensational Truth: God's Plan and Purpose in the Ages,* Philadelphia, PA, 1918, Location 369 Kindle

330) Larkin Charts, https://www.blueletterbible.org/images/larkin/, Accessed 5/21/24

331) Types of Zionism, https://en.wikipedia.org/wiki/Types_of_Zionism, Accessed 5/21/24

332) Theodor Herzl, https://en.wikipedia.org/wiki/Theodor_Herzl, Accessed 5/21/24

333) Star of David, https://en.wikipedia.org/wiki/Star_of_David, Accessed 5/21/24

334) Systematic Theology, https://en.wikipedia.org/wiki/Systematic_theology, Accessed 5/21/24

335) Lewis Chafer, https://en.wikipedia.org/wiki/Lewis_Sperry_Chafer, Accessed 5/17/24

336) David Ben-Gurion, https://en.wikipedia.org/wiki/David_Ben-Gurion, Accessed 5/17/24

337) Israeli Declaration of Independence, https://en.wikipedia.org/wiki/Israeli_Declaration_of_Independence, Accessed 5/17/24

338) Hexagram, https://en.wikipedia.org/wiki/Hexagram, Accessed 5/17/21

339) Ralph Bunche Park, https://en.wikipedia.org/wiki/Ralph_Bunche_Parkm Accessed 5/21/24

340) Ben-Gurion Foresees Gradual Democratization of the Soviet Union, https://www.jta.org/archive/ben-gurion-foresees-gradual-democratization-of-the-soviet-union, Accessed 5/21/24

341) Sun Myung Moon, https://en.wikipedia.org/wiki/Sun_Myung_Moon, Accessed 5/21/24

342) Council for National Policy, https://en.wikipedia.org/wiki/Council_for_National_Policy, Accessed 5/21/24

343) How Did Freemasonry Influence Joseph Smith?, https://www.fromthedesk.org/joseph-smith-freemason-method-infinite/, Accessed 5/21/24

344) Joseph's Temples: The Dynamic Relationship between Freemasonry and Mormonism, https://www.amazon.com/Josephs-Temples-Relationship-Freemasonry-Mormonism/dp/1607813440, Accessed 5/21/24

345) The Untold Story of Christian Zionism's Rise to Power in the United States, https://www.mintpressnews.com/untold-story-christian-zionists-power-united-states-israel/260532/, Accessed 5/21/24

346) Christians United for Israel, https://en.wikipedia.org/wiki/Christians_United_for_Israel, Accessed 5/21/24

347) John Hagee, https://en.wikipedia.org/wiki/John_Hagee, Accessed 5/21/24

348) New Speaker of the House is Zionist Evangelical Christian Who Wants Americans to Believe He was Ordained by God to Support Israel and Destroy Palestinians, https://healthimpactnews.com/2023/new-speaker-of-the-house-is-zionist-evangelical-christian-who-wants-americans-to-believe-he-was-ordained-by-god-to-support-israel-and-destroy-palestinians/print/, Accessed 5/22/24

349) Darby, John Nelson, https://www.encyclopedia.com/religion/encyclopedias-almanacs-transcripts-and-maps/darby-john-nelson, Accessed 5/25/24

350)   Dispensationalism, https://en.wikipedia.org/wiki/Dispensationalism, Accessed 5/21/24

351)   John Darby of the Plymouth Brethren, https://www.christianity.com/church/church-history/timeline/1801-1900/john-darby-of-the-plymouth-brethren-11630602.html, Accessed 5/25/24

352)   Unlikely Zionists: The Fascinating Story of Early American Zionism, https://aish.com/unlikely-zionists-the-fascinating-story-of-early-american-zionism/, Accessed 5/25/24

353)   The Life and Legacy of C.I. Scofield, https://israelmyglory.org/article/the-life-and-legacy-of-c-i-scofield/, Accessed 5/25/24

354)   C I Scofield - Can He Be Trusted?, https://www.scionofzion.com/cis.html, Accessed 5/25/24

355)   Cyrus Ingerson Scofield: Charlatan and Heretic, https://stephensizer.com/2021/06/cyrus-ingerson-scofield-charlatan-and-heretic/, Accessed 5/25/24

356)   Christian Zionism: The series- #7 Zionist funding of the Scofield's reference 'bible', https://www.spreaker.com/episode/christian-zionism-the-series-7-zionist-funding-of-the-scofield-s-reference-bible--51209251, Accessed 5/25/24

357)   Arthur Balfour, https://en.wikipedia.org/wiki/Arthur_Balfour, Accessed 5/21/24

358)   The Scofield Bible—The Book That Made Zionists of America's Evangelical Christians, https://www.wrmea.org/2015-october/the-scofield-bible-the-book-that-made-zionists-of-americas-evangelical-christians.html, Accessed 5/25/24

359)   Masons Warned by Untermyer Against Reich, https://www.jta.org/archive/masons-warned-by-untermyer-against-reich, Accessed 5/25/24

360)   Hermetic Order of the Golden Dawn, https://en.wikipedia.org/wiki/Hermetic_Order_of_the_Golden_Dawn, Accessed 5/25/24

361)   Hermes, https://en.wikipedia.org/wiki/Hermes, Accessed 5/25/24

362)   Hermeticism, https://en.wikipedia.org/wiki/Hermeticism, Accessed 5/25/24

363)   Billy Graham Recalls Help From Hearst, https://www.latimes.com/archives/la-xpm-1997-06-07-me-1034-story.html, Accessed 5/25/24

364) The Sinner's Prayer, https://www.bible.ca/g-sinners-prayer.htm, Accessed 5/25/24

365) Billy Graham and the Pope in 1993, Billy Graham and the Pope 1993 - The Billy Graham Library, Accessed 5/25/24.

366) Billy Graham almost gave up the revival circuit, but L.A. (and Hearst's promotion) became 'watershed', https://www.godreports.com/2018/03/billy-graham-almost-gave-up-the-revival-circuit-but-l-a-and-hearsts-promotion-became-watershed/, Accessed 5/25/24

367) How Christians were duped by the Scofield Bible [Video], 2015, International Solidarity Committee For Islamic Struggle, https://www.youtube.com/watch?v=ROWXV7QJlkY,

368) Study Bibles, https://global.oup.com/academic/category/arts-and-humanities/religion/bibles/study-bibles/?cc=us&lang=en&, Accessed 5/25/24

369) The Jupiter Effect, https://en.wikipedia.org/wiki/The_Jupiter_Effect, Accessed 5/27/24

370) 88 Reasons Why the Rapture Will Happen in 1988, https://www.britannica.com/topic/88-Reasons-Why-the-Rapture-Will-Happen-in-1988, Accessed 5/27/24

371) The Final Shout: Rapture Report 1989, https://books.google.com/books/about/The_Final_Shout.html?id=GCOaGQAACAAJ, Accessed 5/27/24

372) Varner, Kelley, One Reason Why The Rapture Didn't Happen in September, 1988..Another look at Daniel 9:24-27, Richlands, NC, 1989, Praise Tabernacle Press.

373) The Great Disappearance: 31 Ways to be Rapture Ready, https://www.amazon.com/Great-Disappearance-Ways-Rapture-Ready/dp/078525224X, Accessed 5/27/24

374) The Dangerous Teachings of Finis Jennings Dake, https://watchmansbagpipes.blogspot.com/2014/12/the-dangerous-teachings-of-finis.html, Accessed 5/27/24

375) Finis Jennings Dake, https://en.wikipedia.org/wiki/Finis_Jennings_Dake, Accessed 5/27/24

376) Bible Hub, https://biblehub.com/romans/8-1.htm, Accessed 5/27/24

377) EU's top diplomat accuses Israel of funding Hamas, https://www.politico.eu/article/israel-funded-hamas-claims-eu-top-diplomat-josep-borrell/, Accessed 6/2/24

378) Petra the Ancient City, https://www.allaboutarchaeology.org/petra-the-ancient-city.htm, Accessed 6/2/24

379) Desert of Paran, https://en.wikipedia.org/wiki/Desert_of_Paran, Accessed 6/2/24

380) The 12 Tribes of Ishmael, https://nabataea.net/explore/history/12tribes/, Accessed 6/2/24

381) Kaaba, https://en.wikipedia.org/wiki/Kaaba, Accessed 6/2/24

382) Black Stone, https://en.wikipedia.org/wiki/Black_Stone, Accessed 6/2/24

383) Hubal, https://en.wikipedia.org/wiki/Hubal, Accessed 6/2/24

384) Varner, Kelley, Genesis Notes, pg. 59

385) Basilica, https://en.wikipedia.org/wiki/Basilica, Accessed 5/21/24

386) James M. Saslow on Sensuality and Spirituality in Michelangelo's Poetry, https://www.metmuseum.org/articles/james-saslow-interview-michelangelo-poetry, Accessed 6/3/24

387) Michelangelo's Secret Message in the Sistine Chapel: A Juxtaposition of God and the Human Brain, https://www.scientificamerican.com/blog/guest-blog/michelangelos-secret-message-in-the-sistine-chapel-a-juxtaposition-of-god-and-the-human-brain/, Accessed 6/3/24

388) Illuminati Bloodlines: The Orsini Family of Rome, https://www.newsfromtheperimeter.com/home/2019/4/25/illuminati-the-orsini-bloodline-of-rome, Accessed 6/3/24

389) Architecture and Geometry in the Age of the Baroque, https://www.researchgate.net/publication/37693430_Architecture_and_Geometry_in_the_Age_of_the_Baroque, Accessed 6/3/24

390) Basilica of Saint Paul Outside the Walls, https://rome.us/churches/basilica-of-saint-paul-outside-the-walls.html, Accessed 6/3/24

391) Why Is Rome Called 'The Eternal City'?, https://www.ancientpages.com/2024/05/16/why-is-rome-called-the-eternal-city/, Accessed 6/3/24

392) Washington's Hidden Roman Legacy, https://ghostsofdc.org/2014/02/11/washington-originally-called-rome/, Accessed 6/3/24

393) Tiberius Caesar - Bible History, https://bible-history.com/sketches/tiberius-caesar, Accessed 6/3/24

394) The Scandalous Private Life of Tiberius Caesar, https://www.walksinsiderome.com/blog/the-scandalous-private-life-of-tiberius-caesar/, Accessed 6/3/24

395) Distraction, https://webstersdictionary1828.com/Dictionary/distraction, Accessed 6/4/24

396) In Israel, Jews are united by homeland but divided into very different groups, https://www.pewresearch.org/short-reads/2016/03/08/in-israel-jews-are-united-by-homeland-but-divided-into-very-different-groups/, Accessed 6/5/24

397) Chaplains Ordered to Cease Praying 'In Name of Jesus', https://www.toddstarnes.com/faith/chaplains-ordered-to-cease-praying-in-name-of-jesus/, Accessed 6/12/24

398) The Late Great Planet Earth, https://www.goodreads.com/book/show/899325.The_Late_Great_Planet_Earth, Accessed 6/14/24

399) The Transfer Agreement, https://en.wikipedia.org/wiki/The_Transfer_Agreement, Accessed 6/14/24

400) Pompeo visits Israel museum honoring Christian Zionists, Pompeo visits Israel museum honoring Christian Zionists Mike Pompeo administration israel Christians Donald Trump | The Independent, Accessed 6/15/24

401) The Friends of Zion Museum, The Friends of Zion Museum - Wikipedia, Accessed 6/15/24

402) NOW THE GOVERNMENT CAN LEGALLY KILL CHRISTIANS, https://www.spingola.com/Dannemeyer.html, Accessed 6/15/24

403) St. John's Day, Masonic feast, St. John's Day, Masonic feast - Wikipedia, Accessed 6/16/24

404) Saint John, The Apostle and Evangelist, Feast Day of Saint John, The Apostle and Evangelist - St. Boniface Parish - Lunenburg, MA (stboniface-lunenburg.org), Accessed 6/16/24

405) Why does the Church celebrate the Nativity of John the Baptist?, Nativity of Saint John the Baptist | EWTN, Accessed 6/16/24

406) Freedman, Benjamin H, Facts are Facts, Last Century Media, 2023, 1954.

407) Varner, Kelley, Sound the Alarm: The Apocalyptic Message of the Book of Joel, Destiny Image Publishers, Inc, Shippensburg, PA, 2005

408) Defining Antisemitism, https://www.state.gov/defining-antisemitism/, Accessed 7/7/24

409) Anti-Christian incidents are on the rise in Jerusalem's Old City, https://www.americamagazine.org/politics-society/2023/06/29/israel-priest-spit-jerusalem-tension-245604, Accessed 7/7/24.

410) Hellenistic Period, https://en.wikipedia.org/wiki/Hellenistic_period, Accessed 7/7/24

411) A Living Library of Torah, https://www.sefaria.org/texts, Accessed 7/7/24

412) Hoffman, Michael, Judaism's Strange Gods, 2011, Independent History and Research, Coeur dAlene, Idaho

413) The History Of The Fez, https://marktabata.com/2022/05/03/the-history-of-the-fez/, Accessed 7/11/24

414) The Quranic Arabic Corpus, https://corpus.quran.com/, Accessed 7/11/24.

415) Ask the Preacher, http://www.hickoryhammockbaptist.org/quick%20answers/fez.html, Accessed 7/11/24

416) FREE MASONRY'S THE RED FEZ, https://amos37.com/free-masonrys-the-red-fez/, Accessed 7/11/24

417) The History Of The Fez, https://marktabata.com/2022/05/03/the-history-of-the-fez/, Accessed 7/11/24

418) Exposing the Occult in Churches Secret Societies Unveiled: Billy Crone Speaks Out, ID-1014547_TV77 (youtube.com), Accessed 7/11/24

419) Luciferian Jesuits & Deistic Freemasons: The Synagogue Of Satan!, http://www.darknessisfalling.com/darknessisfallingblogblog/luciferian-jesuits-deistic-freemasons-the-synagogue-of-satan, Accessed 7/11/24

420) 2023 Israeli judicial reform, https://en.wikipedia.org/wiki/2023_Israeli_judicial_reform, Accessed 5/13/23

421) Thirty-seventh government of Israel, https://en.wikipedia.org/wiki/Thirty-seventh_government_of_Israel, Accessed 5/13/23

422) WHEN WAS THE TALMUD WRITTEN DOWN?, https://www.kotzkblog.com/2019/08/237-when-was-talmud-written-down.html, Accessed 5/18/23

423) Who Were the Pharisees? The Beginner's Guide, https://overviewbible.com/pharisees/, Accessed 5/18/23

424) Talmud, https://www.biblestudytools.com/dictionary/talmud/, Accessed 5/18/23

425) Pharisees, https://en.wikipedia.org/wiki/Pharisees, Accessed 5/18/23

426) Sadducees, https://en.wikipedia.org/wiki/Sadducees, Accessed 5/18/23

427) Sadducees, https://www.biblestudytools.com/dictionary/sadducees/, Accessed 5/18/23

428) Who was Zadok in the Bible, https://www.gotquestions.org/Zadok-in-the-Bible.html, Accessed 5/18/23

429) Only 4 Percent of Gen Z Have a Biblical Worldview, https://www.impact360institute.org/articles/4-percent-gen-z-biblical-worldview/, Accessed 5/19, 2023

430) Abrahamic religions, https://en.wikipedia.org/wiki/Abrahamic_religions, Accessed 5/25/23

431) What Are The Abrahamic Religions?, https://www.patheos.com/answers/what-are-the-abrahamic-religions, Accessed 5/25/23

432) Stevens, Selwyn, Unmasking Freemasonry, Removing the Hoodwink, Jubilee Resources, New Zealand, 1994

433) Vicomte Leon De Poncins, Freemasonry and Judaism, Secret Powers Behind Revolution, Eworld Inc., Buffalo NY, [No Date], p. 239

434) Schnoebelen, William, Masonry, Beyond the Light, Made in the USA, Middletown, DE, 2020, p. 87

435) Lina, Juri, Architects of Deception, The Concealed History of Freemasonry, Referent Publishing, Stockholm, 2004.

436) Carrico, David L. & Donna M., The Egyptian, Masonic, Satanic Connection, Self-published, Followers of Jesus Christ, Tell City, Indiana, 1994, p. 108-109.

437) McCormick, W.J. Mck., Christ, The Christian, & Freemasonry, National Christian Association, [No Date], p. 37

438) Israel's Religiously Divided Society, https://www.pewforum.org/wp-content/uploads/sites/7/2016/03/Israel-Survey-Full-Report.pdf, Accessed 7/12/24

439) Scicnce and technology in Israel, https://en.wikipedia.org/wiki/Science_and_technology_in_Israel, Accessed 7/13/24

440) Forbidden Chapter of the Tanakh, Forbidden Chapter of the Tanakh | Jewish Voice, Accessed 7/13/24

441) Israel and Anti-Gentile Traditions, Israel and Anti-Gentile Traditions | My Jewish Learning, Accessed 7/13/24

442) The Ben Gurion Canal: Israel's Potential Revolutionary Alternative To Suez – Analysis, https://www.eurasiareview.com/17112023-the-ben-gurion-canal-israels-potential-revolutionary-alternative-to-suez-analysis/, Accessed 7/13/24

443) Horus, https://en.wikipedia.org/wiki/Horus, Accessed 8/22/24

444) Herod the Great, https://en.wikipedia.org/wiki/Herod_the_Great, Accessed 8/23/24

445) The Western Wall: History & Overview, https://www.jewishvirtuallibrary.org/history-and-overivew-of-the-western-wall, Accessed 8/23/24

446) What To Know About The Ancient Tunnels Under Jerusalem, https://www.thetravel.com/ancient-tunnels-under-jerusalem/, Accessed 8/23/24

447) The World's Jewish Billionaires, The World's Jewish Billionaires 2022 - Forbes Israel, Accessed 8/23/24

448) Saint Peter, https://en.wikipedia.org/wiki/Saint_Peter, Accessed 8/29/24

449) Who is Kamala Harris' 'combative Marxist economist' father, Donald J. Harris?, https://www.foxnews.com/politics/who-kamala-harris-combative-marxist-economist-father-donald-j-harris, Accessed 8/29/24

450) St John's: The Oldest Lodge in the United States, https://www.freemason.com/st-johns-the-oldest-lodge-in-the-united-states/, Accessed 9/1/24

451) Take Heed That No One Deceive You, https://www.youtube.com/live/bLoqcU1Uf8s, God's Soldiers Watchmen, Pastor Hank Lee Pogue Sr., Accessed 9/1/24

452) A Journey Through Israel, https://rumble.com/v2bdmuw-march-1-2023.html, Hear the Watchmen & What's Going On, Accessed 9/1/24

453) Breaking: BLOOD MOON Over the Sea of Galilee, https://www.youtube.com/watch?v=d8ZyKWgpOCI, Paul Begley, Accessed 9/1/24

454) You Now Have a Shorter Attention Span Than a Goldfish, https://time.com/3858309/attention-spans-goldfish/, Accessed 9/1/24

455)   The 10 Bloodlines of the Satanic Kings,
https://www.youtube.com/watch?v=hzfhraP4vEI, Underground Church
FOJC, Accessed 9/2/24